The

Wikipedia_REVOLUTION

The

Wikipedia

REVOLUTION

How a Bunch of Nobodies
Created the World's Greatest Encyclopedia

Andrew Lih

First published in Great Britain
2009 by Aurum Press Ltd
7 Greenland Street, London NW1 0ND
www.aurumpress.co.uk

First published in the United States
2009 by Hyperion
114 Fifth Avenue, New York, N.Y. 10011

A catalogue record for this book is available from the British Library.

ISBN 978 1 84513 473 0

1 3 5 7 9 10 8 6 4 2
2009 2011 2013 2012 2010

Book design by Judith Stagnitto Abbate / Abbate Design
Printed by MPG Books, Bodmin, Cornwall

For my wife, Mei

Contents `Go`

Acknowledgments

T he idea for this book started in 2003, when I met Jerry Michalski for coffee at the top of the mountainside campus of the University of Hong Kong. Jerry was a prolific fellow, having served as the first editor of Esther Dyson's legendary Release 1.0 newsletter, and was holding an exclusive freeform technology "unconference." If there was anyone who was looking two steps ahead, it was Jerry.

As we sat overlooking the skyscrapers below, I described my research regarding online participation in journalism. He enthusiastically mentioned Wikipedia as the most interesting collaborative grassroots community on the Internet.

The problem was, I'd never even heard of it.

Out came the laptop computer, and as we were surfing the site, he showed me how anyone could edit any page at any time. No sign-up, log-in, or email required. Every page had an "edit" button. Any passerby could modify any page, making changes live. Like anyone else who first hears of the "wiki" concept, I thought it was a ridiculous idea. But later that week, I took a deeper look at Wikipedia. I started to read the articles in detail. And they weren't junk. In fact, they were good. Really good.

I knew there was something interesting, even revolutionary going on here. As I learned about the online volunteers flocking to Wikipedia, I also became part of the community of editors. Friends and academics used it more and more. They wanted to hear how the site worked—how articles get started, how errors get fixed, and of course about the curious edit wars. After Thomas Friedman, in his book *The World Is Flat,* quoted two pages from an article I wrote about Wikipedia, people kept telling me to put these stories in my own book, since few people had any insight into Wikipedia's inner workings. And that's how the book started.

In 2003, I used Wikipedia as a proving ground for a class for eighty-some undergraduate students. I could not have managed tracking and grading them without the help of graduate students Li Cho and Cathy Ma, who both became experts on Wikipedia because of my coercion. I'm grateful to Ying Chan at the university for providing an environment to experiment with Wikipedia in research.

Two major influences on my life in computer science were Jim Haber of Springbrook High School in Maryland and Chip Maguire of Columbia University and the Royal Institute of Technology in Sweden. I was immersed in the hacker spirit as an undergraduate at Columbia University while working at the Center for Computing Activities (CUCCA, later AcIS). There, I rubbed shoulders with other university instructors (UIs) as consultants and administrators just as the Internet was starting to take root. The most important perk was unlimited access to the university's expensive computing equipment and software, which we could never afford ourselves. Among those full-time employees who allowed us to muck around their offices and computers were Rob Cartolano, Mark Kennedy, Maurice Matiz, and Alan Crosswell. After college, my bosses S. Y. Lee and Peter Ting gave me the phenomenal experience of working at AT&T Bell Labs among incredibly smart folks.

I was lucky enough to launch one of New York City's first dot-com ventures (www.ny.com) with my friends Andrew Denmark, Richard Thor Denmark, Stephen Dossick, and Charles Thayer. I will always cherish riding the dot-com roller coaster with them.

At the Columbia University Graduate School of Journalism, Dean Stephen Isaacs, along with Raph Kasper and Michael Crow of the university's provost's office, supported my initiatives to investigate journalistic practice in the digital age. Professors David Klatell, a keen fan of encyclopedias, and Sig Gissler provided encouragement and support. I'm also thankful to John Kelly when we ran the Interactive Design Lab at the university, along with our bright Ph.D. students Reuben Abraham and Gali Einav. Sree Sreenivasan was my teaching partner for many years at Columbia, and has always been my number one sounding board, cheerleader, and *Seinfeld* trivia opponent.

My fellow podcasters at Wikipedia Weekly were critical in helping me sift through Wikipedia's history and keep up with developments: Andrew Wallwork, Liam Wyatt, David Still, and Nico Montes. Also, fellow Wikipedia-oriented bloggers and editors Ben Yates, Geoff Burling, Brianna Laugher, and Danny Wool were instrumental to my understanding of the community.

The book would not have been possible without extensive interviews with the principal enablers of Wikipedia: Ward Cunningham, Larry Sanger, and Jimmy Wales. Michael Davis, Tim Shell, Terry Foote. Thanks to Wikimedia Foundation board members Florence Devouard, Angela Beesley, and Michael Snow for discussions and insights.

Smart folks who provided insight on the community and wikis included Rebecca MacKinnon, Ethan Zuckerman, Benjamin Mako Hill, Sunir Shah, Mitch Kapor, Jason Calacanis, Ross Mayfield, and Joseph Reagle. Conversations with non-Wikipedia-related people Lokman Tsui, Sasa Vucinic, Paul Denlinger, and Kaiser Kuo helped me crystallize my thoughts.

While the subtitle of the book refers to Wikipedians affectionately as "nobodies," those who gave special insight on the community were real somebodies: James Forrester, Austin Hair, Phoebe Ayers, Naoko Kizu, Revi Soekatno, Evan Prodromou, Mark Pellegrini, Kelly Martin, Kat Walsh, Greg Maxwell, Isaac Mao, Shizhao, Titan Deng, Mingli Yuan, Filip Maljkovic, Kurt Jansson, Arne Klempert, Mathias Schindler, Nina Gerlach, Samuel Klein, and Ray Saintonge. For technical explanations, Domas Mituzas, Mark Bergsma, Tim Starling, and Brion Vibber were invaluable. To the many Wikipedians I've met around the world at Wikimania and at meetups, thank you also for your invaluable insight into the community.

I could not have asked for better people to work with than Will Balliett and Brendan Duffy at Hyperion. I also have my agent, John Brockman, to thank, as he has engaged a fascinating set of authors of which I am privileged to be part. To Will Schwalbe, the original Hyperion editor who first put his faith behind a book about Wikipedia, I owe great thanks.

The book was composed on a combination of open source and commercial software. I'm grateful to the many authors of NeoOffice, Mozilla Firefox, TextMate, Quicksilver, MacJournal, MyMind, TextExpander, and Colloquy as critical tools for writing. For accessing the Internet from China, OpenVPN, OpenSSH, FoxyProxy, Tor, and Skype helped cope with any issues regarding Internet blocking.

Writing a book with a broken arm is no easy task, unless you have friends and relatives to help you through eight weeks of disability. These included Abigail Tay, Joe Merican, and Dr. Mahmoud Merican, who all helped to arrange treatment during holiday season. My doctor Mohammed Azmi was a top-notch caregiver and surgeon. Thariq Ahmad was kind enough to lend a 3G HSDPA modem so I could work, and Joon-Nie Lau and Ken Hwee Tan provided support postsurgery. The poor reputation of mothers-in-law is unfounded, as mine was incredible. Lydia Wong Seet-Wah fed and nursed me back to health, while sisters Cindy, Meng, and Leng ferried me around. Jared and Alison provided needed breaks. It really was a family effort.

I am grateful to my niece Khym Fong, who volunteered to be my assistant, retrieving books and photocopying material in the library. Joyce, Jade, and Tyen Fong have my thanks for accommodating my stays in Singapore during book research.

I have my parents to thank for always providing the optimal nurturing environment, not least of all a house full of books and computers. With my brother, Matthew, and sister, Angela, we made it an all-computer household.

This book is also for my grandmother Katherine Young, who lived to be 104 years old and learned to Web-surf and use email. She also taught me how to type on a manual typewriter, which cured me of my two-finger habit.

And most of all, to my wife, Mei, for putting her faith in the book and being an inspiration. She is not only my partner but also my hero.

To the reader, this book is just a beginning. The story continues to be written at http://www.wikipediarevolution.com/.

magine a world in which every single person is given free access to the sum of all human knowledge. That's what we're doing.

By now, it's hard to use the Internet without experiencing Wikipedia in searches and surfing. It has become an incredibly useful Internet resource in many languages. Yet when you use Wikipedia, you may not understand the philosophy behind it.

What is Wikipedia? Wikipedia is a freely licensed encyclopedia written by volunteers in many languages. That it is freely licensed is one of the most important things.

What do I mean by free? I mean free as in speech, not free as in beer. It means we give people four freedoms. You get the freedom to copy our work. You can modify it. You can redistribute it. And you can redistribute modified versions. And you can do all of these things commercially or noncommercially. When we talk about Wikipedia being a free encyclopedia, what we're really talking about is not the price that it takes to access it, but rather the freedom that you have to take it and adapt it and use it however you like.

And that's really core to our mission, and it's really core to the vision of Wikipedia that gets people to work so hard on it.

How big is Wikipedia? It's now extremely big. It has well over a billion words, making it several times larger than Britannica and Encarta combined.

How big is Wikipedia globally? We've got more than 2.5 million articles in English, but English is less than one-third of our total work. We're truly a global project, in many languages. We have more than 800,000 articles in German, and more than 500,000 in each of the French, Polish, and Japanese editions. In total, there are twenty-five language editions that have at least 100,000 articles.

We have 10 million articles across some 200 languages. We have more than 70 language versions of Wikipedia that have at least 10,000 articles, and more than 150 have at least 1,000 articles. So a thousand articles is not really an encyclopedia—that's just a beginning.

That number is significant, because once we have a thousand articles, we know there's a community there. There are likely five or six people, and they're getting started, they're starting to build, there are regulars there, and that's when it really starts to move.

How popular is Wikipedia? Wikipedia has become a real Internet phenomenon, in the last couple of years in particular. It is now, according to all Internet metrics, a top ten global Web site. And we now have a broader reach, for example, than the *New York Times*.

By reach, I mean the number of unique IP numbers that we see in a given day. We see more people, or more people see us, than the *New York Times;* we see more people than the *LA Times,* the *Wall Street Journal,* MSNBC.com, and the *Chicago Tribune.* The really cool thing is, we see more unique visitors in a day than all of these sites combined.

What is the amazing technology behind Wikipedia? The technology required for Wikipedia is essentially rather simple. You need a database, you need a Web server, you need a Web browser, and you need the wiki editing concept. While the wiki concept was invented in 1995 by Ward Cunningham, Wikipedia didn't start until 2001. So all of the technology, including the idea of a wiki, which is a Web site that anyone can edit, has existed since 1995. Why then, if Wikipedia is a technological innovation, wasn't it developed earlier?

The answer is, Wikipedia isn't a technological innovation at all; it's a social innovation. What we figured out between 1995 and 2001 was not new technology. We had the Web already, but we discovered the basic idea of how to organize a community.

What are the social norms, values, practices that you need within a community? One of the core features that really makes Wikipedia work is the free licensing. This is really empowering to all of the people working on the site.

When you visit most Web sites, if you read the terms and conditions, you'll see that they're really abusive. They basically say, anything you enter on the Web site belongs to us. Sorry. And people have put up with that for a long time, but it does discourage people from feeling really empowered to take control of the site and really care for it. However, under free licensing they realize that if the organization running a site, if the company running this, does a botched job, the community can all leave. They can take the content and go. It really does belong to the community. And if you're going to spend hours and hours and hours contributing knowledge to the world, I think it's really important to have that feeling that it will always be available.

Lots of things come and go in the world, but as long as you put it out there under free license, and you've collaborated with other people, you know it will always be there as a base for someone to move forward on. That's really important.

Within Wikipedia's community, we're actually talking about very old-fashioned types of references. Good writing. Neutrality. Reliable sources. Verifiability. We're talking about people's behavior in the community. We're not talking about some kind of magic process. Quality matters, and a thoughtful community has emerged around that ideal.

I have a philosophy about the design of social software. Imagine that you're going to design a restaurant. Just think about the problem of design for a restaurant. In this restaurant we're going to be serving steak. Since we're going to be serving steak, we're going to have steak knives. And since we're going to have steak knives, people might stab each other. So how do we solve this problem? What we could do is build cages and keep everybody in cages to make sure no one stabs anyone.

Well, this makes for a bad society. We reject this kind of thinking in restaurant design, and yet this is the predominant paradigm for social software design. Traditionally when we sit down to design a Web site, we think of all of the bad things people might do, and make sure that we have controls and permissions, everything to prevent people from doing the bad things.

This has two effects. While you do prevent people from doing bad things, there are often very obvious and direct side effects that prevent them from doing good things. If I look at a Web page and see a small spelling error, but I don't have permission to edit that page, I can't fix it. That's the first order of fact, that by having complex permission models, you make it very hard for people to spontaneously do good.

But the second effect has to do with how human interactions are organized. How do people trust each other? How do people feel about society? Many, many people report that when they've been involved in some kind of online mailing list or other things like that, gee, it's so hostile. There are so many hostile communities on the Internet. One of the reasons is because this philosophy of trying to make sure that no one can hurt anyone else actually eliminates all the opportunities for trust.

These considerations bring us into the nitty-gritty of how the software actually works. All the good intentions in the world, saying "Oh, we love everybody," don't get you very far if you don't really have the software tools to make it work.

So the most important thing about the process is to understand that all of the rules are social. The software does not determine the rules of Wikipedia. Almost everything is completely open-ended in terms of what the software does. There's very, very little in the software that serves as rule enforcement. It's all about dialogue, it's all about conversation, it's all about humans making decisions. So that's extremely important.

Let's take these ideals of Wikipedia and bring them out to lots and lots of people in lots and lots of areas far beyond simply encyclopedias. I think the genuine communities, like Wikipedia, will be built on love and respect. But it's really important, because of all the things I've been saying, to remember that Wikipedia is not about technology, it's about people. It's about leaving things open-ended, it's about trusting people, it's about encouraging people to do good. These communities, I believe, are going to be the norm on the Internet.

People have seen that some of the old models are really unhealthy. Wikipedia shows us a really powerful means to move forward to empower lots of people to do good work, cooperatively.

This book describes the story of how Wikipedia started and evolved along this path, from my company starting a traditional encyclopedia, to how this intricate community emerged and works today.

The
Wikipedia_REVOLUTION

THE WIKI PHENOMENON

"Imagine a world in which every single person on the
planet is given free access to the sum of all human
knowledge. That's what we're doing."
                                              —*Jimmy Wales*

n August 2005, at a modest youth hostel in Frankfurt, Germany, hundreds of
writers, students, computer hackers, and ordinary Internet users from around
the world gathered on the grounds of Haus der Jugend on the bank of the River
Main. Few had ever met in person, and most didn't even know one another's real
name. What they did know was that they had collaborated with one another over
the Internet, across different time zones and continents, toward the same goal:
creating an encyclopedia. They knew one another mostly by their cryptic Internet
personas—Anthere, Cimon Avaro on a Pogostick, Eclecticology—usernames that
projected a quirkier side to an online community that focused on a rather academic task.

There was a curious diversity—they came from different locations, age
groups, and educational backgrounds—but they all referred to themselves with
the same label: Wikipedians. They were there face-to-face for the first-ever

Wikimania conference, bound by a common passion to give away their labor, knowledge, and know-how.

In the hostel's courtyard, over cold beer and cold cuts, they swapped passionate stories. Each person inevitably followed "Hello" with a description of the eureka moment when that person stumbled upon Wikipedia and became an addict. Before long, laptops filled up the outdoor patio as users enthusiastically shared their favorite articles and obsessions. Previously used to editing alone in their homes, Wikipedians found themselves next to others who had the same strange obsessions.

Suddenly talking about digging through stacks of books to confirm one fact, checking grammar for five hours straight, or creating thousands of maps by hand didn't seem so dysfunctional. One user showed how he prevented vandalism to Wikipedia with software he had written, while another demonstrated how he translated articles from Spanish into Portuguese. Into the night, users rearranged plastic chairs and outdoor furniture to cluster around laptops, using the wireless Internet as an umbilical cord to attach to the Wikipedia mother ship, editing, sifting, and adding to the site. Only the hostel's curfew kept them from staying up until sunrise. And oddly enough, this all happened ad hoc, in the days before the conference even formally started.

When it came time for the keynote address, hundreds of Wikipedians and attendees clustered into the modest assembly hall, a space more accustomed to holding amateur youth camp performances than hosting Internet luminaries.

A tall and portly gentleman emerged onstage with the trusty hacker look— gray beard, button-down shirt, round stomach, and tan Birkenstocks. Most barely knew who he was, but without Ward Cunningham they wouldn't have ever found one another. He was the creator of the wiki concept, the radical idea of allowing anyone to openly edit any page of a Web site.

The audience hushed up to hear him speak. But he didn't want the attention. Instead of starting his talk, he turned the spotlight on the crowd of Wikipedians in front of him.

"I know that it's really you guys that made this thing noteworthy. . . . Right now I would just like to applaud *you*. Would you join me in saying thanks to all of you, please? You guys are great."

The Wikipedians grinned and started raucous clapping, looking around at their peers representing fifty-two different countries, basking in the moment. For the first time in Wikipedia's four-year history, the people who created it were able to celebrate their achievement in the same room. By that time in 2005, they had built one of the top fifty Web sites in the world, purely by volunteer effort. (By the end of the year, it would be in the top thirty, and the next year in the top ten.) In the process they had completely revolutionized the notion of what an encyclopedia should be and how it should be created.

In the audience were the folks who built Wikipedia from nothing. There was Florence Devouard, a French housewife with a master's degree in agronomy who spent most of her time taking care of her two children. As a volunteer and recently elected board member for the foundation overseeing Wikipedia, she was one of the early core users who discovered the Web site in 2001. Danny Wool was also an early editor, a former yeshiva student in Israel, turned atheist, who wound up working in publishing, even editing encyclopedias as part of his career. He quickly became known in the Wikipedia community for his omnibus knowledge and photographic memory, a walking institutional memory bank. Then there was Erik Moeller, a German user with the trademark ponytail of a computer hacker and a singular focus on pushing Wikipedians to start bigger and more ambitious projects.

They worked across continents, time zones, languages, and cultures to cooperate online, bound together by a passion for volunteering time, energy, and knowledge. They put together the sum of all human knowledge so others could have it for free—both as in freedom, and as in cost.

History

In less than a decade, Wikipedia has singlehandedly invigorated and disrupted the world of encyclopedias, eclipsing nearly every established tome in every language in the world.

It has become so popular that people casually stumble across its content every day on the Internet, and it is increasingly referred to in books, legal affairs, and pop culture. Yet only a fraction of the public who use Wikipedia realize it is entirely created by legions of unpaid, and often unidentified, volunteers. Every article in Wikipedia has an "edit this page" button, allowing anyone, even anonymous passersby, to edit the contents of any entry.

Unlike most sites on the Internet that solicit "user-generated content," no registration, no email, no identification is needed before someone can change a Wikipedia page. It would seem self-evident that this "open editing" model would lead to uncontrollable chaos and absolute disaster, yet completely counter to intuition, it has produced the opposite—a highly popular, and highly regarded, online reference.

Since 2001, a faceless band of volunteers has self-organized to create an online community working successfully beyond anyone's imagination. Even Cunningham, the creator of wikis, says Wikipedia took the idea further than he could have ever imagined.

The result is that Wikipedia has become the first destination of choice for many and now serves as an integral part of the Internet's fabric of knowledge.

Wikipedia, "the encyclopedia that anyone can edit," is firmly in the ranks of the top ten Web sites in the world,[1] sharing that rarefied air with the dot-com industry elite. No other reference site comes close in terms of traffic or popularity, and very few for-profit sites rack up the same staggering traffic numbers as the nonprofit Wikipedia.

The only "Web properties" that consistently rank above it—Google, Yahoo, and Microsoft—are all multibillion-dollar enterprises with tens of thousands of employees each. Wikipedia had a U.S. dollar operating budget in 2006 of less than $500,000, with fewer than a dozen paid employees.

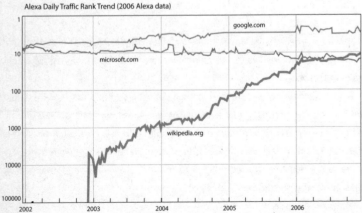

Wikipedia's Massive Growth

Alexa Daily Traffic Rank Trend (2006 Alexa data)

Wikipedia became an instant phenomenon because of both supply and demand. In an information age, with a sprawling labyrinth of information sources, balanced and reliable content is a rare commodity, in high demand. The Internet has a deep supply of volunteers willing to share a deep pool of knowledge, but they are widely dispersed geographically and logistically. Provide an online agora for these two elements to come together, and you have Wikipedia.

The success of Wikipedia is based on simple principles that appear as a radically new phenomenon but in fact extend the long tradition of a "hacker ethos" to a whole new generation of Internet users. Wikipedia built on this hacker culture to establish its principles of making an encyclopedia that is free, open, neutral, timely, and social.

The tech elite who first developed the Internet believed strongly in the freedom of cyberspace, in both aspects of "free"—free as in beer, and free as in freedom. Wikipedia continues that tradition by being disseminated widely and linked to extensively on the Internet. Its direct rivals in the English language, Encyclopedia Britannica and Microsoft's Encarta, started as paid services requiring a log-in and password to access their pages. As a result, they are available only to an elite set of users, and have seen their influence and relevance drop over the years with Wikipedia in the same space. In contrast, no one entity owns a restrictive copyright to Wikipedia's content. Companies and individuals alike are free to copy all of its articles and create derivative works, create new uses, and make money. That's because content in Wikipedia is covered by a "copyleft" license, first pioneered by the "free software" movement, that demands that the information stay free for copying and modification.

Being "free" has unexpected advantages. Wikipedia has evolved from being simply a no-cost alternative into being a superior resource in its own right. Over the years, it has become deeper, broader, and more up-to-date than its traditional rivals. Because of its mission to stay free, it encourages participation—volunteers choose to donate their time and effort without feeling they are making a particular corporation or individual rich. This positive feedback loop has been a large reason for Wikipedia's rapid growth in such a short time.

The Wikipedia project is radically different from other writing methods because it is open. It strives for transparency, to allow inspection for everything within the community. Each article has a complete chronological log of every change ever made, back to its point of creation. The actions of each user (anonymous ones too) are meticulously recorded and tracked in the system and can be observed by anyone else. This feature of "inspectability" is borrowed from the computer programming field, where revisions and decisions are tracked carefully for technical quality.

Openness is also a part of the hacker ethos as a way to inspect others' work, to praise, to learn, to challenge, and to cooperate. It has typically been used by engineers to cobble together electronic parts or share computer programming tips with one another. But the application of this principle to creating content and sharing knowledge through Wikipedia is unprecedented in its scale.

Wikipedia can allow anyone to edit because any action can be easily undone by anyone else in the community. Only in the digital realm is it easier to repair things than to do harm. If Alice incorrectly changes a date, Bob can notice this and change it back with the click of a button. If a vandal attempts to insert incorrect information en masse, other users can thwart it easily and quickly. This crucial asymmetry tips the balance in favor of productive and cooperative members of the community, allowing quality content to prevail.

Most important, the only way to assemble the "sum of all human knowledge," as a collaborative endeavor from many individuals, was to have neutrality as the core editorial policy. Wikipedia founder Jimmy Wales refers to having a "neutral point of view" (NPOV) as the community's only "nonnegotiable" policy, which "attempts to present ideas and facts in such a fashion that both supporters and opponents can agree."

If people on the Internet were to collaborate to create a global distillation of knowledge, there had to be something to bind together their work from very different viewpoints and backgrounds. The founders of Wikipedia had an impetus to be "co-labor instead of anti-labor," to prevent separate agendas splitting the site into polarized factions.

Therefore, it was decided early on that there could be only one version of each article presented at any single time. Participants had to work toward a single common article entry. Differing parallel versions of an article on [[Islam]]* would serve no one well—it would simply be too easy for factions to go off in their own biased corners. The earliest editor and leader of Wikipedia, Larry

---

* Wikipedia uses double brackets to refer to articles with that same name, such as [[Falafel]] or [[Loofah]]. Throughout the book, we will be using the same convention to refer to Wikipedia articles.

Sanger, wisely enforced an NPOV policy, funneling people into the same virtual room to achieve consensus.

Wales acknowledged the impossibility of being truly neutral or objective, but he contended, "One of the great things about NPOV is that it is a term of art, and a community fills it with meaning over time."[2] While it may be impossible to achieve true neutrality, the policy has worked remarkably well. The community has rallied around the idealistic vision of coming up with a single unified treatment of any given topic.

Because it has found a way to be "co-labor," the community has been able to work together around the clock faster than any twenty-four-hour newsroom. Wikipedia wouldn't be as popular today without being timely and cataloging events as quickly as the news happens. In this way, it breaks out of the traditional role of an encyclopedia as a belated summary of history. Instead, it works at the speed of news. As fast as the news happens, like worker bees in a honeycomb, Wikipedians file, edit, and organize up-to-the-second dispatches into the Web site's articles. Whether it was the [[2004 Indian Ocean earthquake]] and resulting tsunami or the [[7 July 2005 London bombings]], Wikipedians were updating articles every few seconds to reflect the latest breaking information. This function as a running log of history is quite unprecedented and uniquely fills a traditional "knowledge gap" created by the lag time between the publication of a newspaper and a history book.

In the English Wikipedia, where activity is nonstop, articles have become an instant snapshot of the state of the world, serving as a continuous working draft of history.

Given all the furious activity it takes to update the site, outsiders are fascinated as to why Wikipedians do what they do. Why would thousands of people flock to Wikipedia to contribute their time and energy for free?

For many, there is the thrill of contributing something that thousands—if not millions—of other people will read, or the satisfaction of helping further the recording of human knowledge. But Wikipedia survives and retains its passionate community also because it is social. You never know whom you will meet, strike up a conversation with, and as a consequence, learn from. Every Wikipedia article has an associated discussion page, to encourage debate and the exchange of ideas with others in the community. Imagine taking an online bulletin board, disassembling it, and spreading it across all the millions of topics and subjects known to mankind, each one with its own discussion group. Conversation among users happens continually when they edit an article, which can serendipitously launch interest in new articles and discussions. It's this strong community of users, all working toward the same goal but in their domains of interest, that spawns new, passionate Wikipedians.

As with most Internet communities, Wikipedia had a dominant set of tech-savvy users at its core in the early days. But as it grew in size and importance, the throng of dedicated users grew to include more and more non-technical types—students, academics, lawyers, and artists. Those who were passionate about donating their labor to the project online found that they wanted to meet in real life. Wikipedia was a virtual product in cyberspace, but it was having implications in physical "meetspace."

This spawned real-life get-togethers. Meet-ups were planned, and starting in 2004, Jimmy Wales, like a prophet visiting his flock, went out to meet as many of the Wikipedians as he could. This fellow from a modest background in Alabama, who had never traveled outside the United States, was seeing the world, with passionate crowds to greet him, first in Europe and North America, then in East Asia and Africa. It was clear Wikipedia wasn't a fad. It was a global phenomenon.

I't all culminated in 2005 at the Frankfurt youth hostel. It was a last-minute affair, typical of how things got done in wiki culture. Following one of the core Wikipedia mantras—"Be bold!"—a group of German Wikipedians decided to organize a conference for editors from all over the world. In a matter of months, what was chatter in a bar became Wikimania, a conference done on a shoestring budget. What could be more wiki than sharing sleeping accommodations with strangers at a youth hostel? But it wasn't just Wikipedians who came to this ad hoc, volunteer-organized summit. Corporations sent employees to see how Wikipedia operated. Internet pioneers came to observe what was happening. Mitch Kapor, founder of Lotus Development Corporation, made the trip on his own time. He had to come see in person what he considered the most exciting project on the Internet.

Press from all around Europe came to interview the minions who participated in the event. Inspired by the Wikipedia model, veteran journalist Danny Schechter showed up with a camera crew to make a Wikimentary about the community—a short video documentary that would be put on the Internet for anyone to alter and edit.

Wikipedia made a major impact that year on the Internet and the media, and accelerated its growth globally. It earned the prestigious Webby and Prix Ars Electronica Awards, and Wales was named one of *Time* magazine's 100 most influential people in 2006.

But as the new elite digerati basked in the Wikipedia phenomenon, the project was not without its skeptics. With an eclectic and mercurial throng of volunteers, Wikipedia has faced its share of crises that come with being big on the radar screen.

In February 2002, just one year after its launch, Wikipedia was rising quickly, but it was still officially an experimental project of the for-profit company Bomis .com. When then-CEO Jimmy Wales mused on the Wikipedia email list whether to put advertisements on Wikipedia's pages to generate revenue, it hit the community like a shock wave.

Influential members of the Spanish Wikipedia were so outraged by even a remote possibility of profiting from volunteer work that within days, they broke off into their own faction. So in 2002, very early in the Web site's history, Spanish Wikipedians copied the entire contents of Spanish Wikipedia onto their own Internet server and asked community members to abandon Wikipedia in favor of this new alternative project, Enciclopedia Libre. It was a jarring setback and a stark lesson about the passionate community Wales had assembled. Despite pleas from Wales, Sanger, and others that advertising was only an idea for discussion, and not in the works, the damage had been done. Most of the Spanish volunteers had left. It would take years for Wikipedia's Spanish-language edition to recover from what is now known as the "Spanish Fork." Some good did result from the episode. It convinced Wales and his partners that they had to spin off Wikipedia into a non-profit entity to convince the community never to doubt its intentions.

Small internal crises were not uncommon. That was to be expected of such a diverse band of global volunteers. Disputes were largely confined within the small Wikipedia community, but with the site's openness, rising popularity, and widespread use, external public relations crises were looming.

The explosion happened in 2005, when veteran journalist John Seigenthaler wrote an op-ed piece in the most popular American newspaper (by circulation), *USA Today,* titled "A False Wikipedia 'Biography.'" The column started out with a punch to the virtual gut of Wikipedians: Someone had edited Seigenthaler's

Wikipedia biography, falsely implicating him in the assassinations of John F. Kennedy and Robert Kennedy.

Seigenthaler thoroughly upbraided Wikipedia and what it stood for, as he described his futile attempt to track down the anonymous contributor who had put in the libelous prank statement. He bemoaned the helplessness he felt as the subject of a Wikipedia article that failed to go through the rigorous editorial process he expected as a journalist.

Wikipedia's honeymoon was over. The embarrassment created a cascade of criticism by the traditional media, and many rounds of self-examination within the community. Wikipedia was no longer just a curious side project and a darling of the tech elite. It was in the big leagues now. People depended on it every day. One very wrong entry could overshadow thousands of great ones, and it affected people's reputations and livelihoods.

And because it has become so influential and powerful, Wikipedia has become a target itself.

The authorities in the People's Republic of China have blocked access to it for Internet users inside the country, ostensibly because the grassroots volunteer community and its content are too unpredictable for a government wanting to maintain control.

Nearly every Internet-enabled student depends on Wikipedia these days, to the dismay of many educators. Venerable study aids like CliffsNotes summaries look like creaky wooden carts next to the supersonic jetliner that is Wikipedia. But Wikipedia's radical working model and uneven quality have resulted in it being "banned" for use in citations by a number of colleges and universities, and there is continual academic debate about the scholarly value of an encyclopedia put together by ordinary, uncredentialed common folk.

There are still enormous questions about the reliability of Wikipedia, though empirical use by millions of people suggests that the site is consistently helpful and, more often than not, accurate. But what about those articles that aren't? How can they be identified? If Wikipedia is a minefield of inaccuracies, should one even be tiptoeing through this information garden?

On balance, it's hard to argue that Wikipedia has been anything but a spectacular success, if only from the volume of visitors who keep returning and the growth of editions in more than fifty major languages. It's easy to concentrate solely on the English-language version—it's by far the largest and most high-profile. But in other languages, Wikipedia's dominance is even more pronounced. In Germany and the Netherlands, the native-language versions of Wikipedia are ranked higher than any domestic news organization's Web site.[3] For many other cultures, in which there are no strong commercial incentives to create an encyclopedia, Wikipedia is the only comprehensive encyclopedia available at all. Therefore, the impact of Wikipedia has been more revolutionary and crucial for those cultures in the "long tail" of the language list.

Wikipedia has likely been introduced to millions simply because they use Google and other search engines. Do a random Internet search, and it's hard not to find a Wikipedia entry in the top five results. The clear, clinical style of its articles on matters whimsical or serious makes it an instant favorite for many Internet users. With blogs and videos overflowing with personal viewpoints, and creative content that challenges one's ability to sift out fact from fiction, Wikipedia has emerged as a respected distillation of knowledge that serves as a touchstone for getting at the truth—a factual yin to opinionated yang.

Wales is more pointed about this aspect of Wikipedia's role: "We make the Internet not suck."[4] In an age with dot-coms, pop-up advertisements, and spam, and with questions of provenance, reliability, and accuracy, people have found Wikipedia to be a haven. It's where anyone can make a contribution to the intellectual commons and depend on reasoned and neutral articles as a result. It is something that by design is empowering and untainted by commerce.

But as it has earned respect as a crucial part of the Internet, even Wikipedia's biggest fans recognize its problems. The Web site may be free of advertisements, but that hasn't stopped entities from trying to exercise influence. Spammers, public relations companies, politicians, and those who can gain from crafting public perception have turned their sights to Wikipedia. Pulitzer Prize–winning columnist Thomas Friedman famously noted this in his book *The World Is Flat*:

> It is not an accident that IBM today has a senior staffer who polices Wikipedia's references to IBM and makes sure everything that gets in there is correct. More young people will learn about IBM from Wikipedia in coming years than from IBM itself.[5]

There is value in trying to influence Wikipedia's articles, transparently or surreptitiously. That has meant legions of volunteers act like street sweepers, constantly monitoring entries for bias.

The story of Wikipedia has inspired businesses, governments, and academics to reevaluate accepted truths about producing works of knowledge. Credentials and central control, once considered the most important parameters for generating quality content, now yield to new terms: crowdsourcing, peer production, and open source intelligence. What was once only done top-down is now being viewed bottom-up.

Books and essays have addressed the impact of projects freely driven by communities of scattered individuals: *The Cathedral and the Bazaar* by Eric S. Raymond, *The Wisdom of Crowds* by James Surowiecki, *The Wealth of Networks* by Yochai Benkler, *The Long Tail* by Chris Anderson, *Infotopia* by Cass R. Sunstein, and *Everything Is Miscellaneous* by David Weinberger.

This book, however, goes in with a deeper focus on Wikipedia, explaining how it evolved to become the phenomenon it is today, and showing the fascinating community behind the articles and the unique online culture the site has fostered. While most people experience Wikipedia in their mother tongue, the impact of the site in other languages reveals a fascinating world of diverse online cultural norms. It's a side of Wikipedia people rarely get to see, and the description of how different language communities have absorbed and adapted Wikipedia's culture is unique to this book. More important, the book takes on an issue few have addressed: where Wikipedia is going and what its challenges are in the future.

In the Afterword, "we" aim to tackle these big questions about the Web site's future. The word "we" is not used in the abstract sense—Wikipedians, scholars, and luminaries were invited to help write this last section as a wiki. What better way to tap the collective knowledge of Wikipedians and thinkers than to put the subject on the Internet for an intelligent "crowd" to map out the future. It promises to be a unique publishing experiment.

A NUPEDIA

"Order, unity and continuity are human inventions just
as truly as catalogues and encyclopedias."
—*Bertrand Russell*

C harles Van Doren captivated the American public in 1957. Americans
were transfixed by the televised game show *Twenty-One,* on which Van
Doren answered question after question correctly for a run of two months
starting December 5, 1956. The clean-cut Ivy League university professor exem-
plified class and scholarship; he was on the cover of *Time* magazine. Before he
left the show, he would rack up $138,000 in winnings,[6] a fairly extravagant sum
in an era when cars cost $2,000.

But then he fell from his pedestal. It was revealed that his wins were a fraud,
that he had been given all the questions and answers beforehand. As dramatized
in the 1994 movie *Quiz Show,* Van Doren testified in front of the U.S. Congress
that he had helped deceive the public.

That's where most people's familiarity with Van Doren ends, leaving him a
disgraced academic who in the aftermath resigned from Columbia University.
What most people don't know is that he resurrected his career to become an accomplished author and an editor at the venerable Encyclopedia Britannica, living
a more modest life of teaching and writing. In 1962, his views on encyclopedias

would be prescient, describing exactly what would transpire on the Internet: "Because the world is radically new, the ideal encyclopedia should be radical, too," he wrote in his essay "The Idea of an Encyclopedia." "It should stop being safe—in politics, in philosophy, in science. . . . But what will be respectable in 30 years seems avant-garde now. If an encyclopedia hopes to be respectable in 2000, it must appear daring in the year 1963."

Of course there was no Internet back then, but Van Doren already envisioned what we see today. His career was made and destroyed with the new media technology of the time—television. He saw the influence that technology was having in the media sphere, and how it would radically change the field of knowledge and how we build it. It is ironic that the vision for Wikipedia, a source criticized for its sometimes dubious contributors, was brilliantly predicted by an academic who was a rehabilitated fraud.

Van Doren's words have turned out to be an interesting touchstone for what has rapidly become one of the most popular sites on the Internet. Wikipedia has indeed been radical and has transformed the world of encyclopedias in just a few years, eclipsing nearly all established tomes in every language in the world. Wikipedia is such a fixture on the Internet today that its mantra, "Anyone can edit any page at any time," is familiar to many, even if they've never edited it themselves. But Wikipedia didn't start out as the radical all-inclusive encyclopedia run by volunteers that we know today.

Its beginnings were entirely conventional. The original project, called Nupedia, was designed as a for-profit venture that specified a regimented screening and production process. It was built around a centrally placed editor in chief managing an inner circle of academically accredited editors to control and direct the work of volunteers. Other than the use of electronic means to promote conversation among participants, its working process was not much different from the encyclopedias of yesteryear.

What Is an Encyclopedia?

We owe the word "encyclopedia" to Classic Greek, *enkyklios paideia,* literally meaning a "rounded education," or something that contains the entirety of general knowledge. Attempts to gather all human knowledge go as far back as Roman times, often taking the form of specific encyclopedias created for particular disciplines and perspectives. Compared to today's classifications of science and history, their manner of organization seems somewhat quirky, if not comical. Some encyclopedias were based around the senses, for example—vision, hearing, smell, taste, and touch. The encyclopedia as a sum of all human knowledge has mirrored the limited known state of the world. So it was not until the era of exploration and heavy trade that the modern idea of a complete recording of the world's knowledge became a reality.

Pliny the Elder, a Roman who lived in the first century A.D., wrote perhaps the first widely recognized encyclopedia in Naturalis Historia, a thirty-seven-book volume that attempted to cover all the known natural world. Its categorization is remarkably modern, with different volumes covering mathematics, geography, ethnography, physiology, zoology, botany, pharmacology, and mineralogy. Showing the Roman fondness for art, there were dedicated volumes just for statuary in bronze and sculpture in marble. Encyclopedias, even back in this era, were compendia of other people's work, so the preface explicitly stated that the Naturalis Historia contained "20,000 facts gathered from some 2,000 books and from 100 select authors."

The Chinese Yongle encyclopedia of 1403–1407 was a massive work, and the largest in the world at the time, using two thousand scholars and eight thousand texts for its creation and covering all matters related to history, literature, medicine, natural sciences, and more. Unfortunately, size was one of this encyclopedia's enemies. It was too large to be block printed and only existed on hand-copied scrolls and manuscripts. Chinese dwellings over the centuries were largely made of wood, unfortunately, and most of the manuscripts were lost to fire. It is said that only four hundred or so volumes have survived to modern times, scattered across libraries and private collections.

But the true mother of the modern encyclopedia was the French Encyclopédie of the 1700s, formally known as "Encyclopedia, or a systematic dictionary of the sciences, arts, and crafts." Originally, Jean Paul de Gua de Malves was hired to create it, but after just a year on the job, in August 1747, he was fired from the position and Jean le Rond d'Alembert and Denis Diderot took over. Most of the world would come to know the name Diderot, as he would spend the next twenty-five years seeing through the Encyclopédie project. Encyclopédie was a powerhouse for the Enlightenment, challenging Catholic dogma by presenting Protestant beliefs and featuring prominent thinkers as authors, such as Voltaire, Rousseau, and Montesquieu.

As was typical of many English-French interactions of the era, the Encyclope-dia Britannica was conceived as a conservative alternative to the more radical Encyclopédie across the channel in France. Proposed by Edinburgh bookseller Colin Macfarquhar and engraver Andrew Bell, the first edition was completed in 1771 and consisted of 2,391 pages, released in weekly installments to subscrib-ers. The most famous was perhaps the eleventh edition, published in 1910–1911 and released as twenty-eight volumes all at once, rather than in weekly editions as in the past. This particular edition became so well regarded that it is still used today, as its copyright has expired and it has passed into the public domain. In the early days of the Internet, this 1911 Britannica was one of the few encyclo-pedias freely available online.

While the content was receiving praise, the business side of Britannica was in trouble, and the owner, Horace Everett Hooper, tried desperately to find a sponsor. The encyclopedia changed sponsors from Cambridge University, whose scholars assisted in reviewing entries, to Sears, Roebuck, before finally gaining its footing again as a separate company in Chicago. The encyclopedia business was a tough one. Academics had to be found and paid to regularly overhaul the content for new editions, and sales of current editions were undermined as consumers waited for the updated ones. Britannica hit its stride with the fifteenth print edition in 1985, after responding to complaints that it had badly fractured information among its three-part structure during the 1970s: the Micropaedia, the Macropaedia, and the Propaedia volumes. The reorganized Britannica went on to be successful, running anywhere from 400,000 topics in 1989 to 700,000 topics in 2007.

A smaller but popular tome in the United States was the World Book encyclo-pedia, which appealed not to scholars but to household purchasers. Its colorful illustrations and hardy pages made it easy to handle, but it had limited appeal because it was not as detailed as Britannica or other "collegiate" or academic encyclopedias.

By the late 1980s, Microsoft was interested in collaborating with Britannica to make an electronic version of the encyclopedia, as CD-ROMs were becoming a popular publishing platform, storing 650 megabytes of data on a disc, consid-ered quite large at the time. However, Britannica declined, deciding its profits were doing nicely and the company could go it alone in creating electronic edi-tions. It would prove to be a fateful call. Britannica print editions were around $2,000 per set, bringing in decent income for the company and making them rather conservative when it came to disrupting a proven revenue stream.

Microsoft still wanted to make an encyclopedia product, and went looking at other encyclopedias using its classic "embrace and extend" model: Identify and follow the lead of a competitor, but establish a superior product. It found a partner in Funk & Wagnalls. It licensed the content from their Standard Encyclopedia to publish the CD-ROM-based Microsoft Encarta encyclopedia in 1993. At first it was considered unimpressive, and not terribly competitive in the marketplace. But because Encarta CD-ROMs were bundled with many new computer purchases of Microsoft Windows it tore into sales of Britannica's print product. Only in 1994 did Britannica come back with a CD-ROM product, which sold for $995 or came bundled for free with a purchase of its pricey print edition. There was also an online edition of Britannica, but subscriptions were $2,000 a year. Britannica tried to hold its own with its deeper and more reputable content, but Microsoft continued to aggressively upgrade Encarta by buying Collier's Encyclopedia and adding more innovative multimedia features. By the time 2000 rolled around, both Encarta and Britannica had disc-based electronic editions for sale and online editions that required subscriptions. Since Encarta was part of the Microsoft behemoth, there was no pressure for it to make money on its own. Britannica was struggling at the time to compete price- and feature-wise with Microsoft.

World Book came out with a CD-ROM edition of its encyclopedia as well, appealing to the same household market, but chose not to have an online version. Among the three big players in the English-language market, there was no complete and modern encyclopedia available for free on the Internet. With content behind the "subscription firewall," Encarta and Britannica had annual prices tailored primarily to big-budget institutions, such as libraries and universities.

At least the English-language encyclopedia market had choices. For many other languages, the choices were even fewer, with one dominant encyclopedia and a smattering of much smaller ones. For Germans, the Brockhaus was the most famous and for the French the Grand Larousse Encyclopédique.

The market was ripe for something to fill the void.

Alabama Rising

With the great encyclopedias of history tracing their lineage back to Rome, Imperial China, France, and Britain, few would guess that Wikipedia's roots could be traced back to Alabama, a U.S. state known more for civil rights struggle than for being a spawning ground for great Internet projects.

Huntsville, Alabama, is where Jimmy Wales hailed from, and the city's growth in the 1960s would have a profound effect on his outlook.

Jimmy's parents, Doris and Jimmy Sr., came from modest backgrounds. The dad, a high school graduate, worked as a grocery store manager in town. His mother and his grandmother Erma had their own ideas on teaching children and started a small private educational establishment in town, House of Learning Elementary School. It was so small that, in the tradition of the one-room school-house, grade levels were clumped together and kids of different ages learned side by side.

Intellectual activity was not Alabama's forte, but during the Cold War, Huntsville suddenly saw itself become a locus of activity. In the ensuing space race between the United States and the Soviet Union, there was a huge advantage in launching rockets closer to the equator, where the rotational acceleration of the Earth helped catapult vehicles into orbit. So immediately, the Southern United States found itself in a prime spot. In 1960, Redstone Arsenal and Marshall Space Flight Center opened in Huntsville, pouring resources and academics into the area. The so-called Rocket City was established in what seemed like an overnight development.

It was in the midst of the town's upsurge that Jimmy Wales was born. Life in town with his brother and sister was exciting, as the innovative energy of the space program was palpable. Rocket tests could be heard in the background of the expanding city. "Growing up in Huntsville during the height of the space program, and all exciting things going on with that, kind of gave you an optimist view of the future, of technology and science," recalls Wales.[7]

Doris, ever the educator, was optimistic too, buying a set of the World Book encyclopedia from a door-to-door salesman not long after becoming a mother. Jimmy, the firstborn, was not even three years old at the time. She didn't know it then, but she was planting a seed that would inspire a phenomenon.

As Wales learned to read, he became fascinated with the encyclopedia, which seemed to put all of human knowledge at his fingertips. World Book was a popular tome for families of the era. Its thick, glossy pages with black-and-white photos made it accessible to children and, more importantly, durable. As opposed to the delicate onionskin-like paper of Britannica and other scholarly sets of encyclopedias, World Book's pages were tactile and withstood rough handling. Kids could read from beginning to end, continually fed by maps and illustrations. The encyclopedia was also famous for its more low-tech "multimedia" features. The "F" volume had transparent overlays for frog dissections showing in vivid color the different organs for the muscular, digestive, and circulatory systems of the amphibian. World Book quickly became a favorite for many children like Jimmy, and its tough pages begged to be turned and dog-eared. It opened up the world of knowledge for kids in an accessible way.

But Wales also learned how inadequate it could be. Things were changing all around him. He was growing up in the Space Age, with new things being tested and discovered. And as a printed tome, the encyclopedia could not keep up with describing the technology he was seeing.

Buying a new set of encyclopedias each year was impractical, and was something only libraries could afford to do. Instead, World Book would send out amendment "stickers" to correct small errors or add new information to subscribers' books. Owners of the encyclopedia would receive updates in the mail and dutifully apply the stickers to the respective pages, something Wales remembers doing with his mom. Of course, this could only be done for so long. At some point an entirely new edition had to be purchased.

Jimmy became a pupil in the House of Learning, under the direction of his mother and grandmother, benefiting from the close nurturing of a parent and learning from older classmates. When it came time to advance to high school, he enrolled at the Randolph School, a private college prep school near Huntsville. One of the great benefits there for Wales was access to computers, somewhat of a rarity back in 1979, when the personal computer was only beginning to blossom. It provided him his first taste of computer programming.

Wales graduated ahead of schedule from Randolph and at sixteen enrolled at Auburn University, a state-funded institution in the east part of Alabama, choosing a practical line of study—finance. He remembers life in college as a time of learning the nuts and bolts of crunching numbers.

After graduating from Auburn, Wales started graduate work in finance at the University of Alabama, and then later at the University of Indiana, in the doctorate degree program. But halfway through that program, he realized finance wasn't his calling. Instead, he went halfway and earned a master's degree, but chose to forgo his Ph.D.

Wales stayed in the Midwest, and with his skills, he wanted to put his talent for numbers into making money. He had written academic papers about financial derivatives and "options-pricing theory," and in the heyday of the 1980s, there was no better way to put that expertise to work than the city of Chicago, a center for the financial trade industry. A friend of his at the time was working at a Chicago trading firm, and knowing about Jimmy's theoretical work in options, she said he should meet her boss.

Jimmy walked into the offices of Chicago Options Associates in 1994 and met the CEO Michael Davis for a job interview. Davis had looked over Wales's academic publication about options pricing.

"It was impressive *looking*," says Wales wryly about the paper. "It was a very theoretical paper but it wasn't very practical." But Davis was sufficiently intrigued, as he wanted someone like Wales to pore over the firm's financial models and help improve them. So he took on young Wales, who seemed to be sharp and had acumen for numbers. Little did either of them know they would have a long road ahead together, with Wikipedia in the future.

Wales's first job was to go over the firm's current pricing models. "What was really fascinating was that it was truly a step beyond what I'd seen in academia," he recalls. "It was very practical, and didn't have a real theoretical foundation." Wales was intrigued that the firm traded on principles that worked in practice, not in theory. (This is something he would say about his future endeavor Wikipedia.) "Basically they just knew in the marketplace that the existing models were wrong."

After working on the analysis side, Wales eventually moved on to perform trades himself. Davis noticed immediately that he was careful and thorough, and Wales quickly gained a reputation for consistently being right on his bets. The legend was that Wales might have made money on every trade he'd ever performed. But in options trading, this was not necessarily a good thing.

Recalling Davis's criticism of him, Wales says, "Michael always said, 'Jimmy could have made so much more money on every trade.' He used to always tease me, 'If every single trade makes money, you're not being aggressive enough!'"

It was an interesting early introduction to Wales's personality for Davis. His new employee was thorough but not aggressive, as a trader needed to be.

Life in Chicago was going well for Wales in the 1990s. He was research director of COA, and at night, on the side, he would draw on his computer hacking interest and hone his programming skills. He freely admits, "I basically had no life at the time."

But he would get a life soon enough. He would cross paths with his future wife, Christine, in June 1996 when a mutual friend arranged for them to meet at a party. "We ended up talking to only each other the entire night and stood in the same place for a few hours," Christine would remember, having been in the dark about the fix-up. A summer of dating was a thrill for the couple.

Four months later they were on a weekend getaway trip to Las Vegas Jimmy had planned. Halfway through the plane trip, Christine opened the lunch bag the airline handed out, and inside was an engagement ring from Jimmy. They resisted the temptation to elope in Las Vegas. Instead, in March of 1997, the couple married in the Florida Keys, with immediate family surrounding them.

During that time, the Internet was starting to blossom. Even while working for the trading firm, Wales still kept up with the mailing lists and discussion groups of his university days. One of the people he knew online was Tim Shell, a fellow member on one of the philosophy subject mailing lists. Working the odd job and studying computer systems in Chicago at night, Shell was on the lookout for breaking into the dot-com business, which was just taking off. He and Wales met in person when members of the mailing list would get together for social functions in the Chicago area.

The two felt it was something they could make a go of, given that start-up costs were minimal, and Jimmy could do it without leaving his COA job. Shell had the time, while Wales worked when he could after hours. Wales put in money from his trading income and Shell took money from his savings, and they were off.

What to call the venture? They jokingly thought of themselves as Bitter Old Men in Suits. What started as an acronym later had appeal in itself, so they stuck with it, officially denying that it stood for anything in particular.

Bomis, Inc., was created in 1996, but as with other dot-coms of the era, the problem was coming up with a viable business model. The sheer breadth of ideas Bomis explored during this period reads like a tour through Internet history. Their first idea was to create an online used-car directory. Shell bought a digital camera, an exotic thing back then, and offered to take photos of cars at different dealers and put the cars up for sale on the Internet. When Shell snapped photos of the cars, the dealers got a kick out of seeing the photo instantly on the camera's screen.

But Wales and Shell quickly found that this enterprise wasn't something that scaled up very well. It took a lot of time to individually photograph and list each car, hoping a buyer would be interested. This was only reproducing what a print catalog would do, and it wasn't really working for them. Moving to something with less legwork and travel, they tried creating an online food ordering service. But to get folks to discover their service required advertising, real-world advertising. Looking at tens of thousands of dollars to get advertising in subways and other venues, they realized that this wasn't going to be a cost-effective model either.

Rather than stick to one business idea, Wales and Shell wanted to keep the firm experimental. There were no proven business models for the Internet then, and they wanted to stay nimble. "Learning from mistakes was the fun part," says Shell.

They started to see what was getting attention—Yahoo!, AltaVista, and Excite were the search engines of the time and were gathering lots of momentum. (It would be a few years before the Google juggernaut would be part of the scene.) It was increasingly clear that transaction services were complex—delivery of goods and handling customer service made such a business hard to start up or scale up. Directory services were much cheaper.

Put listings online, and if people found it useful they would return. Put up some advertising, and you suddenly have a site that can generate revenue without requiring costly customer support.

With that inspiration, Bomis created a Yahoo-style directory for Chicago, which brought about moderate success. It contained listings for links related to the city, and became a place where people would repeatedly return. Bomis signed up advertisers, and with their steady stream of traffic, Chicago suddenly looked like a small market. They then expanded their listings to include anything and everything in the United States, to become one of the many portals that vied for public eyeballs in the dot-com boom.

By 1998, the business was good enough that Wales wanted to leave not just the world of Chicago Options Associates but the city of Chicago too. As a trader, he had made enough money to live comfortably for a while, or as he would say, "I made out OK" and earned "enough." With no incentive to stay in the Windy City, and with the warmer weather of California calling, Wales and Shell decided they could relocate to San Diego and run the business from there. Wales and his wife, Christine, made the move in 1998.

With the basics of directory services figured out, Bomis tried experimenting with other things that were trendy at the time, including creating a special Web browser, which would be known as the Bomis Browser. While the directory service they were building was not as large or as well known as Yahoo, it was well known on the Internet for other smaller innovations.

In an era of incredible Internet growth, it wasn't easy to discover new related sites. One of Bomis's signature features was the use of "rings" to organize chains of Web sites for users to browse. Bomis cataloged and recommended sets of sites, so that after users were done looking at one site, they could press a button to visit the next site in a "ring" of connected and related content. Rings about all sorts of different topics were created—food, travel, cars, business, and the like.

The Mother of All Directories

While dot-com firms in the 1990s became known for their directories and attracting advertising dollars, things started changing as a project with the strange initials DMOZ made an impact on the Internet. It was this project that would give the inspiration for Wikipedia.

DMOZ was shorthand for the site's name on the Internet—directory.mozilla .org. It was started in 1998 by two engineers for Sun Microsystems, one of the powerhouses of the computer industry. Sun was famous for declaring defiantly at the dawn of the Internet, before people could fathom what it meant, "The network is the computer."

Many of the early innovations on the Internet came from Sun, and employees Rich Skrenta and Bob Truel had the idea to create a directory of Internet sites with a radical concept: have it be volunteer-contributed, and openly distributed using a "free license," which meant that users could copy the directory, freely modify it, and edit the listings for their own use.

Would legions of amateur volunteers update and catalog the far corners of the Internet faster than the paid crews of professionals at Yahoo! and other dot-coms? It seemed like a crazy concept. Why should random, anonymous users on the Internet be trusted to work together?

The idea of generating free content was pretty new for the public as well. As the Internet was blossoming, many entrepreneurs and developers were inspired by the free software movement, which had become incredibly popular in tech circles. Free software had as its patron saint a quirky and brilliant man named Richard Stallman, and he was about to make an impact well beyond the small hovel of computer geekdom.

RMS

You can't understand the "free" movement on the Internet without understanding Richard Stallman. A heavily bearded, iconoclastic computer programmer, Stallman became a hacking legend at the Massachusetts Institute of Technology in the 1980s for his programming chops. His experiences as a freewheeling software developer, stifled by corporate usurping of his work, would lead him on a crusade he would pursue the rest of his life: a mission to free up software and content for the masses.

His saga began in 1971 at MIT, which had always been a powerhouse for creating top scientists and engineers. In computer science, it was certainly at the forefront of everything that was happening. It would be instrumental in developing technologies critical for the Internet, such as graphical display systems and standards for networked computing.

Stallman was a whiz, especially with a unique programming language called LISP, which became popular with artificial intelligence researchers. Based on the mathematical principle of the lambda calculus, it was known for its scores of parentheses used while writing computer code. It was simple, powerful, and allowed for creating complex programming. A basic LISP program looked something like this:

```
(defun factorial (n)
(if (< = n 1)
1
(* n (factorial (- n 1)))))
```

It was so easy to learn, though hard to master. Many consider it the most elegant computer language around because of its simplicity.

To understand Stallman's view on the world, you have to understand the computer hacker ethic. The computing culture at MIT and other top scientific schools was one of sharing and openness. These institutions were full of people, after all, who were pursuing software programming not for dollar profits, but for the love of discovery and pioneering new solutions to problems. Worried little about where to live or when the next paycheck was arriving, these students could hunker down in a cloistered academic environment and concentrate on their programming creations.

Hackers would regularly improve how the emerging LISP language and its tools worked, and let everyone in the academic community know by allowing them to share and download new improvements over computer networks that predated the Internet. This was an important part of the hacker ethic: sharing to improve human knowledge. Changes and modifications were put in the public domain for all to partake in. Researchers would improve the work of others and recontribute the work back into the community.

In the 1980s, before it became commercial, the Internet was made up of these educational institutions and research labs in which academics and engineers transferred software packages or improvement "patches" of files back and forth as part of hacker camaraderie. This open marketplace of improvements helped rapidly develop the software that would build the modern Internet.

But Stallman would quickly learn that as idealistic as the phrase sounded, "public domain" was somewhat flawed and fraught with loopholes. "Public domain" meant that intellectual property was not owned or controlled by anyone and, paradoxically, could even be made more restricted.

The problem was that companies could copy computer code found in the public domain, make alterations, but keep these changes secret, not sharing the improvements with the rest of the world. Taking without giving back struck Stallman as especially distasteful and caused many run-ins between him and companies commercializing and hoarding the computer code that Stallman himself helped to write. While he freely gave away his improvements that helped for-profit companies, under public domain they were not obliged to share *their* improvements. In fact, a company could restrict work derived from public domain by copyrighting that modified work, making it no longer free. The freewheeling hacker culture had, as a core belief, the idea that sharing know-how with peers promoted innovation for everyone, but suddenly there were many examples of this breaking down.

As computer software became more widespread, Stallman considered it unethical, antisocial, and harmful to progress to seal up works meant to be free. However, the legal system had no real precedent for solving this problem. "Public domain" sounded good, but it did not enforce sharing, because one could always restrict works derived from public domain works.

So Stallman decided to take this on as his crusade, and in March 1985, he wrote the legendary GNU Manifesto, which appeared in the influential publication for techies, *Dr. Dobb's Journal*. For him, the hacker spirit was about sharing:

> I consider that the golden rule requires that if I like a program I must share it with other people who like it. Software sellers want to divide the users and conquer them, making each user agree not to share with others. I refuse to break solidarity with other users in this way.

Stallman quickly gained a following among academic and professional peers. He proposed a system defiantly called a "copyleft license" (in a play on words and direct opposition to restrictive traditional copyright) ensuring that anyone could study, use, modify, and distribute a work and derivative works. While Stallman was motivated by his experience and passion for computer programming code, he also envisioned that the license could be applied to music, documents, art, or any intellectual property covered by copyright.

At the time, it was a pretty radical idea and was only celebrated by the computer hacking community. It had no immediate recognition or traction outside of that closed culture. This was 1985, after all. The Internet as a conduit for sharing was unknown to the public, and it would be years before music and video files would be transferred via the network as a rival to physical tapes and compact discs.

One of the most important parts of copyleft was the stipulation for derivative works, or the variants people could make based on existing work. A derivative effort in software might be correcting a computer programming error, adding more functionality, or making a smaller version of a program. Stallman's copyleft license stated that any derivative works must also be freely available with the same free license. This clause, effectively a one-way street to free up all computer code that ever touches the original, has been, affectionately or pejoratively, called a "viral license."

(Many years later, Stanford law professor Lawrence Lessig would use a similar observation to start his Creative Commons movement regarding free content. His epiphany came when he saw the same type of phenomenon as Stallman—that derivative works based on public domain content were not required to be public domain. The Disney Corporation is his most famous example of this. Disney can use stories from Mother Goose tales from the public domain, create new works based on Mother Goose, and sue anyone who creates content similar to Disney's movies, specifically because it can copyright the derivative works.)

Stallman's copyleft was not just an abstract idea. To lead by example, he put it into practice immediately by creating the Free Software Foundation, which would be committed to writing free software tools, all created under a new GNU General Public License.

At the time, even Stallman's strident supporters were skeptical. The idea was powerful, but the stark reality was that large computer companies like Sun, Digital Equipment Corporation, Hewlett-Packard, Apple, and Microsoft ruled the landscape. And what could a motley crew of unorganized volunteers around the world achieve that could compete with these multibillion-dollar enterprises? Even more, how would these hackers even earn enough money to eat if they gave everything away?

The FSF started by proposing the creation of a free operating system that could run on a wide variety of different types of computer hardware, and a set of free software tools for programmers. Though it wasn't his favorite system, Stallman chose to base his work on a well-known system used in university settings called UNIX. In a joke typical of his hacking peers, he playfully referred to his project as GNU, using the recursive self-referential phrase GNU's Not Unix.

A GNU operating system would, in a sense, bootstrap a simple operating environment to give folks free tools to make more free software. In a world dominated by computing juggernauts with proprietary software, Stallman saw the Free Software Foundation keeping the hacker flame alive, allowing programmers to inspect the "source code" guts that ran on computers and learn from it. Access to source code (the DNA of computer programs) was something that most companies would either not allow or charge large amounts of money for.

Confusingly, the word "free" has an unfortunate collision of meanings in the English language. Stallman is quick to point out that the "free" in Free Software Foundation is "free as in freedom, not free as in beer." Though having zero-cost software is a good thing, it was not the meaning of "free" for him.

While Stallman's ideas have gained him fame and followers, his mercurial personality and ornery pedantry have earned him a reputation as a person best loved from afar. Notoriously uncompromising, he makes himself known not only in his technology endeavors but also in his commercial consumption. Stallman famously refuses to use Microsoft software because its Windows and Office programs are proprietary. At the many talks he gives, he forgoes the ubiquitous

PowerPoint presentation for other, low-octane alternatives such as plain text documents. At the podium, where he often stands barefoot, he insists on drinking Pepsi, absolutely shunning its competitor in protest of the suspicious murders of unionized workers at Coca-Cola plants in Colombia.[8]

It was perhaps his demanding personality that allowed him to have great success with a few projects at the FSF. Among his most popular were a powerful text document editor called Emacs, a mainstay within the programming community, and the numerous handy software tools called GNU utilities. But by 1992, after eight years of work, Stallman was not pushing forward very well on the elusive goal of delivering a complete operating system free of proprietary software that was "portable" and could run on a variety of computer hardware. He was executing most of this work with a handpicked crew and was particular about who was part of the project. As a result, it was moving forward slowly, while another, more chaotically organized open source project was moving much faster.

Linux on the Scene

The project that did fulfill the goal is now legend—Linux. Started by Finnish hacker Linus Torvalds as a free software project, it grew quickly and gathered volunteers from all over the world, inspired by Stallman's vision for copying, inspecting, and improving software. It all began quite humbly when Torvalds started testing a small, basic operating system called Minix. A computer's operating system acts as the traffic cop to all the hardware resources such as the disk drive, keyboard, graphical display, and networking. All other computer software relies on this "kernel" of the operating system.

Minix was the creation of a computer science professor and was often used in teaching computer science to students. The miniature operating system captured the attention of Linus Torvalds. The free, open source Minix could run on any common Intel microprocessor–based computer that normally ran Microsoft Windows. Minix was small, but that didn't mean it was weak. In its kernel of basic computer code it had all the necessary fundamentals to build bigger and better things. It could easily be loaded onto a floppy disk, and best of all, because it was free, people could inspect the computer code, modify it, and extend its capabilities.

Torvalds learned a lot from "hacking" Minix in his spare time to make it do more. As he improved it, he wondered, like most hackers at the time, why not put the improvements on the Internet to share? So he put them on a computer server and invited people to see his work. Then a curious thing happened. People downloaded his changes, tried them out, fixed some of his errors and bugs, and improved his code. But most importantly, they sent the new code and bug fixes back to him.

He would collect people's contributions, consolidate them, and release another new and improved version for others to download, often within days. In turn, more corrections and improvements were developed and sent back to Linus. Suddenly a critical mass from this process had gathered, and more and more revisions came out in what became a virtuous cycle. Linus didn't author all the improvements; he simply served as the master integrator for this new community of enthusiasts, and the project took on a life of its own.

In contrast to the demanding, controlling, and confrontational Stallman, Torvalds was fascinated by how many folks were pitching in and sending corrections and additions to his computer code. And though he had the ultimate say for these changes being released in his Linux package, he tried to be as inclusive as possible.

Torvalds's mellow and humble style came to codify a tradition in online collaborative projects—that of benevolent dictator. He inspired the project with direction, respected the community of helpers, and exercised authority to solve disputes only when absolutely necessary. His easygoing style and accessibility were essential to the project's success and also set a humble tone for others.

It's important to note that Linux and Stallman's GNU project were not adversarial. In fact, Linux is only one small part of the kernel, the bare essentials necessary for a computer run. The GNU system Stallman created had lots of small computer programs called utilities, which were free through copyleft license. They were modified to run with Linux to create a fully functioning system. In that sense, Stallman has always been insistent that what is commonly known as Linux today should correctly be referred to as GNU/Linux—a hybrid of two systems that work together.

As this GNU/Linux combination started to rise in quality, it also started to challenge the commercial industry heavyweights—Sun, Microsoft, Hewlett-Packard, and others who sold "closed source" operating systems for hundreds or thousands of dollars. Linux wasn't just a free (as in beer) alternative; it was actually a favorite with hard-core programmers because individuals or businesses could take Linux apart and add new functionality, something they could not do very easily with commercial operating systems.

Remember DMOZ

So the long story of Richard Stallman, free software, Linus, Minix, and Linux brings us all the way back to DMOZ.

What did this mean for the DMOZ project?

By 1998 open source software had shown it was a viable competitor to commercial software in terms of quality, something people had not expected from a widely distributed band of volunteers. This inspired people to try the same "free" licensing not just with computer code, but with actual Internet content.

DMOZ was originally started by Skrenta and Truel with the moniker Gnuhoo, a hybrid name that paid homage to Stallman's GNU project and the dominant Yahoo! directory. The idea was to create a directory of Internet sites maintained by volunteers who would participate not because their additions would benefit one company or one person's wallet, but because they would benefit the public at large. This was the hacker ethos again: making information free to allow it to improve more rapidly.

But this was not writing computer code or making technical changes. It was the first large-scale content project of its kind. Contributing required no expertise or tech skills. If you knew of a Web site, and it wasn't in the directory, you could add it yourself.

As the DMOZ project grew in prominence and volunteers, it took off rapidly, formally donning the title of the Open Directory Project. "Open" became the word of the decade: open source software, open content, open formats, and open standards. They all had at their heart the ideas of sharing and the freedom to modify.

Wales was an early Internet user, and remembers when he first ran into Stallman's ideas:

When I entered graduate school at Indiana University, which must have been 1991 or 1992, I was given an account on a UNIX machine and started doing data analysis. I was getting up to speed on UNIX stuff and happened to open up emacs and read the emacs manifesto.* My first thought was, "Wow, what a strange idea." But over time I started to see the sense in it and gradually went from a skeptic to an enthusiast.

When he saw that the same "free" idea could be applied to content, he sensed an opportunity for Bomis. While the company was already providing directory services that it maintained itself, the Open Directory Project was much larger and was updated much more rapidly. Bomis decided, like many other online portals at the time, to start using ODP content. Copying the directory information was completely allowed by a copyleft license (even for commercial use) under the Open Directory license. While Netscape Communications Corporation formally owned the copyright to the ODP content (having acquired it in October 1998), it was "freed" with a clause in the license:

> Netscape grants you a non-exclusive, royalty-free license to use, reproduce, modify and create derivative works from, and distribute and publish the Open Directory and your derivative works thereof, subject to all of the terms and conditions of this Open Directory License.

Rather than just reproduce ODP content verbatim, Bomis tried new things with the directory information. Their own "ring" technology was injected with more sites, and they would find more interesting niches.

Wales describes Bomis's next breakthrough as "a 'guy-oriented search engine,' with a market similar to *Maxim* magazine." Some of its more famous creations were the Bomis Babe Report and the Bomis Babe Ring. Advertising was the Web site's most prominent form of revenue, though they did also manage to create a paid service called Bomis Premium, which had adult photo content for a monthly fee.

Bomis was doing well enough to hire more employees over the next few years, growing to about eight at any given time. By January 2000, Wales was looking at new projects for the company to conquer.

---

* A predecessor of the GNU manifesto.

The Nupedia Idea

The computing power and capital to take on new projects at Bomis made it the right time to fulfill a dream of Wales's: creating an online encyclopedia. He wanted to call it Nupedia, again sticking with a GNU-inspired name, but without wanting to step on Stallman's toes.

Wales had always been a fan of Ayn Rand's objectivist philosophy, and his activities in various Internet forums discussing her ideas would be formative. In addition to the usual Internet bulletin board systems like Usenet, in 1992 Wales announced the creation of his own Moderated Discussion of Objectivist Philosophy, what he described as "the most scholarly of all Objectivist discussions available on the networks."

Rand would inform Wales's thinking on many ideas. He would even name his daughter Kira after the protagonist in Rand's book *We the Living,* Kira Argounova. Gaining objective knowledge from perception by measurement was one of the ideas Wales admired and debated at great length in his online forums. This inspired faith in the idea of measurement by the masses creating an online reference work.

Wales and Shell had originally met via online philosophy mailing lists. And the colloquium of online objectivists would yield another fruitful partnership for Wales. This time it would be with online denizen Larry Sanger, a Ph.D. student in philosophy.

Sanger was born in the state of Washington and grew up in Alaska after the age of seven. He would stay in the Pacific Northwest to attend Reed College, before deciding to study philosophy at graduate school. He seemed straight out of central casting for the role of academic egghead. He would find himself at the much bigger campus of Ohio State University during the years of the Internet boom, studying philosophy and epistemology.

But the short, bespectacled Sanger wasn't just sitting up in the ivory tower studying abstract ideas. He engaged in online discussions about his philosophy interests, in newsgroups and mailing lists, exercising a skill for writing long, detailed essays about his views.

Now, as the year 1999 came around, Sanger wasn't partying. He took on the specter of the most famous non-crisis crisis in modern times: the Y2K bug. In the late 1990s, there was a panic in the information industry about the millions of lines of computer code in various corners of the world that might not be ready for the flip from '99 to '00. Computer code that compared years would suddenly find that 00 was less than 99, and markets would collapse, insurance would be gone, banks would go haywire. Or so the theory went. As companies scrambled to disarm possible ticking time bombs in their computer code, the news reports were getting more urgent. Even the experts didn't know how big a problem it might be.

Seizing on interest in this phenomenon, Sanger, with a friend, created a Web site called Sanger & Shannon's Review of Y2K News Reports. It attempted to aggregate all the reporting on the issue in a digested form. From 1998 to 2000, the Web site gained a healthy following. The good news at the time was that Sanger was gaining a great reputation for it and attracting loyal readers and followers. The bad news was that if the world did not melt down in a computer-induced Armageddon, he would be irrelevant after January 1, 2000.

Well, the world did not implode. In fact, Y2K was one of the biggest nonevents in the history of computing. Within weeks, Larry was looking for something else to do.

Shortly after New Year's Day 2000, Larry sent a private email to a group of acquaintances for feedback on a new "blog" project he had in mind. Wales was one of those recipients, but he had something else in mind for the young philosophy student. "To my great surprise, Jimmy replied to my email describing his idea of a free encyclopedia, and asking if I might be interested in leading the project," said Sanger. "He was specifically interested in finding a philosopher to lead the project."[9]

Wales wanted to build something based on the Open Directory Project idea, but have it be an open source, collaborative encyclopedia, using volunteer contributors on the Internet. But since Bomis was a commercial company, the intention was not simply to give the encyclopedia away, but eventually to generate revenue by selling advertising on the site.

Sanger thought it was a great opportunity, but it would interfere with his ongoing Ph.D. studies at the time. Wales provided some impetus to accept the job. "He made it a condition of my employment that I would finish my Ph.D. quickly (whereupon I would get a raise)—which I did, in June 2000. I am still grateful for the extra incentive," Sanger recalls.

So Sanger piled his belongings into a well-traveled, trusty gray Toyota Corolla wagon, a car he would push to more than 100,000 miles, and drove across the country. Within a month of his email exchange with Wales, he had gone from the cold Ohio winter to the sunny shores of San Diego. The new editor in chief of Nupedia was settled and ready to work. Wales had always thought an academic should head the effort, and he provided Sanger wide latitude.

The idea of an Internet-based encyclopedia was not unique to Wales or Bomis. The most widely recognized early example of the concept was the Interpedia proposed by Rick Gates.

In the 1990s, Gates was a graduate student and lecturer at the University of Arizona's library school, and was seeing the emerging power of the Internet as an information tool. To get people familiar with the new information repository, in September of 1992, for fun, he started a contest called the Internet Hunt that became well known and popular. The idea was to get people to try to use the traditional text-based Internet tools of the time—FTP, Gopher, WAIS—to answer questions posed by Gates. This was the era before the World Wide Web.

The first questions in the Hunt, with the number of points beside them in parentheses, included:

(4) I'm leaving for Japan tomorrow. Approximately how many yen can I get for my dollar, give or take a few yen?

(7) A hurricane just blew in! Where can I find satellite photos of its progress?

(6) I'm taking a job as a social studies teacher at a high school in Denver, CO. Where can I find a list of local environmental organizations that could come speak to my classes?

Today, they seem ridiculously easy to figure out with a quick trip to any Web search site. But in 1992, the term "search engine" was unknown, and it would be a year before ALIWEB and Excite, the first well-known search sites, would be used. Google would not be established for another six years. It took smarts, a lot of scavenging, and a bit of luck to answer these questions. For each set of roughly a dozen, Gates gave people a week to find the answers.

Seeing his scavenger hunt gain popularity, and seeing people flail at finding this information, in October 1993, he circulated his thoughts on a project called "Interpedia," widely seen as the first high-profile proposal to build an electronic encyclopedia on the Internet. In a long post to other citizens of the Usenet system, Gates wrote:

> It can be said that the Interpedia will be a reference source for people who have connectivity to the internet. It will encompass, at the least, articles submitted by individuals, and articles gleaned from non-copyrighted material. It will have mechanisms for submission, browsing, and authentication of articles. It is, currently, a completely volunteer project with no source of funding except for the contributions of the volunteers and their respective institutions. It also has no governing structure except for a group of people who have volunteered to do specific tasks or who have made major contributions to the discussion (see list, below). Everyone is encouraged to make a contribution, small or large.

It sounds remarkably like what we see today, yet this was imagined before the advent of the World Wide Web or wiki software. Because of that, Interpedia was a project perhaps too far ahead of its time and never got out of the planning stages. But it did start circulating the idea that an Internet-based encyclopedia had interest and potential.

In the meantime, other projects that involved harnessing "crowds" would take shape on the Internet. One was related to Project Gutenberg, a movement to have public domain print works available for free on the Internet. Project Gutenberg actually started in 1971 on mainframe computers; now it is one of the oldest online text repositories. The problem it faced was that starting in 1989 it digitized books using optical character recognition systems to automatically turn images of book pages into computer text. The problem was that OCR was imperfect, and there were small, but numerous, errors because of smudges, bad image quality, or dust. That gave Charles Franks the idea to start Distributed Proofreaders in 2000, where people from anywhere on the Internet could help proofread these imperfect OCR texts and fix the problems. It was a good marriage—computers doing the bulk of the data entry, but humans doing the fine-tuning and fixing.

Wales was determined that his encyclopedia project would follow the spirit of open source software, so that everyone could contribute and content could be copied freely. He created a Nupedia Open Content License, based directly on the Open Directory License, that would go quite far in doing this, though, still clinging to his corporate roots, he kept Bomis as the ultimate copyright holder. (This would change eventually to a completely free license.)

Sanger was given freedom to explore specific ways to get the project done, and he discussed his ideas with Wales and Shell along the way.

Nupedia's Rules

The first issue they tackled was the question of "bias" in the encyclopedia. If the project welcomed volunteers from the Internet, they were going to have a variety of viewpoints and opinions. The encyclopedia would have to find a way to integrate those differing points of view.

It was immediately clear to the three, who had met in online forums dedicated to philosophy and objectivism, that a policy of non-bias while assembling knowledge was important. The Ph.D. thesis Sanger was working on at the time, in fact, related to the nature of knowledge. His work encompassed the classic questions of epistemology: What is knowledge, how is knowledge acquired, and what do people know? His doctorate thesis was titled "Epistemic Circularity: An Essay on the Problem of Meta-Justification." In jargon only a philosopher could love, he described it simply as:

> Everybody thinks they know stuff, but how do we show that we know that we know, without going around forever in circles? Or, suppose we wanted to show that what we see, hear, touch, etc., was real. How could we do it without using those same senses?

Compared to that, building an encyclopedia from scratch must have seemed a much easier task.

The three of them were attracted to objectivism for a reason. The objectivist stance is that there is a reality of objects and facts independent of the individual mind. By extension, a body of knowledge could be assembled that was considered representative of this single reality. Put simply, objectivity relates to what is true, rather than ruling whether something is true or false. And their encyclopedia could detail what is true in the world without judgments. Sanger would put it this way: "Neutrality, we agreed, required that articles should not represent any one point of view on controversial subjects, but instead fairly represent all sides."

They saw the Nupedia project as turning objectivist theory into practice; the theory would be the guiding principle to pull it together.

Sanger was determined that even with an open source spirit, Nupedia, like traditional encyclopedias, would require both "management by experts and an unusually rigorous process." Sanger and Wales both saw this as a logical step, as nothing so far in the history of the field informed them otherwise.

As work started in February 2000, Sanger started to draft the operating principles of Nupedia. It would use email correspondence to communicate with volunteers, and he would tap his years of connections in academia and the online world to find them. The idea was to attract a core set of Ph.D.s, professors, and highly experienced professionals to be contributors and editors.

The Nupedians

Ruth Ifcher cannot remember exactly when she first learned of Nupedia, but one thing she does remember—it was Sanger's infectious enthusiasm that hooked her on the project. A computer programmer by day, and a former copy editor and holder of several higher degrees, Ifcher was someone Sanger depended on in his early editorial team.

While Sanger as editor in chief was the sole paid position in Nupedia's ranks, Ifcher agreed to volunteeer as chief copy editor. Even though she was located on the other side of the country in New York, she and Sanger worked closely on Nupedia's early policies and working procedures. She was one of the early ones who signed up for high positions in the newly formed Nupedia Advisory Board to provide direction.

Sanger was given broad authority to set up Nupedia's working process and imagined a tiered structure, combining his vision of an academic quality process with tapping the use of volunteers on the Internet. Among the roles he proposed were writers, editors, and copy editors. In Sanger's vision, he still believed in a top-down structure to manage quality:

> Editors assign topics to writers and formulate any necessary policy and direction with respect to their own categories, though they are expected to follow and enforce general Nupedia policy guidelines.[10]

(It must be noted: This is quite different from the concept of a generic "editor" in Wikipedia, which refers to any individual, even an anonymous one, who simply modifies a page. When talking about Nupedia, "editors" are ones who have been vetted and have extra authority over mere "writers.")

His academic roots compelled Sanger to insist on one rigid requirement for his editors: a pedigree. "We wish editors to be true experts in their fields and (with few exceptions) possess Ph.D.s.," read the Nupedia policy. Editors, in Nupedia's parlance, were "in charge of particular subject matters."

Editors meeting the Ph.D. requirement still had to have some formal way of proving their status, usually by reputation in academic circles or publishing record. Sometimes it wasn't so easy. Building an "academically respectable" encyclopedia would have to rely on bona fides, but when information was lacking, other means were needed. In one case, where the person in question had no Internet Web page as proof, he was asked to fax a copy of his degree to Sanger.

This was something Sanger wanted to emphasize. While the authors were drawn from anyone who wanted to apply, they were subject to review and approval:

> The category editor then decides whether to assign you the article topic (step one). The editor may, in some cases, ask what qualifications you have to write on the article, and therefore it would be a good idea to have completed your member profile. (This is private information.)[11]

The first thing the Nupedia Advisory Board did, by the summer of 2000, after email discussion, was to settle upon a seven-step process for all articles. This consisted of:

1. Assignment
2. Finding a lead reviewer
3. Lead review
4. Open review
5. Lead copyediting
6. Open copyediting
7. Final approval and markup

Before the Nupedia process even started, volunteers were grouped into their subject areas. Three or more people were necessary to make an "active" subject.

Of the dozen or so subject areas active at any one time, biology became known as the deepest and strongest in Nupedia, because of the preponderance of scientists and academics on the Internet.

For an article to start to run the gauntlet, someone first had to create a proposal with a description of one hundred words or less. After review, editors in the proper subject area would hopefully approve the proposal for assignment. The author would then draft the article, whereupon a volunteer editor acting as lead reviewer would review the content and accuracy.

The lead reviewer was responsible for getting the basic information to a level the reviewer was happy with, or in extreme cases the article could be rejected altogether. Correspondence between the reviewer and the author was mostly done by email, though some parts were done via a Web site. Members could not view the articles in the peer review process. Until the material was approved, it was a closed loop between the reviewer and the author.

When the lead reviewer was satisfied, the article was then brought to open peer review, where every member of the community was allowed to comment on it and appropriate modifications would be made.

The entire process to this point would take roughly two weeks, before Ifcher, as lead copy editor, would get her hands on the article. If it got this far in the process, it was probably going to go through all the way. "Very few things were aborted in the middle," she recalls.

With the subject's content and accuracy approved, Ifcher would assign two people to the copyediting task. One would do the heavy lifting of the major copy-edit, to correct footnotes, grammar, punctuation, and style. The second would look over the work of the first. The procedure specifically called for finding folks with a fresh angle on the article's subject.

Concerning copy editor selection, Ifcher wanted diversity: "You were encouraged to pick articles in fields you were not familiar with, on purpose, to make sure the article was clear." The Nupedians made it a goal to create articles a college student could understand if the student had no background in the subject.

The final community step was the open copyedit, when everyone in the community could make final comments and propose fixes. This was the absolute last chance for anyone to raise problems or objections. In general, the copy editor, rather than the author, would answer comments and in the best-case scenario, every change would then be cleared and approved by the author.

The final stage overall was for formal mark-up by the editorial staff to make the article of publishing quality, containing the right headings, spacing, and so on. Sanger would have the final approval and, at last, a Nupedia article would be born.

In September 2000, the first article to completely make it through this process was called "atonality" by author Christoph Hust, a German music scholar of the Institut der Johannes Gutenberg–Universität. It read:

ATONALITY BY CHRISTOPH HUST

Atonality means the absence of a tonal center as the basis for the whole or part of a piece of music. This was one of the radical innovations in music around the second decade of the twentieth century. More specifically, the term is used to describe works that are neither tonally-centered nor use the 12-tone or dodecaphonic [doh"-dek-&-fon'-ik] method of organizing pitch. Although atonality is primarily associated with the composers of the second Viennese School, namely Alban Berg, Arnold Schoenberg [shoen'-beRg], and Anton Webern [vay'-beRn], it was also used by other composers such as the Austrian Josef Matthias [yoh'-zef maa"-tee'-aas] Hauer, the American Charles Edward Ives, the Soviet composers Arthur Lourié and Nikolay Roslavets, and the Pole Józef Koffler. In France, Charles Koechlin's work approached an atonal style as well.

At the end of the article were fourteen footnotes, twenty-seven references for further reading, and a discography reference of recordings. Telltale signs of the rigorous Nupedia process could be found at the bottom of the article:

Posted 2000-09-11; reviewed and approved by the Music group; editor, G. B. Lane; lead reviewer, Edward (Ted) McIrvine; lead copyeditors, Bruce Hamilton and Ruth Ifcher.

The bar for creating an article was set quite high. It was a system managed by elites that demanded high qualifications and a rigorous fixed procedure. As a result, it created a big bottleneck.

"The problem was it took forever for an article to get through," Ifcher recalls with frustration. "The first year, if we produced twelve articles, I'd be surprised."

Sanger seems to remember about two dozen articles with 150 left in draft stage. But all estimates for that first year were measured in "tens" of finished articles. The process was not scaling. They had a very rigorously engineered solution, and it was not clear how to speed it up.

Sanger tried to move away from the "clunky mailing list system" they used for collaboration and turn to a Web-based solution. In the fall of 2000, Nupedia hired a programmer to write custom computer code to manage the encyclopedia's complex process online.

But it proved to be no better than the old method. "By the time the web-based system was ready . . . it had become obvious to Jimmy and me that the seven-step editorial process would move too slowly, even when managed on the web," lamented the editor in chief.[12]

In retrospect, Sanger realized that having both a high bar for contributors and a rigorous process provided a double obstacle. It simply hindered creating the necessary critical mass. "As it turned out, a clear mistake of mine and others was to assume that such a complicated system would be navigated patiently by many volunteers, even if they had clear enough instructions. That is a mistake I doubt anyone designing volunteer content creation systems will make again."

Perhaps the death knell was when one of the founders himself lost faith in the project. Wales wanted to try his hand at what he had funded and took up writing in his area of expertise—he started to pen an article for Nupedia on options-pricing theory, a field he had studied as a Ph.D. student.

The prospect of his work being sent to finance professors for review was the "aha" moment for him. "I had been out of academia for several years. It was intimidating; it felt like homework."[13]

As the first year was coming to a close, it was clear that the process was not going to scale up in a practical manner. Even a tenfold increase in volunteers would not provide a sustainable return for Bomis's time and money. Wales and Sanger were searching for solutions. Bomis partner Tim Shell was glad at the very least that "they were looking for ways to speed it up rather than to shut it down."

Nupedia was too much process, too little volunteer output, and not enough money. And it most certainly wasn't fun.

Something had to change.

WIKI ORIGINS

"Given enough eyeballs, all bugs are shallow."
—*Eric S. Raymond (1998)*

"Our knowledge is the amassed thought and experience of innumerable minds."
—*Ralph Waldo Emerson*

Nupedia was at a standstill at the end of 2000, even though it had gathered a sizeable set of volunteers. Larry and Jimmy knew their concept
was not working, because after a year's worth of work, all the finished
articles bound together would have produced only a booklet. Still believing the
project had to be centrally edited, they were stuck for new ideas.

What the world would come to know as Wikipedia would start just one month
later, but not without some controversy.

Sanger was still new to San Diego, having moved there in February 2000. He
spent that year trying to get Nupedia on track by recruiting Internet volunteers
and ushering articles through the site's rigorous seven-step process. As 2001
started, he was looking for ways to speed things along.

An old friend of his, Ben Kovitz, was arriving in town to take up a job in the
area. Kovitz was a computer programmer Sanger had known since the 1990s,
from their days on Internet mailing lists about philosophy—a common bond

among Sanger, Wales, and many Nupedians. On January 2, 2001, they met up in Pacific Beach in San Diego. At a small Mexican taco house not far from the Bomis office, they caught up on "jobs, techie stuff, and philosophy," Sanger recalls.

While commiserating over Nupedia's difficulties, Kovitz mentioned that he had come across something that might be of interest. Called WikiWikiWeb, it was a Web site built with a simple idea—it allowed anyone to directly edit any page at any time. No special software was needed, and no log-in or password was required. Anyone could alter content on a page, and changes would immediately be recorded. It was a way to collaborate—a way for many people to edit the same documents—and it was extremely easy to use.

Normally, editing Web pages is a complex operation. It requires a tedious cycle of copying the page to your computer, modifying the HTML code of the document, then uploading the changes to the Web server with a file transfer program. It's cumbersome enough that only a fraction of Internet users ever engaged in the authoring of Web pages from scratch.

WikiWikiWeb was different because all the changes happened simply by pressing an "edit" button, and all editing took place within the user's Web browser with a very simple "markup" language to make links within the Web site and to other places on the Internet. This new WikiWikiWeb existed in only a handful of places. The most notable site was created by its inventor, a computer programmer named Ward Cunningham, based in Portland, Oregon.

On the face of it, it was a pretty crazy idea: Open up an entire Web site where anyone, even strangers, could modify any page. The conventional wisdom about Internet safety was that everything had to be locked down. Quality meant being selective and restricting who could participate in editing. But WikiWikiWeb completely tore down this barrier to entry, and encouraged people to create or change information, immediately.

After discussing it for an hour with Kovitz, Sanger thought it was a revelation: "Instantly I was considering whether wiki would work as a more open and simple editorial system for a free, collaborative encyclopedia, and it seemed exactly right."

Sanger was so excited about the idea, the two raced back to his apartment and called Wales with the prospect of using it in Nupedia. Not able to reach him on the phone, Sanger left a voice-mail message. Sanger and Kovitz hung around until Wales called back within an hour, and they talked it over.

"After about a fifteen-minute conversation, Larry had a big smile on his face," says Kovitz. "Larry said that he felt very optimistic that the idea would proceed, and that Jimbo was quite open to it." By the next morning, Sanger had written up a proposal to use a wiki system to solve the problems they were having with collaboration and generating articles at Nupedia.

This is where the Wikipedia history starts to diverge. Each founder claims to have stumbled across Ward Cunningham's creation through a different channel. Wales says he was told of the same wiki concept by fellow Bomis employee Jeremy Rosenfeld. Which story to believe has been a lasting source of consternation between Wales and Sanger in recent years. The earliest press releases and announcements from Bomis on the subject attribute the idea of applying wikis to Sanger. And there is no dispute that it was Sanger who came up with the name Wikipedia, "a silly name for what was at first a very silly project."

In the end, however Wales and Sanger came upon it, it was clear that, through Wikipedia, Ward Cunningham's simple creation was going to make a big mark on the world, far beyond what he'd expected.

Ward's Start

How do people become smart?

It's a strange question, but it's driven Ward Cunningham his whole life. He's always been interested in smart people, and finding how they become that way has defined his career.

The congenial Indiana native with a laid-back Midwestern manner grew up in an era before the Internet, but remembers the next-best communications medium of that era—amateur ham radio. Fascinated by the creativity of the community that had gathered on the airwaves, Cunningham would listen into the night to conversations from all over the United States. Ham radio is a peculiar technology, where the communication waves can be repeated to larger areas, or even be "reflected" off objects such as Earth's moon. As a result, ham radio operators can talk to others around the world.

It was the 1960s and Friday nights often had Cunningham at his radio. One evening, music was aired on a channel for about fifteen seconds, a no-no according to United States FCC rules forbidding such use of the radio spectrum. Ham operators staged a two-hour mock trial to find the perpetrator, which provided "spontaneous entertainment" for Cunningham. Like many other Internet pioneers, this early form of amateur radio "online culture" would make a lasting impact on him.

Cunningham was able to parlay that love for communication gadgets into computers when his high school in Highland, Indiana, started a special program to provide student access to mainframe computers at the Illinois Institute of Technology. A friendly math teacher at the high school let the young student use the expensive hardware through a paper-based Teletype during his free period. And thus Cunningham was introduced to the world of computing in 1966, and he was hooked.

After high school he wound up at Purdue University, and in 1968 he had access to the modern tools of the digital age. When he finished his master's degree in computer science, he wasn't sure what to do next. Computing had been a passion and a hobby, but now it was a matter of employment. At his graduation in 1978, the personal computer was on the cusp of changing the world. Fate would pair him up with a tech firm called Tektronix, well known in the electronics industry as the leader in making instruments for testing other computer components. The most famous was perhaps the oscilloscope, the green screens that displayed wavy sinusoidal signals bouncing around a circular display.

As a fresh graduate, Cunningham joined the computer research laboratory Tek Labs and was hired to help them research how to organize their software projects. Being an engineer himself, he had some insight into how his peers thought. He firmly believed that developers of computer software were conservative. They needed to be shown successful examples to be convinced things could be done. "The only way an engineer would work is if they saw it work in another project," Cunningham says.

But sharing knowledge within corporations was not done particularly well, and especially not in the days before the Internet. In effect, Cunningham was looking for a way to document the people, ideas, and projects within the company, so people across the organization could share in that knowledge.

In his investigation for how to accomplish this sharing, Cunningham drew inspiration from a wide variety of sources one wouldn't immediately link to computer software, such as architect Christopher Alexander, noted museum designer Edwin Schlossberg, and cognitive linguistics professor George Lakoff.

In his book with Mark Johnson, *Metaphors We Live By*, Lakoff explains how humans give words meaning through metaphors, such as when we use spatial words like "high" and "low" to describe a person's mood. To Cunningham, Lakoff's concept resonated as a very powerful idea. In thinking about computers as the conduit for carrying messages around the Internet, he imagined metaphors spreading around and finding the right place on the Net to help. His entire quest was to find a system that supported this function, to create places to allow individuals to teach one another their metaphors.

After a decade thinking about this issue at Tektronix, Cunningham would finally discover a tool to help realize it. He happened across a brand-new software product from Apple Computer called HyperCard, which was given away for free with every Macintosh computer sold in 1987. Very quickly, people started to recognize it was something special. HyperCard was a revolutionary piece of software—it was the first easy way to make free-form hyperlinked content, allowing people to click on items on the screen to bring up other text or multimedia content. Unfortunately, Apple had no idea what a breakthrough product it had on its hands.

The idea of hypertext, or arbitrary linking among electronic documents, is usually dated back to 1945, when American scientist Vannevar Bush published "As We May Think" in the *Atlantic Monthly* magazine. He proposed a memex, a microfilm-based system of documents that would eventually provide inspiration for the World Wide Web. But the most prescient of his predictions was what he foresaw in hyperlinked information.

"Wholly new forms of encyclopedias will appear, ready made with a mesh of associative trails running through them, ready to be dropped into the memex and there amplified." He was basically describing what we know today as Web surfing. But given the vocabulary of the 1940s, he could only express the idea in the language of "microfilm." It's amusing to think of today's Internet activity happening through sheets of microfilm, but Bush was well ahead of his time on the implications of linking together information seamlessly.

As a tool to accomplish this memex function of linking and organizing data, HyperCard had a cult following, as it was easy to use, yet powerful. People could create an interlinked series of documents at the touch of a mouse. This was many years before the first Web browser was even conceived.

Fortunately, Cunningham had early access to HyperCard through a former Tektronix employee named Kent Beck, with whom he had worked. Beck had left to work for Apple Computer and happened to be in Oregon on a visit, and gave his old friend Ward something to see. "Kent Beck showed me HyperCard, which he first got his hands on after joining Apple. It was called WildCard then. I was blown away."[14]

In HyperCard, Cunningham saw a tool that could help him with his knowledge-sharing project. "I wanted something kind of irregular, something that didn't fit in rows and columns." HyperCard used the idea of a "stack" of virtual index cards, in which the user could easily create new cards, create links between them, and place content on them. Putting a picture, sound, or video onto a card was as easy as inserting it and dragging it around on the screen. You could also put virtual buttons on cards that could respond to clicks and other commands.

The brainchild of Apple programmer Bill Atkinson, HyperCard was originally given away for free in 1987 and became incredibly popular with seasoned computer programmers, novice users, and educational institutions. It was easy to understand, easy to program, and incredibly powerful for creating content. No programming experience was necessary, and even kids were getting into the action, creating their own "stacks" of fun content.

Ward got his hands on HyperCard and started a simple database of cards to store written text and diagrams. He started to see the "stack" grow with information about personnel, their experiences, and descriptions of their projects. It became a multimedia scrapbook of company practices.

But there was something Ward didn't like about HyperCard. It was too cumbersome to create new cards and link to them. In the middle of his thinking process, the technical clicks and keystrokes of getting ideas organized in HyperCard got in the way.

To make links between cards, you would bring up the first card, then go to the destination card and tell HyperCard to make a button leading there, then go back to the original card and drop the new button in place.

"In those three simple steps you would have a hyperlink," recalled Cunningham. "But the part I didn't like is you had to go to the card you wanted to end up, because I wanted to write about all these ideas and people and projects, that kind of had no boundary. There was always another idea, always another person. It was a big company. So there was not going to be any completeness. There was going to be this frontier where I was referring to people I hadn't described yet or to projects that I didn't know what they were."[15]

Even though the mechanics of creating new cards and links was simple and straightforward, it was still cumbersome. Even a slight interruption during the creative process meant ideas were lost, as the different steps were disrupting the free flow of thinking and writing.

Cunningham wanted a solution that was transparent and quick—something that wouldn't disrupt his stream of thought.

Because HyperCard was also programmable, he could write new computer code that could extend the functionality of the "stack" of cards beyond what Apple provided. Cunningham decided he could do something better. He created a box on each card into which the user could type a list of titles. Creating a link to a page was as simple as typing the new word or phrase into the list, such as "Project X" or "Joe Smith." Clicking on "Joe Smith" would bring up the card of that same name. You didn't have to manually create a link or even know if that card existed. You simply named the card you wanted, and it would transport you there.

But what if the card did not exist yet? Cunningham programmed the software so a beeping sound indicated a missing card. His innovation? A card could be created automatically simply by pressing and holding down the mouse button. This lingering "click-and-hold" action was programmed to tell HyperCard to create a new card automatically.

"And the effect was, it was just fun to do. You say 'I know something about that,' and you just jam your finger into that screen, with the aid of the mouse, and you made things. . . . Boom there it is, and you start typing." He was like a magician, creating cards on the fly with the long press of the mouse.

Browsing Collaborators

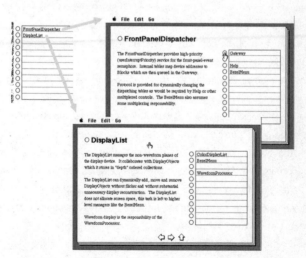

Click to browse a collaborator, press and hold to create and link a new collaborator card.

Reproduced with permission from Ward Cunningham

In creating this simple mechanism, Cunningham enabled individuals to get their thoughts and ideas into the stack in the quickest way possible. Around the hallways of Tektronix, people started to hear about Ward's fun hyperlinked experiment. He got more and more visitors.

"I heard you had that cool HyperCard thing," a colleague would say, appearing at Cunningham's office doorway.

Coworkers would sit in front of his boxy Macintosh II computer and wade through his stack of cards, adding and correcting things on this new fast tool, with nothing more than minutes of training. It was natural, fast, and addictive. "I couldn't get them out of my office.

"We'd get to poking through people and projects and so on when my guests would invariably say, 'that's not exactly right.' So we'd fix it right then and there. And we'd add a few missing links and go fix them too. The stack was captivating. We were often late for lunch."[16]

As Cunningham worked more with HyperCard, it became clear that he had come up with a fast and easy way of organizing this interlinked information. He described his creation as "densely linked," as having multiple paths to arrive at the same data, which made it a powerful tool. The problem was, it remained an island—the "stack" of linked information was stranded on that one computer. This was still the early days of the personal computer; networking was not something widely available.

Sitting in front of the computer and editing the stack was a potent demonstration of the capabilities of hypertext. But you still had to get that person seated in front of the computer. Growing Cunningham's stack of information still meant workmates had to visit his office. Physical movement of information by carrying a floppy disk, comically called "Sneakernet," as opposed to a real networked computing, didn't allow for real-time live collaboration.

Even though Ward knew he was onto something with his creation, it was a temporary dead end. The solution to Sneakernet would require some waiting. It would be another few years before connecting office computers with a network would become commonplace, and the Internet would not become widespread for another few years.

It also did not help that the Macintosh, and by extension HyperCard, was an unconventional choice for the workplace in the 1980s. Apple Computer was locked in a bitter struggle for the desktop computer market with the likes of Intel and Microsoft. While HyperCard was incredibly powerful and critically acclaimed, it was still considered a toy. There were good reasons for this label. HyperCard was designed around the original Macintosh black-and-white nine-inch screen, and was stuck with that small size for many years despite computer displays getting bigger and bigger.

HyperCard was also an odd product for Apple to manage. Because it was given away, something Apple's esteemed creator Bill Atkinson demanded, the company made no direct revenue from it. So while it became quite popular, it was hard for Apple, primarily a computer hardware company, to justify serious resources to develop it further.

The irony is that HyperCard was revolutionary and popular, with entire businesses based on its powerful capabilities, but Apple let it wither on the vine. In the 1980s, Apple was struggling to be relevant in a world with more conventional office productivity software from Microsoft, Novell, and Lotus. HyperCard didn't really fit into the picture.

But despite being ahead of its time, HyperCard and its legacy would have a profound impact on the development of the Web and wikis.

HyperCard's Inspirations

The Internet had been around since the early 1980s, as the TCP/IP networking standard had made it easy to patch together separate networks run by various research corporations and universities. But utilizing the Internet in the early days was not a user-friendly experience. You had to know how to use a "command line" interface to type in cryptic incantations to transfer files or pull information from other computers. And it most certainly did not have anything graphical or visually compelling for the beginner as we have with today's Web browsers.

Until 1990, the Internet was the domain of the geeks—a place for text-based electronic mail, message boards, and file transfers. It was highly biased toward the English language. The Internet's origins in U.S. military research meant there was a lack of standards for dealing with the coding of foreign languages. That made it especially deficient for non-Roman texts such as Arabic and Chinese.

The Internet was powerful in the hands of computer experts, but for pretty much everyone else, it was an unapproachable jumble of codes and procedures.

That all changed in 1990. Tim Berners-Lee, a scientist working at the CERN research lab in Switzerland, was looking for a way for scientists to more easily share documents and collaborate over the Internet. Even though he was not afraid of the Internet's technical side, he knew other scientists and researchers were. He wanted to make a system that was graphical in order to easily share documents.

Tim Berners-Lee used a computer that was the Ferrari of the techno-elite back then. And even though the NeXT computer is a faint memory today, like HyperCard, its impact went far beyond the units shipped. The NeXT cube was the "it" machine of that era. And it would play a pivotal role in the creation of the World Wide Web.

When Steve Jobs was forced out as the head of Apple Computer in 1987, he stayed in Silicon Valley and put his energies into a new start-up called NeXT. This was while Apple was still shipping computers with nine-inch screens and Microsoft's most advanced product was an anemic and stiff-looking Windows 2.0. The NeXT machine, on the other hand, launched in October 1988 and introduced pioneering features we're all used to now: a high-resolution "million pixel" display, a read/write optical drive, and a true multitasking operating system. And in classic Steve Jobs style, it was clad in a sexy all-black magnesium cube form that made it the envy of computer science departments around the world.

The NeXT megapixel grayscale computer display was its most stunning feature. What it lacked in color it made up for in fineness and texture. It was so large and sharp, folks compared it to reading on paper. This was no coincidence—it used PostScript, a special language from Adobe Systems usually reserved for high-end paper printers.

So when Berners-Lee was testing out his idea for a World Wide Web to share documents, he used his NeXT cube computer that was geared toward handling high-resolution documents. The first Web browser he ever built was for the NeXT machine, in February 1991. But he had much grander plans than simply creating a "browser" for reading, and in fact called his program a "browser-editor."

Not only did his program on the NeXT read and display Web pages, it could also alter them and save them. This was a function Berners-Lee had envisioned from the start—a read-write Web of information for sharing.

Given its rich and ambitious origins, it is then quite peculiar that the Web that became popular in the mid-1990s was known only for reading, browsing, and surfing. In the exuberance to push the reading experience, the "write" stuff, which was always meant to be part of the Web, was left behind as a cumbersome feature.

Perhaps Berners-Lee's most important innovation was standardizing how to identify resources located on the Internet. When Rick Gates created the Internet

Hunt contest in 1992, there was a jumble of different "protocols" or methods to access information. In that era before the existence of the World Wide Web, computer servers doled out information using a mix of systems, requiring different text-based and file transfer tools. Until Berners-Lee came along, there was no simple standard way to describe how to access these information sources. The breakthrough came with his creation of the URL, or Uniform Resource Locator. Today, most people know URLs as something like this:

http://www.foo.com/bar/baz.html

The "http" is the Hypertext Transfer Protocol Berners-Lee created for Web pages. After the double slashes was the Internet name or address where the computer is located. The rest of the URL describes the exact path or location on the server for finding documents, images, or other data. Other URLs had protocols such as "ftp" for File Transfer Protocol, or the more obscure "gopher" or "wais" protocols. Today, Berners-Lee's "http" for the World Wide Web dominates for all types of data.

It seems like a simple concept, but the breakthrough allowed any information source to be pinpointed on the Internet using just one line.

While the first Web browser from Tim Berners-Lee gained notoriety, there was a problem. The sexy features of the NeXT were not cheap. They offered only one model, and few folks could afford a $6,500 NeXT cube. Even NeXT's follow-on budget version, the NeXT "slab," was $4,995. It was hardly a computer for the masses.

A Web Browser

If we look under the hood of a Web browser, we see that it's a pretty simple piece of software—it transfers a Web page from a computer on the Internet, known as a server; reads through the contents for images, sound, or other components; and downloads each of those elements. Those parts are then assembled into a page and displayed to the user browsing the Internet.

The language of Web pages consists of computer code called Hypertext Markup Language, or HTML. It's somewhat human readable, with special "markup" used for features on the page—italic, bold, images, and other formatting. But it wasn't meant for human consumption and can become quite cumbersome to read and edit.

The Web became successful because it was an open standard—no one company controlled the specification for it, and it was maintained by a consortium led by Tim Berners-Lee. Since the Web was not tied to one computer company or encumbered by patents, HTML could be generated and displayed by anyone who had the interest and skill to write a program to translate the codes to the computer screen.

Most everything in HyperCard mapped quite well to HTML—text, italics, bold, images, and sounds. And while Ward Cunningham was finding HyperCard easy to use and to derive a prototype from, someone else was also discovering that HyperCard was useful.

Viola

Shipping HyperCard for free on Macs inspired a whole generation of programmers with the power of hypermedia, even if it didn't generate any significant revenue for Apple. In 1989, University of California at Berkeley student Pei-Yan Wei played around with HyperCard and was impressed with Apple's giveaway tool. "HyperCard was very compelling back then, you know graphically, this hyperlink thing, it was just not very global and it only worked on Mac . . . and I didn't even have a Mac."

Wei liked the program so much he replicated it and created a version that ran on the system that was standard for tech types of that era—a UNIX workstation running in the X Windows graphical environment. Wei called it Viola, and when released in 1991, it had all the same type of functions as HyperCard—hypertext at first, and eventually hypermedia, clickable pictures, and multimedia elements.

The university setting allowed Wei to experience the Internet earlier than most. He of course thought of extending Viola not just to link to other cards in the same stack, but to other places on the Internet. Just before creating a "networked hypertext" system, he ran across Tim Berners-Lee's announcement explaining an implementation of a World Wide Web and standardizing everything around something called a URL, or Uniform Resource Locator. It was exactly what Wei was looking for, and he immediately started adapting Viola into what would become ViolaWWW, an Internet-capable hypertext system.

"The URL was very, very clever, it was perfectly what I needed," said Wei. He contacted Berners-Lee about writing a Web browser himself and got a positive response. Four days later, Wei emerged and announced to the World Wide Web community that he had made ViolaWWW.[17]

HyperCard was a product ahead of its time. And even though Apple stopped development and support for it, HyperCard's influence would be much more profound. Its visual interface and hyperlinking were the inspiration for the first popular Web browser, and even twenty years later, after a dot-com boom and bust, people are still trying to replicate the simplicity and power of HyperCard.

HyperCard Revisited

In September 1987, HyperCard intrigued Cunningham, but his work at Tektronix would lead him to study how people design software, and he started to write about something called "pattern languages." Until then, developing software was still considered a complicated and cumbersome task—lots of complexities and intricacies that relied on a guru programmer to work out.

But Ward and others in the software world were starting to recognize that proven methods were reused over and over by engineers. The ability to use these so-called design patterns quickly and reliably was valuable. So the challenge was to spread the individual knowledge in people's heads across different teams and programmers.

There was already a rich tradition in the computer science hacker culture to share and distribute expertise. But the mechanisms to do so just were not easy. That's when Ward remembered his HyperCard project. Even though his "stack" of cards hadn't gone any further than being a cute experiment on one computer, he remembered how empowering it was. As each person sat in front of the computer, gleaned the information, and added content, their eyes lit up. The knowledge base grew, making it more useful for the next person. He would have to wait just a bit longer for the means to free the knowledge from that box.

By November 1991, Ward had left Tektronix, but he stayed in the Portland, Oregon, area, which he would come to call his long-term home. It was a welcoming community to him and his wife, Karen, and they found the lifestyle in sync with both their personalities. They had met as graduate students at Purdue, when they both took the same highly theoretical "advanced compiler" class in computer science. Together, they had the expertise to put Ward's ideas into practice and started a computer programming consulting company named Cunningham & Cunningham.

As Cunningham & Cunningham were applying their expertise to companies, something phenomenal was happening—the Internet that Ward was already familiar with was migrating from universities, military bases, and research labs to the masses. Ward saw what the Internet could do when finally brought out of the university domain, and got to work to put "collaboration" into his easy-to-use tool.

In 1994, Ward started to engineer an Internet version of his HyperCard experiment that he worked on at Tektronix. Ward would come to utilize something called Perl to create a prototype. Perl was one of the first widely recognized curious creations of the Internet that quickly became a Swiss Army knife of the dot-com industry. Perl is an acronym for what was originally the "Practical Extraction and Reporting Language"—a tool to glean numbers and create reports from volumes of numerical or text data. But it was so useful, people starting adding more features to the language to do more things. And as an open source program, it grew rapidly, as people shared the new features with the rest of the Perl users in the world.

The most interesting aspect of Perl was that it was a computer "scripting" language, meaning it could be used to quickly create a proof of concept. In contrast to the hammer and chisel of normal computer programming languages, using Perl was like using clay—it might not hold up well long-term or perform the best, but it was incredibly fast to test out ideas and make quick changes.

So with a few hundred lines of Perl code, Ward was able to create a site where it was easy to edit the very pages people were browsing. It sounds rather dangerous, but if it was managed correctly, the worst thing the user could do was mess up that one page, and not inflict any permanent damage to the computer system. In the early 1990s the vast majority of Web servers ran on the heavy-duty UNIX operating system. Popular versions of UNIX came from Sun Microsystems, Hewlett-Packard, and IBM, but the Linux operating system was getting increasingly popular. The Web "server" software they ran during that time was something called "httpd" or HTTP daemon, a program that ran all the time and served up Web pages.

Cunningham was getting the fundamentals down, but he was looking for a name. For that, he would think back to 1982, when he and Karen were on their honeymoon trip to Hawaii. He recalled sidling up to the counter at the airport, to ask how to travel between airport terminals. When the agent said to take the "*wiki wiki*," Ward did a double double take. "I asked for that direction to be

Andrew Laing

repeated three or four times until the airline representative took the time to define the word wiki for me."[18]

Wiki was the Hawaiian word for "quick" with *wiki wiki* meaning "super quick." The airport's Wiki Wiki bus, a Chance RT-52 shuttle bus to be precise, was their quick transport between terminals.

"I did pick up a book about the [Hawaiian] language before my return home. I learned many things from this, but wiki wiki is the word that sticks the most." Cunningham had found the perfect word for his new creation. "I wanted an unusual word to name what was an unusual technology."

He wanted editing text on a wiki page to be simple. To make something italic, you could type in two single quotes, and to make a new paragraph you typed in two returns. Making a link to another page was done by putting two CapitalLetters in a single word. On a Web page, any word showing up in ThatFormat would automatically link to another Web page with that name.

The "wiki markup" that read like this:

Please ''try'' to assemble a TodoList

displayed like this on the Web browser:

Please *try* to assemble a <u>TodoList</u>

Pushing words together with double capital letters was a bit unusual, and surely made grammarians cringe. But Ward wanted to get people thinking, typing, and linking quickly, without having to learn fancy codes or worry about how to create Web pages.

"I needed some way to make a link, and then got the idea of actually taking characters out, so the markup size was negative," meaning you actually typed fewer keys to make a link. "I said, 'Oh yeah, that's good.'"

Ward's curious creation of a HumpintheMiddle would affectionately become known as CamelCase. For the tech-savvy folks who first experienced Ward's wiki, it was rather familiar—it closely mirrored the conventions used for keywords in computer programming. In time, CamelCase would become quite commonplace even in the commercial world. YouTube, MySpace, LiveJournal, and other arbitrary mixes of upper- and lowercase have become part of the dot-com lexicon.

On March 25, 1995, Cunningham launched his WikiWikiWeb creation on c2 .com, and invited folks to visit. More importantly, he asked people to edit and contribute to the site what they knew about programming and software engineering. They would not need an account or password, which was quite odd even for computer veterans.

There would be no gatekeeper, no central editor to submit to. Ward firmly believed that wikis would work because, "People are generally good."

The wiki quickly started to grow, as folks started adding their experiences and recommendations to the site. Tracking what was going on would have been impossible without some way of learning what was changing or being added. One of Cunningham's innovations was the Recent Changes page, a running log of every change in the site. In one glance, you could see who was doing what.

- <u>UsingWikiInEducation</u> at 3:22 pm (3 <u>changes</u>)......<u>HelmutLeitner</u>
  new page
- <u>StewartMader</u> at 3:19 pm (3 <u>changes</u>)......<u>HelmutLeitner</u>
  new page
- <u>WikiPatternsBook</u> at 3:15 pm (1 <u>change</u>)......<u>Helmut Leitner</u>
  new book wiki & patterns
- <u>DanPupek</u> at 5:02 am (2 <u>changes</u>)......166-27-62-86.digitalskys.com
  Added my website and new homepage URL

"There had to be a public sense of what we were talking about, and where people's interest were," he recalls. "And that's when I decided we needed Recent Changes. It would serve the need of showing people where we were working."

Even more importantly, on Ward's wiki every version of every page was saved, providing a complete trail of changes and, in effect, the ability to easily inspect or undo any edit. People weren't afraid of trying to edit the wiki, because nothing was ever permanently lost or destroyed. Pages could be resurrected and reverted back to their original state.

Finally, after eight years of waiting, he had an easy to edit, networked, collaborative resource that people could share in creating.

Cunningham's WikiWikiWeb (more affectionately known as Ward's Wiki at http://c2.com/cgi/wiki) became a curiosity and a central location for programmers interested in patterns in computer code. He would later dub it the Portland Pattern Repository, as it allowed people to individually contribute to it.

WikiWikiWeb became popular not just for the computer programming knowledge that accumulated, but also because of the wiki community that arose from it. One of the folks who discovered this was Sunir Shah, who described his first experience:

> While searching for information on Design Patterns, I stumbled onto WikiWikiWeb. At first I dismissed it, but it was only a matter of time before I found the next online community to suck me in wholesale. It was an amazing conception: the web with write permissions, just like Tim Berners-Lee always wanted. It was stable. It was high signal. It was great.[19]

People interested in the "wiki culture" came to observe what was going on but found that Ward's Wiki wanted to keep its focus on pattern programming and that there was tension among users. Shah proposed a separate endeavor altogether:

> As readership/contributors went up, quality went down. Flame wars ensued. Meta-wiki discussions about the nature of Wiki itself consumed the community. I did what I thought was natural: with the help of Clifford Adams, I precipitated the formation of a separate wiki, MeatballWiki, precisely to talk about meta issues of online community. . . .

I'm going to build a community. Not only that, a community that builds communities. And damn us if we don't change the world.

Shah spawned the MeatballWiki as a "friendly fork" of WikiWikiWeb, as a way to create a specific wiki community to discuss online community and culture.

MeatballWiki would prove to be instrumental in documenting online practices and, specifically, the new emerging wiki culture. Shah saw MeatballWiki as unique among other technology-oriented groups. "What differentiates Meatball-Wiki from many online meta-communities is that participants spend much of their time talking about sociology rather than technology, and when they do talk about technology, they do so in a social context." It would prove later to be a rich resource for Wikipedia, as that nascent community started to run into issues that MeatballWiki had documented and discussed at length.

One of the folks who stumbled across the new WikiWikiWeb creation was Ben Kovitz, who was working as a programmer at the time.

Remember him? He would provide the lifeline to Nupedia.

WIKI INTRODUCED

"Every artist was first an amateur."
— *Ralph Waldo Emerson*

"History is too serious to be left to historians."
— *Ian Macleod*

After both Larry Sanger and Jimmy Wales found out about WikiWikiWeb software and its use for collaboration, both were keen on it helping kick-start Nupedia's lackluster pace. Nupedia was simply not working, because people were not collaborating efficiently and articles were not being generated fast enough. The wiki software might just get existing Nupedians to work better, while also allowing more participants from the outside world.

On January 10, 2001, Wales installed the same wiki software that Ben Kovitz described at the time—a "script" called UseModWiki that ran on a Web server.

Surprisingly, it was not a complex software system. UseModWiki was a simple program that did just the most basic things for a wiki Web site. By merely placing the program file on the Web server, you immediately created a fully functioning environment where anyone could edit any page. Pages could be created very easily and stored as simple files on the server.

The provenance of UseModWiki is a classic example of how open source software works—building something better on top of other people's work and releasing for more improvement. UseModWiki traces its heritage back to Ward's original wiki software through many intermediate modifications:

Clifford Adams started developing UseModWiki in 1999 for his Usenet Moderation Project (Usemod).

UseModWiki was based on the code of AtisWiki 0.3 by Markus Denker.

AtisWiki was based on CvWiki by Peter Merel.

CvWiki was based on Wiki Base, the wiki engine of the WikiWikiWeb by Ward Cunningham.

Just like Ward's original wiki, UseModWiki was meant to be quick and easy to learn. Anyone could edit any page by simply clicking on the edit button. Creating a username and logging in were entirely optional. As for making the page look more interesting, bold text could be created by placing three single quotes around a word; italics by putting two single quotes:

'''Bold text'''
''Italic text''

The magic of creating a link to another page was performed by using Camel-Case, by removing spaces and "pressing" words together. A small letter followed immediately by a capital letter would be interpreted as a link word. If the Use-ModWiki software saw this, it would create a link automatically to a page of that name. This was the easy-to-use, "accidental linking" that Cunningham liked. If the page did not exist, there would be a question mark next to the name, indicating that clicking on it would create the page.

For programmers, CamelCase was an acceptable shorthand, but for the kind of contributors writing a credible encyclopedia, it was ghastly. Kovitz recalled how the CamelCase word abominations made the academic, exacting editor in chief Larry Sanger "cringe."

Despite the wiki project's tech roots, Sanger and Wales launched it knowing it was an experiment, even with the bizarre CamelCase. But it wasn't simply a bit odd. There were real practical problems. While it's quite obvious CamelCase works fine for articles like AlbertEinstein, it required Nupedians to be imaginative for article names that were short. For one-word articles, funny-looking titles like NepTune and MatheMatics started to crop up. The CamelCase titles for even shorter articles looked more ridiculous, like ApE or EgG, but it was the only solution with the UseModWiki software, out of the box.

The wiki experiment was done under the auspices of the Nupedia project and was originally meant as a development proving ground for Nupedia. Sanger made an announcement to the Nupedia mailing list, called Nupedia-L, with the title "Let's make a wiki":

> No, this is not an indecent proposal. It's an idea to add a little feature to Nupedia. Jimmy Wales thinks that many people might find the idea objectionable, but I think not.
>
> . . . What it means is a VERY open, VERY publicly-editable series of web pages. For example, I can start a page called EpistemicCircularity and write anything I want in it. Anyone else (yes, absolutely anyone else) can come along and make absolutely any changes to it that he wants to.
>
> (The editing interface is very simple; anyone intelligent enough to write or edit a Nupedia article will be able to figure it out without any trouble.) On the page I create, I can link to any other pages, and of course anyone can link to mine. The project is billed and pursued as a public resource. There are a few announced suggestions or rules. The concept actually seems to work well, as you can see here with the original wiki:
>
> http://c2.com/cgi/wiki
>
> Links are indicated by using CapitalizedWordsBunchedTogether LikeThis.
>
> If a wiki page exists, the word is underlined; if not, there is a question mark after the word, which is clickable, and which anyone can use to go and write something about the topic.[20]

After hearing positive feedback, later that day Sanger announced to the mailing list

> Here's the URL for Nupedia's wiki:
>
> http://www.nupedia.com/cgi-bin/wiki.pl?NupediaWikiHomePage

Told you we could make it fast. It hasn't yet been linked from the website, so if you're very concerned that we're going to make utter jackasses of ourselves and you want to stop us from doing this, speak up! :-)

Larry

Nupedians started to trickle in to try the new creation. At first it looked like the wiki experiment would be just the right thing to help Nupedians to generate more content. But this didn't last long.

Whether it was the offputting CamelCase, or the wiki's radical inclusiveness, allowing anyone into the inner circle of creating encyclopedia articles, the Nupedians generally didn't like the new wiki project. Sanger saw that his elite editors were not happy sharing their project with the masses. "They (some of them) evidently thought that a wiki could not resemble an encyclopedia at all, that it would be too informal and unstructured."

After vigorous complaints from the Nupedia advisory board, just one week after the wiki project began, it would have to be spun off into its own parallel project. Even after the split, Wikipedia was still viewed as simply a breeding ground for content to be eventually moved into the commercial Nupedia. It was launched as Wikipedia.com on January 15, 2001, and Sanger took to promoting it in the mailing lists and Internet forums.

The first article to be created on the new Wikipedia.com was about the letter "U"—the origins, history, and significance of the twenty-first letter of the English alphabet. But how do you apply CamelCase to a single letter? They settled on the bizarre convention, naming it "UuU"—which contained consecutive lowercase and uppercase letters to indicate a CamelCase link for the software. It was the simplest solution even if it was not pretty.

Articles started to take shape with the Nupedians who chose to help out, and by people who heard about Wikipedia from the mailing lists that Sanger posted to. Back then, the tools for tracking what was happening on the site were fairly primitive, but the most important tool was the Recent Changes page listing all edits in reverse chronological order. Each line read like an entry in a logbook:

* SunirShah at 13:32:34 (1 change) . . . . . SunirShah
   12:30am, January 23, 2001

* EnglishWikipedia at 08:06:38 (1 change) . . . . . BrianKeegan
* Update article number

Each entry contained the name of the page, the time of the edit, and the associated person making the edit, or the Internet address of the computer making the edit.

The irony was that "anonymous" editors who did not have a username and instead had their Internet protocol addresses recorded actually revealed quite a bit about themselves. This IP address provides the identification of a computer on the Net, and consists of four numbers (each up to 255) separated by dots (e.g., 128.59.192.114). One could usually figure out what country the IP address came from, and in many cases the city and company associated with it.

After a few weeks, legions of folks started to visit the site, and it was clear it was going to be more than just a small silly project. A spot check on January 30, 2001, saw 224 IP addresses as visitors to the site, and 4,871 accesses that day. Not bad for less than a month of operation.

Larry worked on both Nupedia and Wikipedia at the same time, though he was increasingly spending more time on Wikipedia, with its more chaotic and loose structure needing oversight. The pressures of this dual role were evident in the message that had to be posted to the Nupedia Web site:

> Please note: the editorial processes and policies of Wikipedia and Nupedia are totally separate; Nupedia editors and peer reviewers do not necessarily endorse the Wikipedia project, and Wikipedia contributors do not necessarily endorse the Nupedia project. Larry Sanger is working on both projects, as are a number of Nupedia members. The projects might eventually develop a very interesting symbiotic relationship. But nothing along those lines is official, and no changes are anticipated in the near future.

As more people came to the Wikipedia site and started to contribute, there was a pressing need for the editors to comment on and discuss each other's changes.

That's where there was a bit of a culture clash.

Ward's Wiki had been designed as a scratchpad for discussion and consensus, not for displaying "finished" work as with Wikipedia's encyclopedia articles.

The established wiki tradition held that people would engage in dialogue directly on the page, with all the scribbles and casual conversation visible. Later, someone would come to "refactor" or summarize and consolidate the viewpoints into the prose. This was clearly not a good model for writing an article that was expected to be coherent and readable at any given time. It would be like seeing all the editor's marks, pencil scratches, and Post-it notes all over a finished work.

Tim Shell, Jimmy Wales's original Bomis partner, who was active in the early days of Wikipedia, pointed this out on the mailing list within weeks of the project starting:

> If Wikipedia is to be an encyclopedia, then it probably is not appropriate to have threaded discussions on a subject page. See for example AlTruism, where one person gives a flame bait description of the concept, and numerous people then argue back about that description. If a discussion is appropriate, perhaps there should be a standard discussion page, as AltruismDiscussion or AltruismDebate, that is linked to from the subject page.

Editors familiar with the established wiki culture felt that discussions should stay on the page. It's a wiki after all, and that's how wikis are done. This led to serious discussion within the group about the nature of Wikipedia: Was it going to be a wiki, strictly adhering to the existing wiki culture and conventions? After all, many of the early contributors were attracted because of their familiarity with wikis. Or was Wikipedia simply launching with wiki software and then evolving its own norms for encyclopedia writing?

Fortunately, UseModWiki creator Clifford Adams was a subscriber to the Wikipedia mailing list, watching intently as Wikipedia started. He had no qualms about jumping in to help customize his program for Wikipedia's needs.

The use of CamelCase, while familiar to note-jotting techies, was entirely a bad fit for an encyclopedia shooting for accuracy and readability. "Someone unfamiliar with the local wiki conventions," Adams says, "might guess otherwise on another page and link to a separate 'DemoCracy' or even 'DeMocracy.' Ick."

Adams proposed a new "syntax" that he called free linking. Instead of writing links in CamelCase, this new convention would use double brackets around the words, as with [[George W. Bush]] or [[Ski]].

Out of the blue, he posted a note to the Wikipedia mailing list on January 27, saying he'd been watching the Wikipedia community struggle with CamelCase and had created a solution:

> To make a longish story short, I added code (about 150 new lines of Perl) to my development copy to allow (site-optional) "Free" linking within [[double brackets]]. You can use spaces, numbers, commas, dashes, and the period character in these kinds of links. Valid link names include [[George W. Bush]], [[China-Soviet Relations]], [[Physics]], [[music]], and [[Year 2000 bug]].

Adams did something unexpected for the academic community, but common in open source culture—release early and release often. Within weeks of its launch, one of the biggest annoyances of Wikipedia was resolved directly by the software's author. It was not because of monetary compensation or any formal request, but simply because the author was interested in solving it on his own time, and sharing it with others. It was the hacker ethos, and it had crossed from the domain of tech programmers into the world of encyclopedias.

At the end of the month, Wikipedia managed to accumulate an impressive six hundred or so articles. There were some missing pieces, certainly. It was still largely a text-only project, as there was no way to upload pictures to Wikipedia. Also, the so-called housecleaning chores, such as renaming, moving, or deleting articles, required someone with the master "administrator" password, something not many people were allowed access to.

Nevertheless, Wikipedia achieved more in weeks, by volume, than Nupedia had in one year. It was a profound message.

"Wikipedia has definitely taken [on] a life of its own; new people are arriving every day and the project seems to be getting only more popular. Long live Wikipedia!" announced Sanger. He also set a goal: "I predict 1,000 [articles] by February 15."

In fact, they hit it three days early.

Slashdotting

If there was ever a salon for the technical elite and a grand senate of the computing community, it was Slashdot.org. Started originally as a user-contributed news site, Slashdot boldly proclaims as its pedigree: "News for nerds. Stuff that matters." It lists significant technology stories in a blog format to foster discussion, but it started even before blogging became part of the Internet lexicon.

What makes Slashdot more than just a blog is its unique community formula. A handful of the site operators serve as editors, sifting through user submissions to post on their front page taken from important technology stories from other outlets. But the story is simply a starting point. The real interesting content comes from the community discussion that ensues. Slashdot has become so popular that discussions are overrun by hundreds and thousands of comments, some pure gold, but many more pure crap. How do you sift the good from the bad when there are thousands of comments each day?

Slashdot pioneered a way for self-policing the community with an innovative solution. In an era before the interactive and participatory Web 2.0 movement, Slashdot experimented with using something called meta-moderation. The system employed moderation techniques by tapping readers from time to time, not unlike the random marketing surveys found on many Web sites. These selected readers were asked to help rate the merit of individual comments. They were given five "moderation points" to dole out to comments they thought merited attention. As moderators, they could rate comments a number of ways, including positive "insightful" or "interesting" ratings, or negative ratings, such as "flame-bait," to flag disruptive comments that should be ignored.

Comments with more positive ratings bubbled to the top. This way, readers could browse the comments at levels ranging from -1 (reading everything) to 5 (where only the top rated comments would be shown).

As comments were rated up and down the scales, writers of those comments got more or fewer "karma" points, which became a tangible metric as an indication of social capital within the community. The Slashdot model worked very well, to the point where after a decade of operation, it still retains a large, high-quality community, able to keep the "signal" high and the "noise" low.

But the next step was more interesting. To guard against bogus "mod points" and gaming the system, other users were also tapped to "watch the watchers" by performing "meta-moderation." That is, users were asked to rate the ratings. Users were selected to view certain ratings at random without knowing who was involved in giving out the moderation points in the first place. In effect, it was an audit of the ratings being dished out.

The result was a community that could scale up to handle dozens of stories a day, deal with thousands of comments, yet maintain an extremely high signal-to-noise ratio because of legions of community members who participated in this so-called meta-moderation.

In fact, the discussion areas have likely usurped the stories as the centerpiece of the site. Articles have become a sort of MacGuffin—not particularly important in themselves, but they serve to drive an interesting conversation. In fact, diving directly into the conversation without bothering to read the original story is such a typical action, one of the most common exclamations by regulars is "RTFA"—long-standing Internet jargon for "Read the friggin article!" Conversations in Slashdot are laced with inside jokes, ranging from bad 1980s Yakov Smirnoff laments about Soviet Russia, to cherished *Simpsons* quotes like "I for one welcome our insect overlords," when talking about the risks of technology.

Slashdot gained an intense following in the technology crowd because of its high caliber of contributors. It was a lively community that grew in size, but maintained quality as well. Slashdot became the tech elite's peanut gallery and salon. If you won the hearts of Slashdot readers, you captured the in-crowd and gained extremely influential technology street cred.

While Slashdot's editing system was very different from Wikipedia's free-form system, it did provide an important seed. It was a tight community of readers and editors familiar with rating one another's work. They worked together to sift the good from the bad and to filter out disruptive behavior. The usefulness of Slashdot was entirely in the hands of the individuals who volunteered to do meta-moderation. It was like a community garden. People were stakeholders and invested their time and energy in preserving something special in their corner of the Internet.

When Slashdot editors reported on the launch of Wikipedia in January and February of 2001, it resonated. Their readers were introduced to a site that aspired to take the contribution of the masses, be it writing, editing, correcting, or sifting out junk. It was a perfect fit.

The first wave of editors from that tech community had such a great influence that Wikipedia has often been dubbed the "Encyclopedia That Slashdot Built."[21] As Wikipedia chugged along, it was to benefit greatly from the Slashdot veterans. To this day, pretty much any story about Wikipedia is treated favorably on Slashdot, with many of the users speaking knowledgeably about the project because they are themselves editors at Wikipedia.

Contributing the Meaning
of Everything

While the use of wiki software to form Wikipedia was a breakthrough in allowing anyone to edit any page at any time, the assembling of a reference work from distributed strangers is actually not new.

The venerable *Oxford English Dictionary* (*OED*), the history of which is masterfully documented by Simon Winchester in *The Meaning of Everything* and *The Professor and the Madman*, was in fact possible only through the soliciting of contributions, and the receipt of thousands of "slips" of paper, each with words and definitions found by readers and volunteers.

The *OED* didn't start out with such a grand title, and was first a project of the Philological Society in Great Britian, as a response to what they saw as the popular dictionaries of Noah Webster and Samuel Johnson not doing the "English language justice."[22] In 1857, it was started as the Unregistered Words Committee, and the job was to comb through all forms of media of the era (printed matter, song, spoken word) leading to the inventorying and cataloging of English words. The three founders, Chenevix Trench, Herbert Coleridge, and Frederick Furnivall, sent out a notice in November of that year: "AN APPEAL TO THE ENGLISH-SPEAKING AND ENGLISH-READING PUBLIC TO READ BOOKS AND MAKE EXTRACTS FOR THE PHILOLOGICAL SOCIETY'S NEW ENGLISH DICTIONARY." Specifically, it described the project thusly:

> Accordingly, in January 1859, the Society issued their Proposal for the publication of a New English Dictionary, in which the characteristics of the proposed work were explained, and an appeal made to the English and American public to assist in collecting the raw materials for the work, these materials consisting of quotations illustrating the use of English words by all writers of all ages and in all senses, each quotation being made on a uniform plan on a half-sheet of notepaper that they might in due course be arranged and classified alphabetically and significantly. This Appeal met with generous response: some hundreds of volunteers began to read books, make quotations and send in their slips to "sub-editors" who volunteered each to take charge of a letter or part of one, and by whom the slips were in turn further arranged, classified, and

to some extent used as the basis of definitions and skeleton schemes of the meanings of words in preparation for the Dictionary.[23]

The notice was sent to "bookshops and libraries across the English-speaking world" and, under the direction of Scottish lexicographer James Murray, saw its growth blossom. In 1879, Oxford University Press formally agreed to be publisher and employed Murray to take on the editorship. Slips sent in to the effort were filed away in pigeonholes at the Scriptorium, a corrugated metal building Mill Hill School erected specifically for the effort of sorting and housing the staff to work on the dictionary.

The *OED* story compares with the Wikipedia story in some interesting ways. First, discrete pigeonholes for slips was the best that could be fashioned as their primitive database before the electronic information age. Winchester described Murray's first custom oak arrangement as "six square holes high, nine across—giving him a total of 54 pigeon holes, with some 260 inches of linear space, that were thought sufficient to hold comfortably between 60,000 and 100,000 slips."[24] It's hard to imagine today dealing with that many items by hand. The Scriptorium handled so many slips of paper, up to 1,000 a day by post, that there was a special pillar-box erected by the city's post office just for the dictionary makers.

The acknowledgment, by name, of volunteers in the preface sections of the *OED* is akin to Wikipedia's edit history, where one can inspect who contributed to each article. Some Oxford contributors were professors, some royalty, but most were ordinary folks who answered the call. Winchester, in *The Professor and the Madman: A Tale of Murder, Insanity, and the Making of the Oxford English Dictionary*, tells the story of the "madman" William Chester Minor, a U.S. Civil War survivor whose "strange and erratic behavior" resulted in him shooting an "innocent working man" to death in the street in Lambeth. He was sent to Broadmoor asylum for criminal lunatics. He discovered the *OED* as a project around 1881, when he saw the "Appeal for Readers" in the library, and worked for the next twenty-one years contributing to the project, receiving notoriety as a contributor "second only to the contributions of Dr. Fitzedward Hall in enhancing our illustration of the literary history of individual words, phrases and constructions." Minor did something unusual in not just sending submissions, but having his own cataloging system such that the dictionary editors could send a postcard and "out the details flowed, in abundance and always with unerring accuracy."[25] Until Minor and Murray met in January 1891, no one working with the *OED* knew their prolific contributor was a madman and murderer housed at Broadmoor.

As we will see in later chapters, a common question of the wiki method is whether one can trust information created by strangers and people of dubious background. But the example of the *OED* shows that using contributors rather than original expert scholarship is not a new phenomenon, and that projects built as a compendium of primary sources are well suited for harnessing the power of distributed volunteers.

The GFDL

Just before Wales and Sanger created Wikipedia, they happened to adopt a new license covering its content. Originally Nupedia used the Nupedia Open Content License, which allowed people to copy and modify content. However, with that license Bomis, Inc., was still the legal copyright holder.

In January 2001, after some exchange of emails with Richard Stallman, Jimmy Wales was convinced to move to the GNU Free Documentation License (GFDL). This was similar to Stallman's GNU General Public License, but it applied to written content, such as computer documentation. This meant that Bomis would no longer be the ultimate copyright holder for the site's content.

The GFDL at its core shared the same free and also "viral" property of the GPL. As stated in the License text:

> The purpose is . . . to assure everyone the effective freedom to copy and redistribute it, with or without modifying it, either commercially or noncommercially . . .
> This License is a kind of "copyleft," which means that derivative works of the document must themselves be free in the same sense.

This meant that no text could be contributed to a GFDL-licensed work unless it complied with all these terms, hence its reputation for being a "viral" license. Anything that was incorporated into a GFDL work had to abide by the free license terms.

The GFDL did come with some caveats. It had requirements meant for printed computer documentation, but it did not transition well into the collaborative online electronic text of Wikipedia. The license refers to "Title Page," "Acknowl-edgements," and "Dedications," showing how rooted it was in the book writing mindset. When printing anything covered by the GFDL, users were required to include "this License, the copyright notices, and the license notice saying this License applies to the Document." With the text of the License at over 3,000 words, printing a short Nupedia or Wikipedia article would be oppressive, as the license would often be longer than the content itself.

Another difficulty was the requirement to list "at least five of the principal authors of the Document." Since Wikipedia articles were the product of editing by dozens or even hundreds of people, determining "principals" was not a trivial task. Was this determined by number of edits, or the substantiality of the edits, or the most recent relevant edits? In practice, the GFDL was welcomed since it was the only well-known "free" license without the copyright being held by one single entity.

No doubt, a big reason Wikipedia had traction with the Slashdot community in those early days was its use of Stallman's GFDL, showing that it had the right pedigree and philosophical roots in the hacker community.

UseMod Grows

As Slashdot provided an influx of volunteers, Wikipedia was evolving quickly. Clifford Adams created a more elegant way of pointing to pages by using free links in double brackets. Now Wikipedia looked more like a proper work, and not one littered with strange CamelCase.

To move forward with its popularity, it would need to get more features.

It was clear that the UseModWiki system, as a humble little program, was coming to the end of its useful life. Wikipedia was by far the largest wiki installa-tion using UseModWiki, and its design was starting to show cracks. It was always meant as a simple script, so it kept each page as a separate file on a computer server. It did not have a proper "database" per se, meaning that searching and managing revisions of each page was very inefficient. Even in the early days, folks knew that the project was taking off and that UseModWiki would not be able to keep up with tens or hundreds of thousands of pages. They needed a solution fast.

That's where Magnus Manske took up the challenge. A German programmer who was involved with Wikipedia from the start, he knew a real full-fledged database was needed. A database organizes data in a way that makes it efficient for computer programs to store, search, retrieve, and modify its contents. It's the difference between, say, a library storing books in random piles, versus having a method of shelving and retrieving tomes quickly.

Keeping with the open spirit of Wikipedia, Manske's solution was to build a new wiki engine using some of the most tested open source tools around—the MySQL database and the PHP programming language. The MySQL database system is used for storing and retrieving data quickly, and the PHP programming language helps format and display pages for Web browsers. The beauty of open source systems was that people could "port" or convert information to different computer systems, allowing for more widespread use. On Wikipedia, the spirit of Stallman was present both in the software and the content.

Manske started from the UseModWiki model and added lots of new functions, to create a system called MediaWiki. One of the most important new features added was the watchlist, a way for each person to track articles.

Each user in Wikipedia could put articles on a watchlist that would be retained by the system. It was a sort of bookmark system to help people track articles they were interested in or had edited. Instead of sifting through all the recent changes in Wikipedia, people could simply click on the "Watchlist" button and see all the recent changes to the articles on the user's own custom watchlist.

The ability to monitor articles of interest, seeing what modifications had been made, promoted the tracking of articles and maintaining quality by imbuing individuals with a type of oversight.

To figure out what has changed, one of the most important tools in Wikipedia is called the "diff." Long ago, in the early 1970s, clever programmers found a way to automatically compare two text documents and identify the differences between them. Originally meant for computer programmers to highlight changes in their computer code, the method has been coopted as an essential tool for Wikipedia contributors to inspect one another's changes in written articles.

The diff is absolutely crucial to the second-by-second operation of Wikipedia. When one looks at the edit history of an article in Wikipedia, one can instantly compare any two revisions of the article by doing a diff. The output will show additions, deletions, and modifications, to assist users in tracking changes. Oftentimes, the diff will be something trivial, like the fixing of a typo or the addition of a word. Regardless of how big or small, the diff function will display the change to the user.

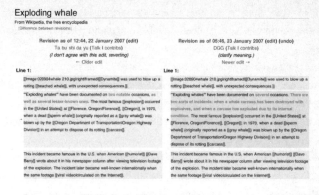

Example of a diff display between two versions.

Give Me More Space

One of the additions of the MediaWiki software was the creation of "namespaces." The bulk of Wikipedia's pages are in the "article" namespace, as actual entries one would find in an encyclopedia. Pages are named like the article itself, like [[Dog]] or [[George Washington]]. But as the community grew, contributors needed pages not in the article space but in another administrative space, to discuss and coordinate with other Wikipedians. As a result, other namespaces were added to separate out non-article content.

The most important was the "talk" namespace. Every article in Wikipedia has an associated Talk page, such as [[Talk:Dog]]. This provides a way for people to discuss, debate, or coordinate editing of the Dog article in Wikipedia. Think of it as a bulletin and discussion board for each individual page.

The Talk page was an innovation that was quite different from the original wiki concept, but it drew praise from Ward Cunningham. He was fascinated to see his creation adapted for use by Wikipedians, even when he was skeptical.

"I was afraid. . . . I thought of an encyclopedia as stuffy, and wiki as kind of being freewheeling, as this continuous distillation of thought," he remembers. "Then I saw that just by pairing those two pages that you could have the free-wheeling and the stuffy at the same time, I said, 'Ah that's brilliant!'"

Talk pages are simply regular wiki pages that anyone can edit, but people quickly adapted them to act like "threaded" discussion boards where comments and responses were posted to make up full-fledged conversation and debate.

Another namespace was the "user" namespace, a page for describing each registered user in Wikipedia. For example, [[User:Jimbo]] was dedicated as a sort of home page allowing Jimmy Wales to post personal details. Similarly, [[User talk:Jimbo]] was a page that allowed other users to engage in discussion with Jimbo.

The "main community" namespace was created under the moniker "Wikipedia" to house policies, essays, and community pages that were not meant to be part of the collection of articles. They made up the behind-the-scenes housekeeping and community of Wikipedia, and even though they were publicly accessible, most passersby didn't often see them.

As more people joined Wikipedia in 2001, there was a desire to have a virtual town square to discuss general issues, so the [[Wikipedia:Village pump]] was created, in homage to the water source of a small community square where people would mingle. One of the more famous policy pages was [[Wikipedia:Ignore_all_rules]], an essay written by Larry Sanger to encourage folks not to get too hindered by rules and conventions:

> If rules make you nervous and depressed, and not desirous of participating in the Wiki, then ignore them and go about your business.

Ignoring rules was a nod to Wikipedia's culture of "radical inclusion," something that helped the young project get new participants editing, and a stark contrast to Nupedia's detailed submission guidelines.

Because MediaWiki was designed around the needs of Wikipedia specifically, it provided a good platform for growth. Magnus Manske was not the only one who did the coding. With the Slashdot effect came more and more programmers to the cause.

One that stayed and became employed full-time specifically for Wikipedia was Brion Vibber. In a project full of volunteers, he was one of the programmers paid to do the crucial heavy development on features that could simply not wait for a volunteer to pitch in.

Server Load

The first year of Wikipedia's existence, the encyclopedia was growing quickly, but by technology standards it was not too demanding on computing resources. It had grown to 20,000 articles in one year, but it was still a project largely known only to the tech elite. Wikipedia basically ran on one large computer for the first two years of its life, since the wiki software really couldn't benefit from having more hardware. But in 2003, Manske and others started to see the cracks form as the English language Wikipedia chalked up more than a hundred thousand articles, and more than a dozen other languages were growing quickly. The traffic was climbing, the demands getting more complex, and there were brief outages and slowdowns, as the system could not keep up with the traffic.

They started to look into other solutions. At the very least, they could split the load of the wiki between two computers—one for the Web server and one for the database. In combining their computing horsepower, the two machines would talk to each other over a high-speed network connection.

As Wikipedia's traffic climbed even higher, in January 2004 a major change was made to make a drastic bump in the site's capabilities. Nine new server computers were purchased. One served as the database server, while the other eight serviced requests from Web visitors. It was a major upgrade in quality for the public, as 2003 had seen some major multi-day outages of Wikipedia, something hardly imaginable today. While there was eight times the capacity to serve visitors, having only one machine handling database functions did prove a bottleneck. In the art and science of Web server solutions, you don't always get proportional bumps in capacity if you "throw hardware at the problem."

That year, Wikipedia followed an exponential growth curve, such that more than thirty machines were purchased to serve the load. Even then, the additional hardware could not speed up the database significantly.

At the end of the year, the volunteers who helped do system administration had an idea from seeing what other major Internet sites were using. By doing a clever job of caching, or storing frequently used information in computer memory, and not taxing the database and computer processors, you could get a manyfold increase in speed. One of the major improvements was the installation of what the volunteers call "squid" servers.

Normally when one visits a Web site, the Web server makes a computationally demanding request to fetch you the desired page. For Wikipedia it's a pretty taxing operation if it accesses the database and has to compete with other people's requests as well. A peculiar thing about Wikipedia, and most Web sites, is that 90 percent or more of the queries are simply requests to read articles. "I want to see the article on Dog," for example. In these cases, if the page for [[Dog]] can be serviced without hitting the database, it's a faster response for the user, and it reduces the load on the database server.

This is essentially what the clever Wikipedia developers did with two technologies—squid servers and memcached, both open source software packages. A squid is a very lean Web server that tries to serve Web requests very quickly from what is stored in memory, and memcached is a program to help groups of squid computers share their memory to store information efficiently. They work as a team to avoid putting a load on the database servers.

This allowed for a team of machines to respond to a page request quickly if that page had been accessed recently. If the page could not be found in the memory of the squid/memcached system (a "cache miss"), then a normal request would be sent to the database server. But more often than not, requests had a "cache hit" and the page was sent quickly.

The results were dramatic. The developers reported the news:

[Squids] are currently running at a hit-rate of approximately 75%, effectively quadrupling the capacity of the Apache servers behind them. This is particularly noticeable when a large surge of traffic arrives directed to a particular page via a web link from another site, as the caching efficiency for that page will be nearly 100%.[26]

By putting up a "front line" of computers that handled user requests, Wikipedia was able to get an instant boost in performance because the bulk of page requests were being serviced from the cache, and not bothering the database server.

It was a godsend. Through the squid and memcached software, and some slight modification to the wiki software code, the exact same hardware was able to handle many times the number of visitors as before. And even better, with this solution, throwing more hardware at the problem helps. More machines means more memory and more computing power to service requests.

It's this industrial-strength caching solution, and a clever crew of volunteer programmers, that allowed Wikipedia to scale to become a top ten Web site, with a budget of less than a million dollars.[27]

It should be noted, as a historical footnote, that Richard Stallman, who inspired the free software and free content movement, also proposed his own encyclopedia in 1999, and attempted to launch it the same year that Wikipedia took off. Called GNUpedia, it coexisted confusingly in the same space as Bomis's Nupedia, a completely separate product. Keeping with tradition, Stallman renamed his project GNE—GNU's Not an Encyclopedia. But in the end, Wikipedia's lead and enthusiastic community was already well established, and Richard Stallman put the GNE project into inactive status and put his support behind Wikipedia.

COMMUNITY AT WORK (THE PIRANHA EFFECT)

"History will be kind to me, for I intend to write it."
—*Winston Churchill*

"The only thing that will redeem mankind is cooperation."
—*Bertrand Russell*

When we want to understand how communities cooperate, we are compelled to look at examples in the animal kingdom. How do teams of organisms hunt, build, feed, and survive together as a clan? Behavioral scientists work for years, homing in on the minutiae of group dynamics in animals, looking for clues as to how they cooperate, especially because they don't have the benefit of spoken language.

What kind of systems in nature help describe Wikipedia's dynamics?

Many have likened what happens in Wikipedia to a giant ant farm, with worker ants, drones, and a master queen. Different ants identify themselves for the tasks at hand and interact without instructions "from the top." There are no ant middle managers directing the others.

In his book *Emergence: The Connected Lives of Ants, Brains, Cities, and Software,* Steven Johnson provides a compelling spectrum of scientific examples to describe how individual parts of an aggregated whole interact to form a collective "intelligence." He shows that ants (despite our erroneously ascribing a mode of "royal command" to the queen) in fact operate in a distributed and decentralized way. There is no hierarchical command structure for ants, and the intelligent survival of the colony is in fact "emergent behavior" made up of small, simple, individual decisions and signals communicated on an ant-by-ant basis and by a trail of pheromone markers left behind as they move about their living space.

The term "stigmergy" has been proposed as a biological term to describe this behavior, derived from the Greek words *stigma* ("sign") and *ergon* ("action"). Academic researcher Joseph Reagle, a doctoral student who wrote his Ph.D. thesis about Wikipedia collaboration, describes the phenomenon:

> Stigmergy is a term coined by Pierre-Paul Grasse to describe how wasps and termites collectively build complex structures; as Istvan Karsai writes, it "describes the situation in which the product of previous work, rather than direct communication among builders, induces [and directs how] the wasps perform additional labor."

This implicit communication by modifying one's environment, within the "virtual ant colony" becomes a rather useful model to describe Wikipedia. Individual users are informed about environmental changes through the Recent Changes page, article edit histories, and watchlists. The states of these continually change, and relay valuable signals used to understand the activities of others in the community. It's what has allowed a largely anonymous cluster of volunteers to build an encyclopedia with millions of entries without any type of top-down command structure.

A functional community emerges from simple directives agreed upon by those who choose to participate: maintain a neutral point of view, assume good faith, and don't bite the newbies. Forceful enough to give clear direction, but loose enough to be flexible and evolve.

Basic sets of guidelines, acted upon by individuals at a micro level, wind up feeding into a larger phenomenon of emergent behavior, such as creating decent encyclopedia articles. Like the pheromones left by ants for their workmates, Wikipedia depends on signaling of actions from one user to others and encourages vigorous action by being bold.

If we look to the behavior of fish, we also find a useful metaphor for describing Wikipedia's operation, at least that's how the Francophones see it. "In French Wikipedia they came up with a fantastic phrase, they call it the piranha effect," says Jimmy Wales. "You start with a little tiny article and it's not quite good enough so people are picking at it and sort of a feeding frenzy and articles grow."

The piranha is a small, rather innocuous-looking individual fish. A single animal might give you a nasty bite, but collectively a group is able to make short work of a cow on an unfortunate stroll in the river. The carnivorous fish swarm and work as a team, each one attracted by the activity of another. They are predators, attacking what comes their way, yet they are also scavengers, roaming and devouring what they find scattered about.

Wikipedia took off in 2001 with this piranha effect almost overnight. But it depended on a rich existing online Net culture accustomed to collaboration and group behavior.

Usenet's Legacy

One of the earliest online community message systems was Netnews, which ran on a system called Usenet. This USEr NETwork, started in 1979 by two Duke University students, predated even the Internet and goes back to the era of old computer "bulletin board systems."

Usenet worked on a simple principle. BBS systems were small communities of users who would connect (usually by a modem and phone line) to a central computer and engage in typed discussion about common topics such as computer hackery, sports, or whatever the sysop, or system operator, allowed to happen on the computer.

One computer system might have served a virtual island of a few dozen or hundred users. Another system might have a community of another set of users. To relay bulletin board postings, the computer systems would contact each other periodically and exchange text information. In the 1980s, before the high-speed Internet, this would usually be by an automated phone call. A computer system contacting another computer system (often at night when toll costs were lower) to exchange messages might take minutes or hours to settle all transfers of text messages, pictures, or other data back and forth.

By a kind of digital osmosis, computers would relay their messages to other computers, and so on, with information hopping across to different enclaves of users. It was not "live" or instantaneous like Internet systems that we know of today, so discussion happened not so much in real time, but rather over hours or days at a time.

While not immediate, it was useful enough for folks to start creating a system called Netnews, which provided a global discussion system where topics were organized in a treelike fashion. Comp.sys.mac, for example, would be about Macintosh computer systems, while rec.sports.skiing would be about skiing.

Most of the bulletin board posts on Usenet were ephemeral conversations among users, but over time, the system started to see the same types of information being requested over and over again. In an era before the Internet and the World Wide Web, there was no readily available repository for accumulated knowledge. Therefore, users on Usenet created FAQs, or frequently asked questions, which were normally initiated and maintained by an enthusiastic volunteer for that subject. Rec.food.chocolate, for example, would have questions (and answers) like:

THE OFFICIAL REC.FOOD.CHOCOLATE LIST OF FREQUENTLY ASKED QUESTIONS
This FAQ is posted on the sixth day of every month . . .

1. General
1.1 What is chocolate?
1.2 What is the history of chocolate?
1.3 How is chocolate made?
1.4 What is conching?
1.5 What kinds of chocolate are there?
1.6 What is this white, blotchy stuff on my chocolate bar?
1.7 I just bought a whole bunch of chocolate. What's the best way to store it?
1.8 What is lecithin and why is it in my chocolate?

2. Cooking with chocolate
2.1 What is tempering?

2.2 What is couverture?

2.3 How do I melt chocolate and what's the best kind to use?

2.4 I was melting some chocolate, and suddenly it changed from a shiny, smooth liquid to a dull, thick paste. What happened?

2.5 How do I make chocolate covered strawberries?

2.6 Where can I get some chocolate?

3. Chocolate trivia

3.1 Hey! Did you hear about this lady at Neiman Marcus who wanted to buy a cookie recipe . . . ?

3.2 Is chocolate really an aphrodisiac?

3.3 Can I give chocolate to my dog?

3.4 How much caffeine is in chocolate?

3.5 Doesn't chocolate cause acne?

With information accumulated in FAQs, encyclopedia-like content was starting to emerge on Usenet. But without any type of universally accessible "persistent storage" in the early 1980s, readers were relegated to monthly updates posted to the entire discussion list. The maintainer of an FAQ usually welcomed outsiders' contributions and edits, but out of necessity, control over editing the document was held by a handful of people.

At the same time, a select group of universities and research institutions were connected via an experimental network called ARPANET, which was a project started for the Advanced Research Projects Agency of the U.S. Department of Defense. This was the precursor to today's Internet and was a "live" connection of computers around the United States. Eric Raymond, in *A Brief History of Hackerdom,* describes the creation during the ARPANET days of the Jargon File, another precursor to Wikipedia's group-edited document:

> The first intentional artifacts of the hacker culture—the first slang list, the first satires, the first self-conscious discussions of the hacker ethic—all propagated on the ARPANET in its early years. In particular, the first version of the Jargon File (http://www.tuxedo.org/jargon) developed as a cross-net collaboration during 1973–1975. This slang dictionary became one of the culture's defining documents. It was eventually published as The New Hacker's Dictionary.

The Jargon File was much beloved by the hacker community and passed along like a family heirloom, with prominent computer scientists such as Richard Stallman, Guy Steele, and Dave Lebling all having a major hand in its editing. ARPANET was for the elite set—those who were lucky enough to work for a research institution, or straggled around as graduate students at engineering strongholds like MIT or Carnegie Mellon University.

For most people it was Usenet that provided their first entry point into a global online community.

Users could read Usenet's Netnews through one of many different types of newsreader programs since the way messages were stored and transferred was a widely published standard for all to use. There was not just one program for reading news. People were encouraged to create other reader programs with better enhanced features. Even today, Netnews still exists and is used by many in technical circles. While the likes of Web-based sites like Digg.com and other dedicated discussion forums have dominated the landscape, a user-friendly version of this system can be found in Google Groups (formerly DejaNews).

A peculiarity of Netnews was that users were not authenticated in any central way. That is, anyone could post what he or she wanted under whatever alias the user chose, and the community was generally trusted to behave nicely. There was no central control as to who belonged or not, and real names were optional. It was, after all, just a general agreement for disparate systems to exchange their latest messages with one another.

People generally respected the Netnews netiquette because it made the community better for everyone. But as with anything that gets popular quickly, the dynamics changed. You had people who would not stay "on topic" within the purpose of the newsgroup, would send heated emails or would harass others. It was in reaction to this that Netnews culture generated many of the Internet norms we know of today—writing in ALL CAPITAL LETTERS was considered the equivalent to shouting, and sending scathing emails was considered "flaming." Both were considered bad form. Acerbic dueling users engaging in "flamewars" would at times plunge entire discussion boards into crisis.

Fortunately, there was a simple remedy for dealing with annoyances—the ominous-sounding "kill file." In actuality, it was simply a list of word patterns you could instruct your particular Netnews reader to ignore. The contents could be the username of someone you didn't want to hear from again, or a topic that you never wanted to read about. So one's kill file might read "JohnnyAppleseed" or

"JFK" if a particular user sending assassination conspiracy theories annoyed you. Anything that matched your kill file words would simply not show up on your screen.

With the kill file, most problems could be screened out on the reader's end, but in the case of system-wide disruptive behavior, other community action was needed.

The massive waves of unsolicited and unwanted emails we know as "spam" had its origins in Netnews in the 1990s. Because there was no central authority, and anyone could post, marketers and scam artists certainly saw Netnews as a target-rich environment.

This was the case in 1994 when two immigration lawyers, Canter and Siegel, discovered the Internet and Netnews. Seeing an opportunity, they initiated a slew of advertisements to pitch their services for obtaining permanent resident "green cards" to stay in the United States. Ignoring all accepted "netiquette," they sent postings to thousands of newsgroups with the title "Green Card Lottery" and a description of their services. The community was immediately enraged. The duo was spoiling their digital commons with their unsolicited blanket messages. Within a few hours, Usenet veterans assembled software programs called "Cancelbots" to counter the spam messages. These were like Usenet cruise missiles—computer programs specifically combing the newsgroups to look for and destroy messages titled "Green Card Lottery." It was an example of how the community could pull out the heavy artillery when needed. Their software "bots" dished out vigilante justice, zapping Canter and Siegel's messages on sight.

The community decided to react quickly, so as not to give the spammers any kind of reward for their actions. Canter and Siegel would enter the history books as the ones who brought about the end of Usenet's age of innocence. As the Internet became more commercial and allowed in individuals and corporations looking to make a buck, the hacker ethos would no longer be dominant.

Lessons from Usenet

Why is the story of Usenet and Netnews so important? Because so many things pioneered by Usenet have become foundations for the Wikipedia community and its resulting success.

If we fast-forward to Wikipedia today, much the same dynamic exists as did with

Usenet. The power of Wikipedia's model is that it is free-form—anyone can edit any page at any time. Contributors work on a micro-level, adding a fact here, changing punctuation there. The community trusts individuals to behave responsibly. Lessons learned from dealing with vandals, troublemakers, and noisy individuals in Usenet were applied by Wikipedia's toolmakers and community members. Obnoxious users could be blocked from editing, and articles could be locked to prevent vandalism. And changes to whole sets of articles could be done through software robots, not unlike the Netnews Cancelbots.

Fortunately, though, as Wikipedia took off, the community found most people were remarkably well behaved and productive, something not everyone would have thought about a site that encouraged anyone to edit any page at any time.

"Generally we find most people out there on the Internet are good," says Jimmy Wales. "It's one of the wonderful humanitarian discoveries in Wikipedia, that most people only want to help us and build this free nonprofit, charitable resource."[28]

Growth

When Sanger and Wales decided to start what would become Wikipedia in January 2001, it was always thought that it would be a proving ground for articles to feed into Nupedia. As Slashdot and other tech communities noticed Wikipedia, the academic Nupedians who were the first Wikipedians suddenly found many computer programming types joining the ranks. By itself this was not a bad thing. Suddenly articles about engineering, computer science, and general science were shaping up quite nicely, a result of the expertise of the newcomers. But it was certainly a change from the early days.

By January 2002, one year after launch, Wikipedia had gone from zero to twenty thousand articles. This was far beyond the imagination of even the most optimistic of the bunch.

The press release from Bomis read:

At present, nearly 200 people are working on the project daily, from all around the world; organizers estimate that the project has had well over a thousand contributors. The success of such an open project, staffed by such a large and diverse body of writers, is a puzzle: how can so many people with so many different backgrounds collaborate with such little oversight? Project organizers say that it is partly because the participants can edit each other's contributions easily, and partly because the project has a strong "nonbias" policy; this keeps interaction relatively polite and productive. Sanger explains: "If contributors took controversial stands, it would be virtually impossible for people of many different viewpoints to collaborate. Because of the neutrality policy, we have partisans working together on the same articles. It's quite remarkable."

What was even more remarkable was that within one year, the number of articles would double yet again.

Wikipedia could not have grown so quickly without a good mix of both stigmergic effects (picking up on changes in the environment) and explicit communication channels. The electronic mailing list established early in 2001 was invaluable for coordinating initial activity among folks who were just starting out with the wiki culture. Not long after launch, much of the communications activity was on the talk pages of articles and user pages. A dialogue about how to structure the article [[University]] was better done in [[Talk:University]] than on a list with all Wikipedians. Instead of a single mailing list, discussions were spread across the wiki, alongside the relevant articles. Both of these were non-real-time communication tools that benefited people working across different time zones and provided a forum for longer, more thoughtful discourse. But as work started to get more rapid, leaving messages on talk pages and waiting for replies became inefficient for quick collaboration.

As 2001 progressed, the community experimented with trying out a form of online communication in the form of Internet relay chat, or IRC. As a simple, open standard, IRC was a group chat space that preceded today's modern "instant messaging" such as AOL, MSN, Skype, or Jabber. With IRC, users could run a program to connect to the central machine operated by Freenode, one of the largest IRC servers, and chat in real time with other Wikipedians. It was a new experience for Wikipedians to converse synchronously, and it provided an even faster feedback loop with which Wikipedia could evolve. The downside was that more communications channels lead to more partitioning and a greater chance of forming disconnected cliques.

How Wikipedia Works

To outsiders, how articles get created and grow on Wikipedia is a bit of a mystery. It's actually simpler than one would think. The original wiki software conceived by Ward Cunningham indicated missing pages by presenting a clickable question mark after the page name. The MediaWiki software created for Wikipedia presents links that are red in color. By clicking on the red link, you can immediately start editing.

Wikipedia has established a style that basically follows an "inverted pyramid" writing formula, by having the most important facts at the top of an article. The Wikipedia article [[Dog]] for example reads:

> The **dog** (Canis lupus familiaris) is a <u>domesticated subspecies</u> of the <u>wolf</u>, a <u>mammal</u> of the <u>Canidae</u> family of the order <u>Carnivora</u>. The term encompasses both <u>feral</u> and <u>pet</u> varieties and is also sometimes used to describe <u>wild canids</u> of other subspecies or <u>species</u>. The domestic dog has been one of the most widely kept <u>working</u> and <u>companion animals</u> in human history, as well as being a <u>food source</u> in some cultures. There are estimated to be 400 million dogs in the world.

The basic markup language called WikiMarkup gives simple ways to add features to the text. Making text bold, italic, or a link to another page is as simple as surrounding the text with single quotes or brackets. Different sections within the document can be delineated with multiple equal signs, such as:

> == Main Section ==
> === Subsections ===

Not only does this provide visual separation between sections, it also helps to automatically create a table of contents for the article, properly numbered with hyperlinks to jump directly to their place on the page.

Other features of WikiMarkup that help make a Wikipedia article look more professional are bullets and numbering, which are inserted simply by using * or # before a sentence.

Along with the article page are other "meta pages" that are unique to Wikipedia. The most important is the Edit History page, which shows each and every revision ever made to the page. This is the indestructible audit trail of every wiki page, the "infinite undo" that makes experimentation safe. It's also allowed for Wikipedia to declare to users since its earliest days to "Be bold."

Larry Sanger put it this way in February 2002, when the project was still young: "Wikis don't work if people aren't bold. You've got to get out there and make those changes, correct that grammar, add those facts, make that language precise, etc., etc. It's OK. It's what everyone expects. So you should never ask, 'Why aren't these pages copyedited?' Amazingly, it all works out. It does require some amount of politeness, but it works. You'll see."[29] The page in Wikipedia encouraging such boldness reads:

Be bold in editing, moving, and modifying articles, because the joy of editing is that, although it should be aimed for, perfection is not required. And do not worry about messing up. All prior versions of articles are kept, so there is no way that you can accidentally damage Wikipedia or irretrievably destroy content. But remember—whatever you write here will be preserved for posterity.

Perhaps most endearing to readers is when the clinical, just-the-facts style of Wikipedia is applied to subjects never having received such treatment. Consider the case of [[Beer goggles]], a subject almost always discussed churlishly after too much celebration:

> **Beer goggles** is a slang term for a phenomenon in which consumption of <u>alcohol</u> lowers sexual inhibitions to the point that very little or no discretion is used when approaching or choosing sexual partners.

And if you've ever had a tough time explaining what came first in philosophical terms, the chicken or the egg, Wikipedia explains it in [[Chicken or the egg]]:

> The **chicken or the egg** <u>causality</u> dilemma arises from the expression "which came first, the <u>chicken</u> or the <u>egg</u>?" Chickens hatch from eggs, but eggs are laid by chickens, making it difficult to say which originally gave rise to the other. To ancient philosophers, the question about the first chicken or egg also evoked the questions of how life and the universe in general began. Cultural references to the chicken and egg intend to point out the futility of identifying the first case of a <u>circular cause and consequence</u>.

In the process of cataloging human knowledge, the Wikipedia community has dedicated an entire page to documenting these more amusing anecdotes, called [[Wikipedia:Unusual articles]], a Ripley's Believe It or Not–style museum showcasing the community's quirkier contributions.

Very few articles start out as masterpieces in Wikipedia. In fact most start very humbly as one-line "stubs" that may barely even qualify as coherent prose.

Stub articles, in Wikipedia parlance, are short, incomplete articles that need attention and development by the community. It's a situation peculiar to Wikipedia, as no published encyclopedia would ever leave such half-baked works-in-progress intact and visible to the public. But in Wikipedia's culture, leaving stubs visible provides an inducement to help bring in more editors, to help expand and contribute to the project. Again, this is the stigmergic effect, modifying the environment, leaving stubs out in the open for others to build on.

As articles grow in Wikipedia, so does the edit history, as the running log of all changes to a page. Every change is saved in Wikipedia—every addition, deletion, or modification. For each page, there is a button that's labeled "History" that reveals the complete lineage of an article. The [[Emperor Penguin]] article, for example, shows an edit history that contains entries such as this:

- (cur) (last) ○ 15:34, 21 January 2007   Shimakaze (Talk | contribs) **m** *(grammatic error fixed)* (undo)
- (cur) (last) ○ 23:29, 23 December 2006   90.14.8.164 (Talk) (undo)
- (cur) (last) ○ 23:13, 18 December 2006   Tregoweth (Talk | contribs) (undo)
- (cur) (last) ○ 14:43, 15 December 2006   Ais523 (Talk | contribs) **m** (→*History: "data" is plural*) (undo)
- (cur) (last) ○ 16:01, 4 December 2006   212.100.3.56 (Talk) (→*Appearances*) (undo)

While it may seem a bit overwhelming, displaying the edit history has evolved quite a bit since the first wiki software of Ward Cunningham. The newest revision is at the top of the list, and older ones are listed below it. The "cur" and "last" links are very useful for inspection. The "cur" button is a simple way to see all the changes that have happened between the current version of the page and the one in the list, using the diff function. The output shows changes in red links and will show which paragraphs have been completely added or deleted. Similarly, the "last" button shows the differences between the current version and the one before it. While those buttons give the technical output of the diff command, the human editors can also leave notes as to what they did. That's where the comments in parentheses, the edit summary, comes into play. Editors are encouraged to leave useful descriptions of what they've done, to help other community members, such as "spelling corrected," or "grammatic [sic] error fixed."

The time and date of each edit is noted with exact precision, along with the name of the editor, which includes some convenient shortcuts. There are links to the talk page of the user who made the edit, and one can quickly check the complete list of contributions from that user as well. In the latest incarnation of the software, there is the "undo" function, which allows people to quickly unwind the changes of a user. Normally "reverting" a user's changes without comment is frowned upon, but for fixing vandalism, it's invaluable. Finally, in the case of users with special "administrator" status, there is a "Block" button, which gives the administrator the ability to lock out someone for a period of time if it's determined the user is disrupting Wikipedia, especially if the user is refusing to talk or discuss changes with others.

Administrators first came about because of a quirk with how wikis work. Anyone can edit any page at any time in a wiki, but deleting a page is rather problematic. Letting just anyone delete articles means information would simply disappear, and go missing from the work space. If people took issue with the deletion, where would they go to retrieve it? How would they even know it was gone? As a result, deletion was seen as a technical tool that not every person should have.

There was another more urgent issue with deletion: Sometimes it was important for information to be completely destroyed and wiped from Wikipedia's public space. This is especially the case for a copyright violation, libelous speech, and inappropriate private information about someone. Leaving this information in would have serious legal ramifications. Therefore, it was decided that users designated as administrators, proven members of the community, and only they, would be allowed to delete and undelete articles. Later on, there would be additional powers called "oversight" that would not just put the deleted info into a virtual dust bin, but actually wipe them from the database itself for legal reasons. Understandably, oversight was something only a very elite set of trusted users had.

Despite the important-sounding title, Jimmy Wales was quick not to put too much weight behind the "administrator" role, which was also nicknamed "sysop" from the old days of computer bulletin boards when "systems operators" had extra privileges:

I just wanted to say that becoming a sysop is *not a big deal*.

I think perhaps I'll go through semi-willy-nilly and make a bunch of people who have been around for awhile sysops. I want to dispel the aura of "authority" around the position. It's merely a technical matter that the powers given to sysops are not given out to everyone.

I don't like that there's the apparent feeling here that being granted sysop status is a really special thing.[30]

Though they were the ones entrusted with "potentially harmful tools" of Wikipedia, users were quick to point out that administrators had no more extra editorial authority than anyone else. Deletion of articles still had to adhere to the community guidelines and be done through a process of consensus (detailed in later chapters). To emphasize humility, the role was often referred to as being a Wikipedia janitor, with the greeting to newly minted sysops being "May you wield the mop and bucket with equanimity."[31]

Once the administrators were established, it was natural to entrust them with more privileged operations in Wikipedia. As the project got more popular, the front [[Main Page]] of Wikipedia was constantly being vandalized, so it was eventually locked down using a "protection" feature, so only administrators could edit it. The protected page feature proved useful enough that it was extended so any administrator could lock down any page in Wikipedia. This was usually done in the case of a particularly popular page that kept getting vandalized or to stop an edit war between users who would not compromise.

Users who were truly disruptive could be completely blocked by administrators as well, for arbitrary durations.

In the early days of Wikipedia, prior to 2003, admin requests were made on the group electronic mailing list, and were usually granted right away. If you were seen around the project and no one could see any reason not to, you were given "adminship." It was, as Wales wanted, "not a big deal."

By March 2003, the English edition had more than 100,000 articles, putting it on par with commercial online encyclopedias. It was clear Wikipedia had joined the big leagues. As the community was scaling up that month, there were roughly 480 active editors, 100 core editors, and 48 admins.

Because the community was growing so quickly, the process of forming consensus by email did not scale. What was once an intimate group who all chatted on the mailing lists, while also encountering each other on the wiki, had ballooned into a much larger community. People who stumbled upon Wikipedia, registered, and became the new generation of editors didn't necessarily partake of the mailing list.

Instead, the adminship process was moved onto the wiki itself, with a page called [[Wikipedia:Request for Adminship]] which was a forum for nominating potential admins. This was an important turning point where the small community practices had to be upgraded to a formal voting system. Wikipedia was not a small village anymore, and as it grew to become a metropolis, more bureaucratic methods of promotion were employed simply because people were not as familiar with one another as in the past.

In the fall of 2006, Wikipedia was just breaking into the top ten most popular Web sites in the world (according to Alexa.com)[32] and was getting an increasing number of citations in the media. In August 2006 the number of active editors in English Wikipedia had reached a new high of 44,193,[33] with 10 percent of these having the distinction of being "very active"[34] core editors, who made more than 100 edits each per month. Serving as "janitors" were roughly 1,000 active administrators, tending to the duties of deleting, blocking, and protecting resources.

Urban Jungle

The plight of Wikipedia growing from small community to larger digital metropolis is something both Joseph Reagle in his Ph.D. work on Wikipedia and Steven Johnson in *Emergence* note as being similar to problems of urban planning. There is no better historical example than that explored in Jane Jacobs's book *The Death and Life of Great American Cities*, her critique of the modernist planning policies of the 1950s and 1960s, an era when New York City developer Robert Moses was razing entire swaths of neighborhoods for planned housing projects and communities. Jacobs argued for preserving her small neighborhood on Hudson Street and resisting massive urban renewal, because the intimate sidewalks served an important social function. She argued that sidewalks provided three important things: safety, contact, and the assimilation of children in the community. In the summary of Jacobs's vision of the sidewalk, there are parallels to wikis and how to build community:

> Street safety is promoted by pavements clearly marking a public/private separation, and by spontaneous protection with the eyes of both pedestrians and those watching the continual flow of pedestrians from buildings. To make this eye protection effective at enhancing safety, there should be "an unconscious assumption of general street support" when necessary, or an element of "trust." As the main contact venue, pavements contribute to building trust among neighbors over time. Moreover, self-appointed public characters such as storekeepers enhance the social structure of sidewalk life by learning the news at retail and spreading it. Jacobs argues that such trust cannot be built in artificial public places such as a game room in a housing project. Sidewalk contact and safety, together, thwart segregation and racial discrimination.[35]

Similarly, a wiki has all its activities happening in the open for inspection, as on Jacobs's sidewalk. Trust is built by observing the actions of others in the community and discovering people with like or complementary interests. Some

Wikipedia users take up editing; others emphasize new article creation, or map creation. But each Wikipedian self-identifies for tasks, much like what Jacobs describes as the "self-appointed public characters."

> A final function of sidewalks is to provide a non-matriarchy environment for children to play. This is not achieved in the presumably "safe" city parks—an assumption that Jacobs seriously challenges due to the lack of surveillance mechanisms in parks. Successful, functional parks are those under intense use by a diverse set of companies and residents.

It is perhaps an interesting coincidence that the wiki page where new users are encouraged to experiment and "play" safely is called the Sandbox. Johnson perhaps put it most eloquently when he said, "Sidewalks work because they permit local interactions to create global order. . . . The information networks of sidewalk life are fine-grained enough to permit higher-level learning to emerge."

Signaling One Another

As Wikipedia grew larger, editors found that there were messages and phrases that kept repeating themselves. In response, they came up with a new idea called "templates," which allowed for a shorthand phrase to be expanded into more text. Templates are designated by putting double curly braces {{}} around a word, which will replace it with another chunk of text. For example, typing {{stub}} into an article would, upon saving, actually show a message at the top of the page:

This article is a <u>stub</u>. You can help Wikipedia by <u>expanding it</u>.

The {{stub}} template not only adds a caution/help sign to readers, but it also triggers another action—the addition of the article to a "category" for stubs. Wikipedia Categories allow different pages to be placed in one of many different classifications. Stubs in Wikipedia, for example, are put in Category:Stub. This way, anyone clicking on the page [[Category:Stub]] will get a list of all pages in Wikipedia that have been placed in that category. One of the exercises for people looking for some way to contribute to Wikipedia is to start with the list of stubs, and see if they can help expand or fill in any of the articles. This template and categorization system becomes a way for people to signal to one another about the coming and going of new information in Wikipedia.

But how exactly do users pick up on these signals? With so much activity going on in the virtual space, how do users see all this? In the early days of low traffic, or on wikis with a smaller number of users, Cunningham's recent changes page was the hive of activity. When there were a few edits each minute, users could simply inspect the list of recent changes like an old stock ticker tape, and inspect the changes. By 2008, on the English Wikipedia, there were dozens of edits recorded every second. It would be impossible to track or sift through all these changes by hand.

Instead, this is where the watchlist came into play. The watchlist is a customized list of articles that each user maintains. They might be articles the user is interested in, has edited before, or wants to keep an eye on. Like a filtered recent changes page, the watchlist shows a reverse chronological log of changes but only for the articles the user is interested in. While most people have hundreds of articles they are watching, it's not unusual for others to have thousands of pages on their list. Any modification to a "watched" page or to the associated talk page will be displayed in a refresh of one's watchlist.

Wikipedia could not handle millions of articles and edits without the watchlist function. Each user observes an arbitrary portion of the article space with his or her list, with different people redundantly checking and correcting information.

The output of the watchlist is similar to that of recent changes, listing the page name, author of the last edit, and convenient links to leave a note with that editor or to inspect the editor's contributions. If a user watches the page [[Disc golf]] then any change to [[Talk:Disc golf]] is automatically noted as well, because it is useful to track conversations about certain topics, or with certain users. For each page, there are "diff" and "hist" links, allowing one to show the difference with the previous version or to inspect the entire edit history of the page.

11 May 2008

    m   23:29 Talk:Mainland China (diff; hist) . . (+68) . . Pyl (Talk I contribs I block) *(forgot to sign)*
          22:04 Talk:Keith Olbermann (diff; hist) . . (+10) . . Roox1963 (Talk I contribs I block) *(→ "I'm a liberal")*
          21:46 HTML editor (diff; hist) . . (+3,534) . . 69.40.60.71 (Talk I block) *(Undid revision 211620477 by 85.15.57.55 (talk))*
    m   18:13 Ruben Barrales (diff; hist) . . (+212) . . Optigan13 (Talk I contribs I block) *(Tagging or repairing external links using checklinks tool)*
    mb 17:51 Talk:Disc golf (diff; hist) . . (+245) . . SineBot (Talk I contribs I block) *(Signing comment by 75.60.110.2 - "- →Removed American Football reference: 2234 /1/ ~~~~")*

Because the watchlist is packed with so much information and so many links, users can quickly pick up on the environmental changes of other users in the system and act on them. In fact, the number of words that are clickable in the watchlist display far outnumber the ones that are not.

Enhancements were added to the watchlist over the years, such as a number indicating how many bytes (or characters) had been added or removed from the article, in parentheses next to the page name. A large number meant a wholesale change to the article, and when taken with an edit comment like "undid" or "revert," it signaled simply undoing the previous action. Just by glancing at the list, without even doing a "diff," it's possible to understand the nature of many edits very quickly.

Experienced users have made their watchlist their first stop of the day, browsing the log of changes to search for telltale clues of activity. The watchlist has become an essential tool, a zeitgeist of Wikipedia's hive of activity custom-made just for the user.

Then Came the Bots

It was incredible what the Wikipedia community achieved with individual volunteer editors. But in terms of enforcing any kind of uniformity (making changes across all the animal-related articles on site, for example) it was a much harder slog.

As Wikipedia got bigger, it was even harder to coordinate going through thousands of articles to make sure each one was consistent with the others. Is the spelling correct? Is punctuation used the same way? Do all the articles about animals have genus and species defined?

So while Wikipedia didn't depend on users having advanced computer skills, people who knew how to write computer programs had a major role to play. And perhaps that's one of the most brilliant parts of Wikipedia's culture. It may have been inspired by earlier online communities, but it remained an inclusive, human-oriented endeavor, allowing tech elite and tech averse to work side by side toward the same goal of building an encyclopedia. There was no better example of this than when software "robots" came onto the scene after Wikipedia got too big to maintain simply by hand.

In October 2002 Derek Ramsey was at the center of the most controversial move in Wikipedia history. Wikipedia had been growing slowly, and its

English-language edition was starting to gather impressive attention. It had roughly 50,000 English articles, while other languages were just getting off the ground. With just a few thousand articles were the nascent communities of German, French, Dutch, Polish, and Esperanto.

Ramsey was a skinny computer science student, recently graduated from the Rochester Institute of Technology when he discovered Wikipedia in September 2002. Always interested in mathematics and statistics, he noticed that Wikipedia had a smattering of articles about big cities and towns in the United States, but it was by no means comprehensive or complete. He signed up as User:Ramman, and started work on the articles related to geography, something he had always loved.

Being a numbers wonk, he saw that the United States Census data was on the Internet for anyone to download. Performed once every ten years, the U.S. Census attempts to record every single living person in the United States for the purpose of determining how representation for each state is divided in Congress. Along the way, census takers capture detailed statistics for individuals in each town, city, and village. Ramsey thought the publicly available census data would certainly be valuable to help fill in Wikipedia articles.

Fortunately, copyright issues about the numbers and statistics were not a problem. Works by the United States government are not protected by copyright, and are considered public domain. In the early days of the Internet, before Wikipedia was created, *The CIA World Fact Book* was one of the most popular references on the Internet. Despite its ominous title, the collection of detailed country profiles by the top U.S. intelligence organization was public domain and could be freely copied and published on the Internet. The same was true of the census data from the year 2000, which could be downloaded from the U.S. government Web site.

When Ramsey discovered Wikipedia, he was a new graduate, recently married but unemployed. "After the dot-com bubble bursting and September 11," he says, "software engineering jobs were more scarce, so I didn't find a job until November 2002." In the intervening months, he took the time to experiment with Wikipedia. After dabbling with a handful of articles, he saw the power of creating pages. But being a computer scientist, he was irked by the haphazard nature of Wikipedia.

"I discovered that most of the cities that I wanted to work on did not exist.

I didn't want to create an article with one sentence with some little bit of trivia. I also discovered that many other people were shy about creating such articles. I wanted to create an article on every U.S. city and county so that people would have stubs to work from and not feel daunted by article creation."

Ramsey thought, why not insert all the census data into Wikipedia? A visit to the Census Bureau's Web site showed a bounty of statistics and geographic data. But it was like a jigsaw puzzle. It contained a hodgepodge of information and uncorrelated data in different formats. Seeing it as a challenge to get it unified and inserted into Wikipedia, Ramsey plowed in and got to work.

He spent hours sifting through the numbers and cross-referencing the information from multiple databases. The job wasn't without "contradictions and difficulties." Longitude and latitude coordinates, postal zip codes, and Federal Information Processing Standard codes made up a maze of numbers that needed to be sifted and correlated. After dozens of iterations and using his computer programming skills, Ramsey eventually generated a unified database that could be processed and systematically inserted into Wikipedia.

At first he started with the 3,000 counties in the entire United States and inserted each one of them by hand, manually copying and pasting the articles into newly created Wikipedia articles.

"I was unemployed, so while I was not job hunting, I was working on Wikipedia during the day, for many many hours."

Finishing the 3,000 entries kicked off something in Ramsey's pleasure center. He had his first whiff of "wiki-crack," the irreverent jargon Wikipedians have used to describe their addiction. So he set out on the next task—adding 33,832 city articles to Wikipedia. The problem was, at the same rate of entry, he calculated it would take months to hand-edit and create all those articles.

He saw that other Wikipedians had instead crafted software programs to act like human editors to insert data into Wikipedia. These "software robots," or bots, mimicked what a human editor would do but never tired or asked for a break. Bots were usually created using a simple scripting language like Perl or PHP, the same system used for creating Wikipedia's software, and were hopefully well tested lest they wreak havoc on the articles.

Until then, these robots had done rather small, repetitive tasks like fixing punctuation or reformatting pages, things that were easily interpreted as being useful to Wikipedia.

Ramsey thought, why not use this method to insert the census data into Wikipedia? Putting his programming skills to work, and reviewing the work of previous bot creators, he created his own version to do the job. His bot did exactly what a human would do: create an article, load numbers from a database, copy the prepared text in, save the article, and go on to the next one. But it wouldn't get tired or bored and, as a result, wouldn't make sloppy mistakes.

After some "massaging" of the census data so it was all consistently formatted and bot-friendly, Ramsey was ready to fire. This bot was going to be a bit different, though. In an English Wikipedia with just over 50,000 articles, he was about to push the button to add 33,832 more, all in one shot. He would instantly be responsible for 40 percent of all the Wikipedia articles.

Such mass creation of articles had never been done before. He wasn't sure how the community would react. But in the spirit of "Be bold," one of Wikipedia's core mantras, he hit the "Start" button.

From October 19 to October 25, the bot operated under the auspices of his User:Ram-man account as it plodded through the list, starting with [[Autaugaville, Alabama]] and working tirelessly for a whole week to finish. The articles all followed a similar format, taking raw numbers and putting them into slightly more palatable human-readable prose:

Autaugaville is a town located in Autauga County, Alabama. As of the 2000 census, the population of the town is 820.

GEOGRAPHY

The town has a total area of 20.5 km² (7.9 mi²). 20.0 km² (7.7 mi²) of it is land and 0.4 km² (0.2 mi²) of it is water. The total area is 2.15% water.

DEMOGRAPHICS

As of 2000, there are 820 people, 316 households, and 219 families residing in the town. The population density is 41.0/km² (106.1/mi²). There are 384 housing units at an average density of 19.2 persons/km² (49.7 persons/mi²). The racial makeup of the town is 32.32% White, 65.98% African American, 0.24% Native American, 0.00% Asian, 0.00% Pacific Islander, 0.24% from other races, and 1.22% from two or more races. 0.98% of the population are Hispanic or Latino of any race.

There are 316 households out of which 34.5% have children under the age of 18 living with them, 39.6% are married couples living together, 25.0% have a woman whose husband does not live with her, and 30.4% are non-families. 28.5% of all households are made up of individuals and 13.6% have someone living alone who is 65 years of age or older. The average household size is 2.59 and the average family size is 3.18.

In the town the population is spread out with 31.1% under the age of 18, 8.9% from 18 to 24, 26.5% from 25 to 44, 20.2% from 45 to 64, and 13.3% who are 65 years of age or older. The median age is 33 years. For every 100 females there are 86.4 males. For every 100 females age 18 and over, there are 78.8 males.

The median income for a household in the town is $22,563, and the median income for a family is $35,417. Males have a median income of $29,688 versus $19,821 for females. The per capita income for the town is $12,586. 27.1% of the population and 27.4% of families are below the poverty line. Out of the total people living in poverty, 31.2% are under the age of 18 and 23.2% are 65 or older.

As it chugged along, people started to notice the gradual accumulation of articles, almost like a slowly rising flood within Wikipedia. Some thought it was a great deed, adding the crystal seeds needed to spur more activity for individual towns.

But it wasn't all a warm reception for Ram-man.

Others viewed his work as an abomination—an unintelligent automaton systematically spewing rote text, fouling the collection of articles. Wikipedia was supposed to be a project started by humans and controlled by humans. Was an article where every other word was a number or a statistic a well-crafted start or simply a data dump?

There was no doubting the good intentions of Ramsey, a convivial programming whiz and part-time Church of the Brethren preacher. But debate would brew in the community about this massive bump in article count. Was it healthy to preen about the number of entries, knowing few of the new articles had been seen by human eyes or would be edited anytime soon? Some were skeptical about the value of entries on tiny towns of only a hundred or so people.

"According to [[Wikipedia:What Wikipedia is not]], Wikipedia articles are not 'Mere collections of public domain or other source material.' This article is a mere collection of the US census information. No links to this page, except the county page. I believe the demographics information to be useful, however, without some history, and intelligent writing to go along with it, it is quite useless," said user David Grant.[36]

Even though he faced vocal criticism for his mass addition, and did for some time, on balance Ramsey has no regrets.

"The rambot article spurned lots of policy discussions about what Wikipedia was: Should certain stubs be allowed? What types of articles are acceptable? Is a town of 1 person notable? Is a ghost town of 0 people notable?"

Subsequent discussions to try to delete or prune back the "Census articles" were heated but ultimately unsuccessful. The concept started to grow on people, and the novelty of finding one's previously insignificant hometown in Wikipedia likely gave the project a boost as well. In the end, the majority of Wikipedians found the articles to be a huge step forward, providing the starter seeds for more activity.

"The point is that I wouldn't have bothered to write any [of] my contributions, and probably many other users wouldn't either, if Rambot hadn't given me a starting point and some organization," said User:Meelar.

Ramsey's 33,832-article addition, causing a 60 percent growth in one week, was by far the largest bump Wikipedia had seen or has since. Historic charts graphing Wikipedia's growth always have a distinctive "Rambot spike" showing the one-week leap that English Wikipedia undertook in 2002.

The benefits didn't come without some confusion. Ram-man's human edits were lumped together with edits made by his software robot. Because other Wikipedians could not tell which was which, they really weren't sure whether to criticize the person or the bot. Also, when people were reading the Recent Changes list to track community activity, it was completely flooded by Ram-man's bot edits.

This spawned a new policy as a way to distinguish between humanity and the automatons: Special "bot accounts" would be registered to do bot actions. It was a good idea, as it would make it easier to identify, filter, and undo the mass edits.

Between them, Ram-man and Rambot chalked up more than 100,000 edits by the end of 2004. Ramsey's additions and subsequent follow-up additions made him the top editor in Wikipedia by far.

Rambot has inspired many other bots to not just add articles, but also help to do mundane, repetitive tasks. Bots have been modified not just simply to work on their own in isolation, but also to be "manually assisted" by humans. Spelling is a good example of where the community of people managing bots in Wikipedia stated that the bots should not run on their own.

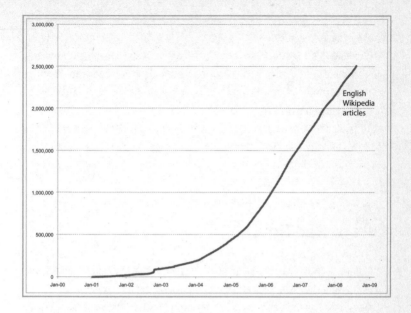

"There should be no bots that attempt to fix spelling mistakes in an unattended fashion. It is not technically possible to create such a bot that would not make mistakes, as there will always be places where non-standard spellings are in fact intended."[37]

Spellbots were one of the first developed to do automated checking of articles en masse. Volunteers were asked to help monitor Spellbots' alarms and, by hand, approve or deny their spelling recommendations.

In practice, bot-assisted editing is somewhat like a hamster feeder, with an endless supply of food (or in this case, spelling mistakes) and Wikipedians scurrying about, grabbing pieces and processing each one.

One user, Lupin, programmed a live spellcheck to check spelling on every new article that was saved in Wikipedia. Users could volunteer to watch the output and correct any that caught their eye. The bot output looked like this:

Josiah Tongogara matched <u>consistant</u> . . .
Dana International matched <u>wich</u> . . .

Clicking on the errant word would allow one to correct the mistake manually. It's hard to imagine that Wikipedia could have scaled past 100,000 articles without the assistance of bots automating the tasks of filtering and sorting, and assisting the human editors.

Similarly, it's hard to imagine today's massive auto industry still requiring hand-assembly of autos as Ford did with the Model T. Repetitive tasks left to robots (or software robots in this case) allow human beings to do what they're good at—decision making, redesigning, and adding new features.

The side effect, or piranha effect, was that Rambot's additions did not just sit there gathering digital dust, entertaining occasional visitors. The basic county and town articles inspired others.

Lots of Red Dots

Seth Anthony was one of your typical Wikipedians, a student living in North Carolina, with a passion for sharing information and time to exercise it.

He was surfing through Wikipedia one day in March 2004, when he stumbled on a Rambot-created page for his hometown. When he pulled up [[Apex, North Carolina]], he saw the top of the rather dry entry:

Apex is a town located in Wake County, North Carolina. As of the 2000 census, the town had a total population of 20,212.

GEOGRAPHY

Apex is located at 35°43'55" North, 78°51'10" West (35.731952, -78.852878).

Typical of Rambot's creations, it had no additional info other than the raw statistics on population. Someone had added the exact coordinates of the town. The article was pretty accurate, but not terribly useful for a human being.

Seth logged into Wikipedia as his online persona User:SethIlys, and added a few paragraphs about the history of his small town—how it was incorporated in 1873, had been consumed by fire but was rebuilt, and how Keith Weatherly was the current mayor.

He left it at that. It was a nice enhancement for a Rambot article that had been sitting there for over a year largely untouched. But a few months later, after spending more time adding prose to articles, Seth had an idea.

Keen to showcase his hometown, he started up his computer graphics program that could pinpoint longitude and latitude, and grabbed the geographic information system (GIS) data for North Carolina. He put a red dot on the map where Apex was located, saved the picture file, and uploaded it to Wikipedia.

A few keystrokes later, and he had added his own handmade map to the article. Now anyone in the world who looked up Apex in Wikipedia would see his visual creation and know where he lived. Who would be looking up Apex? Probably no one anytime soon, but if only one other person saw it, it would be worth it. After all, if Seth had visited the page on a whim, surely someone else might.

Without having to create an entire Web site, without having to advertise his new addition, he was able to contribute his knowledge of his corner of the world for everyone to see.

For Seth, it was empowering. And he found himself strangely addicted:

> Then I decided, what the heck, since I've done that and have the graphics program open, why don't I make maps for every town in the county? That afternoon, I did about a third of the state and it didn't make any sense to stop there, so, like Forrest Gump, I just kept on running. Eerily enough, other people started running, too, and before long nearly all of the User:Rambot U.S. census location articles will have maps.[38]

There's a famous saying in the tech world: When you have a hammer, everything looks like a nail. If there was ever a project that had unhammered nails, thousands and thousands of them, it was Wikipedia.

And best of all, Wikipedia welcomed anyone with Internet access to start hammering.

When non-Wikipedians hear of folks like Ram-man and SethIlys, they often ask, "Who would choose to do such things on their own time?"

If they're not paid for what they are doing, what is the motivation? Why would so many folks converge on this strange project to do what they do?

Peer Production

Noted Yale law professor Yochai Benkler has a theory. In a widely circulated and famous essay on the Internet called "Coase's Penguin," he offered his thinking on why people participate in efforts such as Linux and other "free" projects. There was already a culture, before Wikipedia, of folks donating their time, effort, and skills to the collective good for no monetary gain or immediate compensation. Benkler observed this part of the hacker ethos and was curious to know what the common thread was.

He dubbed it "commons-based peer production." It's a fancy moniker for the phenomenon of people working together toward the same end—creating computer code or content that is free to be copied, distributed, used, and modified by others.

Benkler believes the Internet and the "free culture" movement have allowed individuals to connect and combine their efforts in ways unprecedented in history. The legal academic is not shy to combine scholarship outside his area of training by drawing on economics, sociology, and technology to form his theory.

According to Benkler, if monetary rewards and the creation of corporate firms have been the accepted driving force for human innovation and progress, there has to be something else driving volunteers in Linux, Wikipedia, and other "free" projects that have become so pervasive and monumental in the digital age.

He asserts the motivation comes from two main things other than money: the "socio-psychological" reward of interacting with others, and the "hedonic" personal gratification of the task.

Wikipedia's magic occurs when these two things come together. One person's personal affection and indulgence—mapmaking, grammar checking, baseball statistics, history of stamps—easily finds a home in Wikipedia's amalgam of topics, where it also feeds into and inspires activities by others.

There's never a dearth of things to do—fixing spelling, grammar checking, statistics, sorting, categorization, list making. There is also no deadline, and no pressure to work at a particular pace. In this sense, Wikipedia is the obsessive-compulsive's dream come true. It has a bottomless pit of source material with which to indulge one's pet peeves or obsessions.

But it doesn't stop there, with an individual's work. One person's edits are not confined to a garage or a back room. In the open and transparent Wikipedia universe, none of the actions people take are in isolation. They show up on the Recent Changes page; they trigger notices on other people's watchlists; they're seen by hundreds of passersby who happen to find them by browsing. Hence the piranha effect or, more specifically, the stigmergic effect. One person's change to the environment inspires another to something greater, and the effects cascade through the community.

Sethllys's project was one of them. He became obsessed with dot maps. He created a "subpage"[39] of his own Wikipedia user page and dedicated it to making a dot map for each and every town and city in the United States. Doing this by hand seemed clearly insane to most folks. But on Wikipedia, instead of being a fool's quest, it was a magnet for other like-minded people. Ramsey had already shown it would take months to create city articles by hand, so doing maps would be even harder.

What's strange to observers is that creating maps by hand is a job many wouldn't do even if you paid them. Yet in Wikipedia, here were a dozen folks willing to take up the dot map cause, doing repetitive tasks on their own time for no money.

So, oddly enough, Seth Anthony suddenly saw people appear on his virtual doorstep wanting to create maps as well. To take in these newfound volunteers, he formed an ad hoc support group for people who shared his dot map obsession and dubbed it the Dot Project.

Dot Map Obsession

One of the kindred spirits with an itchy dot-mapping finger was User:Bumm13, a Wikipedian who joined in 2002, well before Sethllys showed up in the community. Bumm13 took some time to work up to the community, editing for a long time as an "anon" with no username, preferring to let his edits speak for themselves and not conversing with others. But eventually, Bumm13 registered a name and was intrigued when he came across the article for [[Cary, North Carolina]] and saw one of SethIlys's dot maps.

He had seen SethIlys before in the IRC chat room, the online lounge where Wikipedians would message one another about everything under the sky—the latest community happening, gripes about articles, or preening about their latest edits. He saw SethIlys talking about his dot maps, and Bumm13 wanted to try it for himself.

Two and a half hours later, after some instruction from SethIlys on how to make maps in software, Bumm13 started his own path to obsession and created a dot map for [[Hatton, Washington]]. Then he made dot maps for the towns of Lind, Othello, and Ritzville, at a rate of one every few minutes.

Now, anyone even slightly knowledgeable about maps and computers is likely asking, "This is the twenty-first century. Aren't there automated programs that can make maps faster, more easily, and more accurately than using human hands?" Absolutely.

But instead of waiting for someone with the programming knowhow, interest, and time to do it, Wikipedia's community encouraged folks to use human hands to act first, without thinking much about efficiencies or potential duplication of effort.

"It's a lot of work that is exceedingly repetitive and tedious, but it beats waiting for someone to come up with a fancy GIS software–based method," says Bumm13.

Programming a solution to dot maps wasn't a choice for him. As he proclaimed on his user page, "I have been fascinated with computers and how they work, etc. Unfortunately, my one shortcoming is that I cannot program. Anything!"

Bumm13 couldn't write software, but what he could do was contribute his time and mouse clicks, generating the dot maps for all the towns of Washington, Wisconsin, Nevada, Delaware, Oregon, and Nebraska. Wisconsin alone required 1,720 individual maps. He only managed to finish Northern California, but he made up for his shortcomings by turning his sights to Australia and making maps for Western Australia and the Northern Territory.

There is a special bond that is forged between a maker and his handmade product. Making dot maps may be an act of absurd inefficiency, but the showcase of the human spirit provided inspiration for others. Standing as exemplars, the dot maps encouraged bigger and better things by folks who didn't know such things were possible.

It's one reason why Wikipedia is considered one of the most important showcases in the Web 2.0 "movement" that has started at the turn of the twenty-first century. Wikipedia is a human-centered endeavor that invites participation on a massive scale. It usurps top-down authority, empowers individuals, and harnesses previously untapped labor of individuals previously isolated in separate social networks, but brought together by the Internet.

You don't need to be a technical whiz; you don't need a computer science degree. You don't actually need to know anything else other than how to hit "edit this page" and make a fix here and there.

For many Wikipedians, the act of participating in article making is also an act of learning. This is a dynamic most outside readers don't often see or experience. Writing about subjects while abiding by Wikipedia's neutral point of view (NPOV) requires research, critical thinking, and weighing the facts. Contributors often find themselves learning by editing, simply because they are required to cite sources, read others' contributions, and decide how the article can be reshaped or balanced to adhere to NPOV. Even Ram-man, SethIlys, and Bumm13 had to learn new skills to execute their projects.

The community also reinforces another Web 2.0 value—reuse and remix. If you can build and learn from the work of others, this unbridled content can evolve much faster.

In the process, almost every Wikipedian gets a crash course in intellectual property law just by contact. Creating new features requires learning about copyright, fair use, and other legal issues surrounding the incorporation of existing works. Wikipedia is rather strict about staying legal and not violating the copyrights of others. Anyone who spends time as a Wikipedia editor will immediately need to become well acquainted with U.S. copyright law (with the servers being physically located in Florida), public domain works, and "free" licensing. It's part of the "commons-based" system that Benkler describes. Free content begets more free content. And it's a formula Wikipedia has thrived on.

SethIlys and Bumm13 found a calling, and its legacy lives on in Wikipedia's thousands of dot maps. Was it completely free, though, or was there a cost? Years afterward, SethIlys has no regrets and is proud of his work. But there was a cost of sorts, he admits. He was spending so much time on the dot maps, it indirectly caused his breakup with his girlfriend at the time. Maps are a tough mistress.

Essays, Guidelines, and Policy

When Wikipedia was launched, it started out with very few fixed rules. The wiki culture was still new to everyone involved, and Larry Sanger was simply trying to gather critical mass for the project. One of the most famous original and innovative rules was his: Ignore all rules (IAR). It is not as nihilistic as it sounds. The earliest incarnation read:

> If rules make you nervous and depressed, and not desirous of participating in the Wiki, then ignore them and go about your business.[40]

Sanger was simply saying that people shouldn't let the rules intimidate them into leaving and not getting interested in the project: "I thought we needed experience with how wikis should work, and even more importantly at that point we needed participants more than we needed rules. . . . I always thought of the rule as being a temporary and humorous injunction to participants to add content rather than be distracted by (then) relatively inconsequential issues about how exactly articles should be formatted."

The wiki culture at the time trusted in community members to make reasoned decisions. Wikipedia evolved along these lines, to emerge with three main developments: essays as nonauthoritative writings that contain insights and exhortations; guidelines, or what Joseph Reagle described as "actionable norms approved by general consensus"; and policies, which have "wide acceptance among editors and are considered a standard that all users should follow."

Early on, three core policies emerged for the Wikipedia project that were formed by Sanger as being absolutely necessary: neutral point of view (NPOV), verifiability (V), and no original research (NOR). Wikipedia considers them as the three fundamentals for editors:

> Wikipedia:Neutral point of view is one of Wikipedia's three core content policies. The other two are Wikipedia:Verifiability and Wikipedia:No original research. Jointly, these policies determine the type and quality of material that is acceptable in Wikipedia articles. Because the policies are

complementary, they should not be interpreted in isolation from one another, and editors should familiarize themselves with all three.[41]

NPOV is the only nonnegotiable policy in Wikipedia, according to Jimmy Wales. It's what makes people work together: converging while collaborating.

Verifiability is about "whether readers are able to check that material added to Wikipedia has already been published by a reliable source." Wikipedia's popularity has meant verifiability has been taken much more seriously in recent years. This has led to adoption of stricter standards when adding material to articles, including requiring citations to sources on the Internet and more stringent requirements when it comes to writing about living persons, because of concerns over libel. One of the more often used templates in Wikipedia is {{citeneeded}}, which places a small [citation needed] message next to unsourced statements to warn readers of dubious content and to prod editors into citing or removing such claims.

No Original Research (NOR) was crafted to keep with an encyclopedia's role to reflect a summary of what is established in writing and scholarship. "Wikipedia does not publish original thought: all material in Wikipedia must be attributable to a reliable, published source. Articles may not contain any new analysis or synthesis of published material that serves to advance a position not clearly advanced by the sources," reads the policy.

Much later, after four years and many policy pages, User:Neutrality reconceived what he saw as the sprawling set of policies to make it simpler. He wrote, "All of Wikipedia's 28 official policies and 35 semi-policies are really based on five unchangeable pillars that define Wikipedia's character." Today, these "Five Pillars" read:

I. Wikipedia is an encyclopedia.
II. Wikipedia has a neutral point of view.
III. Wikipedia is free content.
IV. Wikipedia has a code of conduct.
V. Wikipedia does not have firm rules.

To achieve the piranha effect, Wikipedia encourages users to "be bold." Sanger embraced this side of the wiki culture, even to the point of saying, "Do not worry about messing up." But being bold can easily escalate into aggressive editing when dealing with other editors. Therefore, a soft code of conduct developed as a counterbalance to govern community-oriented interactions. A core idea Wikipedia embraced, borrowed from the original MeatballWiki, was to assume good faith (AGF) when interacting with others. The guideline promoted optimistic production rather than pessimistic nay-saying, and reads, "Unless there is strong evidence to the contrary, assume that people who work on the project are trying to help it, not hurt it; avoid accusing others of harmful motives without particularly strong evidence."

Because Wikipedia relied on typed text communication for article writing, talk page debates, and email list discussions, it was prone to all the problems that plagued Usenet, with sarcasm, compassion, and humor often lost in transmission. AGF was an important principle to maintain a stable community culture. Wikipedians were also reminded, "Don't bite the newbies," as the next new user you meet could be the next great Wikipedia convert and supreme editor.

Fix It Yourself

Since the Web 2.0 era is about user-generated content, it can be a shock to newcomers who are not used to the idea when they come to Wikipedia. The community practice of not waiting for a fancy solution and just getting your hands dirty has spawned a special mantra (or admonishment): SOFIXIT.

Don't like the way things are done? Annoyed how dates are missing in an article? Think there's a better way to display images? Those articles are missing maps?

"SOFIXIT, it's a wiki after all" became the standard reply on the mailing lists or talk pages to newbies. It's even become a standard response to critics.

"SOFIXIT" came into being as a response in the early days of Wikipedia, when people might not have realized they could edit Wikipedia's pages. A visitor might complain something was misspelled or a fact was incorrect. In response, the administrators were so tired of repeating themselves incessantly, they created a special boilerplate message, like a form letter, something they could easily leave as a note to others.

Adding {{sofixit}} as a template to the talk page of a user would expand to become a full message explaining that users could in fact edit Wikipedia themselves.

When it was first created on April 10, 2004, {{sofixit}} read:

Hello, welcome to Wikipedia! We welcome your contributions. Wikipedia is a wiki, and anyone—including you!—can edit nearly any article, at any time, by clicking the **Edit This Page** link at the bottom of the article. You don't even need to login, although there are several reasons why you might want to. So, feel free to make this correction yourself! If you are unsure about how to edit a page, try out the Sandbox to test your editing skills.

But what happens when people take SOFIXIT too much to heart?

Wikipedia invites people to "Be bold," but what happens when people are too bold, and they start to clash?

The calls for volunteers inevitably create some contentious conflicts. And in Wikipedia, the ultimate battleground is over what articles should stay and what should go.

What to Include

One of the most heated perennial debates in Wikipedia is the question: Which articles should be included in Wikipedia? When Jimmy Wales and Larry Sanger started the project, they wanted it to be an encyclopedia in the tradition of the great print encyclopedias in history—Diderot's Encyclopédie and Encyclopedia Britannica. Because both were paper-based, they were necessarily limited by shelf space, printing costs, and other practical physical limits. Human editors, starting from a hierarchical taxonomy of what to include, centrally organized them to encompass the topics of the known world. To plan out the volumes, they needed a system of classification.

Unlike other encyclopedias throughout history, Wikipedia has no physical limit on how many pages it can contain. Every year, computer disc space grows in size and shrinks in cost, so storage space is not a scarce resource.

Also, in the age of Google search and hypertext, people can come across Wikipedia's content through any number of avenues.

The idea of a "volume" or "alphabetical order" is completely irrelevant to a modern Internet encyclopedia. Although Wikipedia maintains a rough hierarchical classification of subject areas, few people use it as an entry point. It's maintained as a relic of history.

So given that space is no constraint, what determines what gets included in an encyclopedia? It's a continuously shifting standard in the Wikipedia universe, and varies greatly across languages as well.

One faction believes Wikipedia should contain pretty much anything, as long as it's factual and verifiable. "Wiki is not paper," so why not include everything under the sky? This is a unique opportunity in human history. In the absence of any physical limitations, why *not* include anything and everything, since the presence of one article in cyberspace does not affect your finding or reading another one? Wikipedians who subscribed to this thinking quickly became known as the "inclusionists" of the community. When in doubt, include it. Why not? Wiki is not paper. Disc space is cheap.

On the other side of the debate are the "deletionists," although this somewhat unfairly characterizes their view in a destructive way. Some prefer the word "exclusionists." This camp believes it is important to strictly determine not only whether something is factual, but whether it is notable, whether it is worthy of being included in the pantheon of human knowledge. They believe that selectivity equals quality. Keeping stringent standards provides for a more useful encyclopedia, so you're not constantly intermixing prominent subjects with minutiae and irrelevant topics. When you're looking up [[John Brown]], you should get the American of the 1800s who fought to abolish slavery, and not some random John Brown who's someone's local barber or a telephone repairman.

Wikipedia has reached an equilibrium point where there is a consensus that extreme inclusion is not tenable because it will indeed gum up the virtual works. Even the most staunch inclusionists know that while [[War of 1812]] is appropriate, [[Jane Smith's waffle breakfast of January 12, 2003]], even if verifiable, factual, and referenced, is not.

So at the center of this debate is notability, which is where inclusionists and deletionists in Wikipedia have their skirmishes. The community has converged on a definition, for now:

A topic is presumed to be notable if it has received significant coverage in reliable sources that are independent of the subject.[42]

This description illustrates something that Wikipedia established early on: Wikipedia itself is not a primary source for information. It should depend on facts and figures published first in reliable, independent primary sources of information.

Wikipedia should not be original research. Wales has said this policy prevents Wikipedia from being "novel narrative or historical interpretation."

No original research, neutral point of view, and verifiability form the three content policies of Wikipedia that are immutable. Everything in the editorial guidelines hinges on those three ideas.[43] Even after many years, the constant struggle between inclusionists and deletionists over these three ideas has not ended. And the consequences show up in all corners of Wikipedia.

There are articles everyone can agree should be in the collection of all human knowledge. No one would dispute Wikipedia should have pages on common general knowledge subjects such as [[Napoleon]], [[elephant]], and [[tsunami]].

The reader might be surprised that over the years, Wikipedia has come to consensus to include a number of articles unlikely to be found in any other encyclopedia. Among these articles are the following actual seriously written pages from Wikipedia's own list of "Unusual articles" (http://en.wikipedia.org/wiki/List_of_unusual_articles).

Festivus	December 23: a fictional holiday celebrated by the Costanza family on the television show Seinfeld
Year zero	Was there a year between 1 BC and AD 1?
Bushism	Any of a number of peculiar words, phrases, pronunciations, malapropisms, semantic or linguistic errors that have occurred in the public speaking of United States President George W. Bush.
Buttered cat paradox	If a cat always lands on its feet and toast always lands buttered-side-down, would a buttered cat simply levitate above the ground?
Five-second rule	The belief that food dropped on the floor is safe to eat only as long as it's picked up within five seconds.

Infinite monkey theorem	An infinite number of monkeys typing on an infinite number of typewriters will produce all possible written texts.
All your base are belong to us	A phrase that originated in the 1989 video game Zero Wing and sparked an Internet phenomenon in 2001 and 2002.
Croydon facelift	A hairstyle peculiar to parts of England.
Jumping the shark	Metaphor for the point at which one can speak of a TV show as having had its best days behind it.
Exploding whale	Real whales exploded in Oregon in 1970 and Taiwan in 2004.
Chewbacca Defense	A satirical term for any legal strategy that seeks to overwhelm its audience with nonsensical arguments.
You have two cows	The beginning phrase for a series of political joke definitions.
Flying Spaghetti Monster	A satirical religion created to make fun of Intelligent Design. Its supernatural creator is a monster which resembles spaghetti and meatballs.
Anti-tank dog	Failed Soviet weapon of the Second World War.
Boston molasses disaster	Twenty-one people die in 1919 when a huge tank at a confectionery factory bursts, sending a wave of molasses down the streets of Boston.

There are a range of topics, however, that are always being disputed between inclusionists and deletionists. It's the borderline cases that are the hardest. A long-running battle has been about whether or not to have an article about each and every school that exists. Each college or university certainly deserves one, but what about each and every middle or elementary school in the world? In 2001, there was a debate about having an article for each and every victim of the World Trade Center September 11 attack. After much debate, articles about 9/11 victims were moved to a separate memorial wiki.

The primary battledome where inclusionists and deletionists duke it out, every hour of every day, is a page called Votes for Deletion. It's the place of final judgment, where the community gathers to decide the fate of Wikipedia articles nominated for removal. (Today, it is known as Articles for Deletion, for reasons detailed later.)

While most everything else in Wikipedia works based on being bold and taking direct action, this is one area that depends on a bureaucracy. Votes for Deletion, or VfD, became an important forum in Wikipedia because only administrators could actually delete articles. The problem was that if administrators were the only ones that could perform deletion, it was certainly not "consensus" of the community to determine what stays and goes.

As a result, VfD was set up as the public chopping block, allowing the community to review requests for deleting articles, and to voice opinions on whether to keep or delete entries. Putting an article on VfD was like a "Hear ye, hear ye" announcement requesting consensus on a proposed deletion. People could chime in on the article's merits. Most comments were terse and direct: "Delete. Nonnotable," or "Keep, important historical figure." The more complicated cases spawned vigorous debate.

As people registered their views, usually a consensus would form. After a specified number of days, the "closer," an administrator volunteering to do the task, would determine the sense of the community and act accordingly.

Therefore the original title of the process, "Votes for Deletion," which stayed in place for years, was a misnomer as it wasn't truly a straight vote. The "closing" administrator hoped to see a strong consensus one way or the other. If the administrator was lucky, it was 90/10 or 80/20 in favor of a certain action. It was never considered a binding vote in order to discourage gaming (to artificially induce an outcome that is not genuinely the sense of the community). In fact, Wikipedia took its stance from the original MeatballWiki culture, where online communities have discouraged outright voting. Wikipedia's stance was very similar:

Don't vote on everything, and if you can help it, don't vote on anything.

The original name of the policy page was more emphatic: VotingIsEvil.

Given Wikipedia's increasing popularity, it is not surprising that true consensus has had difficulty scaling up, and in fact in close cases, straight voting has become a more common occurrence out of necessity.

While deletionists felt that notability and verifiability were important, some on the extreme went even further, listing articles for deletion that were poorly written, even if the topic clearly belonged in an encyclopedia. In that sense, VfD was also seen as a way to bring about action:

> I included Talossan language on VfD because the article, as written, was nonsense. It has since been modified to make it a legitimate topic. VfD frequently serves such a useful purpose.—RickK

This particular strain of deletionism held that an article should either be written well, or not written at all. Wales disagreed and thought poorly written articles should be kept:

> The benefits are easily identifiable—these are topics that are of ongoing interest to people, they have historical relevance in the long run, wiki is not paper so they don't hurt anything, and so on.[44]
> But the costs are harder for me to identify. These aren't appearing on the front page. They will only been seen by people who are looking for them. Given the mechanics of VfD, it's a lot more work to delete them than to just ignore them or (better) throw in a couple more lines to improve them.

Wales's opinion carried weight and was indicative of the major ideological difference between an academic stance ("edit then write") and the wiki stance ("write then edit").

This bright-eyed hope in the future for articles has been dubbed "eventualism." An article may not be great now, but even without a deadline, it will eventually be made better in the future by someone else. It was a sign of faith in the piranha effect taking hold, eventually. The problem is that the piranha effect requires a critical mass of people and attention. For RickK and others, putting an article on VfD was putting the ultimatum out—piranhas come feast, or we're throwing it out.

Eventualism has become an accepted norm in the community, because by default since the beginning of the project, starting from nothing, articles have overwhelmingly benefited from multiple eyeballs (and edits). Entries have generally increased in quality over time, giving more and more faith to the theory that articles by and large attract more content.

For some, eventualism is a fancy name for "passing the buck." It is being lackadaisical in doing something right now to fix things. For professional writers, editors, and academics, leaving things in a half-baked state was a clear departure from their comfort zone. But given the masses of wiki, Slashdot, Usenet, and open source software veterans, eventualism remained the prevailing attitude, at least in the early days.

However, as Wikipedia's articles matured and became more popular on Google, got closer to some complete state, or were given "featured" status as the cream of the crop, this faith in eventualism started to get some reconsideration.

Gaming the Vote

Wiki communities are designed to foster discourse and consensus, and to avoid being battlegrounds for binding votes. In reality, Wikipedia's VfD was mostly a straight vote. Most cases were an easy call to either keep or delete. Staying away from calling it a formal "vote" provided some latitude to administrators in case there was evidence of questionable outside influence, like vote stacking or canvassing.

Because VfD serves as a public square, and public spectacle, Wikipedia has been subject to crowds from bulletin board systems, email lists, or other forums on the Internet stampeding to Wikipedia to vote a certain way.

Fake grassroots voting, or "astroturfing," is not unique to Wikipedia. Nearly every news or entertainment Web site with a vote option sees this problem. But when a site encourages anyone to "edit this page," the problem is magnified. Wikipedia has seen a series of political groups, religious groups (Scientologists being of particular note), or simple pranksters line up to game the vote.

As a result, Votes for Deletion was redubbed Articles for Deletion, to remove any supposition that it was a vote and to cut through the noise of these canvassing efforts. But for all practical matters, it is still a vote, or rather a referendum with room for interpretation.

Discussions can get heated in the Articles for Deletion forum, but at least it's in the virtual town square of Wikipedia. Because it happens in plain sight, you have hundreds or thousands of folks watching, reinforcing, debating, and creating consensus. People come together; decisions are made with diverse collective input.

Small Ball

By contrast, the tough cases of Wikipedia are not in the big forums, but really in the trenches, when skirmishes happen in small corners of the community, away from the collective eyeballs. Here at the article level, it's editor against editor, a clash of wills among individuals usually unfamiliar with each other, who find themselves treading in the same virtual space.

In order to attract and elicit contributions from users, Wikipedia charges visitors to "Be bold," but as a consequence it also encourages (nay, depends on) conflict. BEBOLD and SOFIXIT directives provide grist for this virtual mill. And too often, it's not a pleasant interaction.

This is where the real latent problems of Wikipedia hide, in these contentious, hard to track disputes happening at the article level, and they create the real scourge of Wikipedia community: the edit wars.

An edit war happens when two different sides are both determined they are right, and will not yield, compromise, or arrive at consensus. In Wikipedia lore, there is no more famous example of the edit war than the curious case of Gdansk and Danzig. Even the order in which they are mentioned in this text might cause a ruckus among Wikipedians at the heart of this debate.

First, a whirlwind introduction to this subject.

Gdansk/Danzig Wars

The city Gdansk (also known as Danzig) in present-day Poland lies on the mouth of the Vistula River on the south part of the Baltic Sea. Over the last few hundred years it had the unique (and as we'll see, unfortunate) privilege of being variously ruled over by the Teutonic Knights, the Prussian Confederation, the Polish Crown, the Kingdom of Prussia, nobody at all (when it was the Free City of Danzig), the German Empire, and today's Republic of Poland. As a result, this city has seen its classification shift over the last half dozen centuries, creating an all-out, millennium-long identity crisis.

At least this is the case for the Polish, German, and self-appointed history-minded editors in Wikipedia.

It started out innocently enough in the first year of Wikipedia's existence, when User:H.J. created an article [[Gdansk]] on December 24, 2001:

> **Gdansk** is a city in <u>Poland</u>, on the coast of <u>Baltic Sea</u>.
> Its German name is **Danzig** and it was usually called by that name in English until <u>1945</u>. In Latin it was called **Gedanum.**

It seemed like a good start.

Because Gdansk/Danzig had changed hands so many times through history, it posed a conundrum not just to writers of this article, but to writers of any other articles that referred to the city. Is it a Polish or German city? Should other articles refer to it as Gdansk or Danzig? What about people born there, were they of Polish or German ethnicity?

The article quickly gathered Poles, Germans, and anyone else who cared to chime in with their own interpretation of what was right. "Neutral" was unfortunately a casualty of the conversation, as it had broken down into a test of wills and strong points of view.

One of the most obstinate and persistent users was one User:Nico. An especially contentious editor, he held the firm belief that all German-related articles should have German names prominently mentioned. That put Gdansk (nee Danzig) and many other Polish (nee German) cities in the crosshairs. On the other side of things was User:Wik, someone quite famous in Wikipedia for not shying away from making a point and being heard. They were not the only ones involved, but they were the most vocal and the most uncompromising.

The Gdansk article had been the subject of dozens of adjustments and skirmishes, but on October 16, 2003, it began a descent into prolonged, sustained conflict. It was the beginning of perhaps the most famous "edit war" in Wikipedia history, in terms of profile, duration, number of users, and ultimately, the final remedy.

One glance at the edit history of the article shows a nasty exchange between two sides, neither willing to compromise.

In the article history for [[Gdansk]] in October 2003, the trail of usernames and "edit comments" left by Nico and Wik showed the ugly details:

16 October 2003
   20:45 Nico (fmt)
   21:42 Wik (rv)
   23:07 64.175.121.242 (See "Talk")

17 October 2003
   07:56 80.213.15.39 (Revert to the last edit by Nico)
   08:06 Wik (rv)
   09:14 Ruhrjung m (links)
   13:05 Nico m (Reinsert deleted paragraph)
   14:05 Ruhrjung (shortening)
   14:08 Ruhrjung m (link)
   16:44 Wik
   16:45 Wik
   19:22 Nico (Revert to the last edit by Ruhrjung)
   19:38 Wik
   19:42 Kpjas m (some typos and one sentence added to give context)
   19:45 Wik (rv)
   19:51 145.254.119.100
   20:18 Kpjas m (this edit corrects typos and adds one sentence if you don't
   agree with it discuss it in Talk: don't revert discriminately)

18 October 2003
   16:55 Nico m (Revert to the last edit by Ruhrjung)
   17:27 Wik (Revert to the last edit by Kpjas)
   17:43 Nico m (Revert to the last edit by Ruhrjung)
   17:51 Wik (rv)
   19:49 Nico (Revert to the last edit by Ruhrjung)
   19:54 Nico m
   19:56 Wik (rv (are we having fun yet?))
   20:12 Nico (Revert to the last edit by Ruhrjung)
   20:15 Wik (rv (someone protect this please))
   22:40 Nico (Revert to the last edit by Ruhrjung (What do you have problems with, Wik? Why just tell us at the talk page?))
   22:42 Wik (rv (same problem as with Poznan))
   22:43 Nico (Revert to the last edit by Ruhrjung)

22:45 Wik (rv)

22:48 Nico (Revert to the last edit by Ruhrjung—if you not are willing to discuss the case you will be reverted again and again)

22:50 Wik (rv (see Talk:Poznan))

22:53 Nico (What about Talk:Poznan? Nothing there about Danzig. You should visit Talk:Gdansk—again reverting to Ruhrjung's latest edit)

22:55 Wik (rv (you're just trolling now, this is exactly the same case as Poznan, just exchange the names))

22:59 Nico (It's a fact that the city also is known as Danzig to English speakers. I reinsert Ruhrjung's note about that. You can discuss the article at Talk:Gdansk if you want, and maybe you will be able to conv)

23:00 Wik (Danzig is known as a former name, nothing else)

23:03 Nico (No, Danzig is surely the actual German, Danish, Swedish name of the city, and is actually also used by many speakers of English. Reinsert Ruhrung's note again.)

23:04 Wik (the first paragraph says all there is to say about the name)

The repeated series of "revert" or "rv" edits are the telltale signatures of an edit war.

In Wikipedia, a revert means the only change is to undo the work of someone else. In essence it is a repudiation of another Wikipedian by removing that user's particular contribution from Wikipedia. Reverts have their place, to undo vandalism or to correct a small mistake by someone else. But a revert duel can be a bitter spectacle.

Wikipedia's edit war guidelines admonishes revert warriors, "This is generally considered a useless practice. Please don't do it."[45]

If no one can talk the warring parties out of an ongoing dispute, an administrator usually has to step in to protect the article from all editing until the situation cools off. In extreme cases, one or more "warriors" could even be blocked temporarily from editing anything in Wikipedia.

Not long after this edit war broke out, Wikipedia administrators stepped in to protect the article and to avoid this rapid reverting between versions. However, the problem with protection is that it doesn't solve the root cause, it just prevents further flipping of the article. Once an administrator thinks the warring has cooled down, the article can be unprotected, but in the case of Gdansk/Danzig, the situation did not stabilize.

Outbreaks of edit warring would occur again on October 28, November 18, and November 30 of 2003, and spill into 2004, on January 21, January 31, and February 3.

Users with names such as User:PolishPoliticians, User:Gdansk, and User:Emax would join the fray, stoking more debate and keeping the issue simmering for months on end. It was widely known in the Wikipedia community that the Gdansk/Danzig debate was a festering wound, but if there was no party to reconcile the differences, it would keep going on.

As 2004 was beginning, Wikipedia was making big strides and becoming widely recognized by the mainstream public, having been written up in *Discover* magazine, *Popular Science, The Wall Street Journal,* and the San Jose *Mercury News.* As Wikipedia passed the 200,000 article mark in February 2004, it was still accelerating in terms of article and community growth.

While the community celebrated the external recognition and accomplishments, it knew internally there were trouble spots, like Gdansk/Danzig, where contentious edit wars were cropping up more and more and creating angst and burnout.

Wikipedia experimented with some ways to quickly defuse situations. One measure was something called Quickpolls, an ad hoc "night court" for the community to quickly decide, in twenty-four hours, how to discipline problem users. It was made specifically for four types of cases:

1. someone violates the three revert guideline
2. a sysop repeatedly misuses a sysop capability
3. a signed in user goes on a "rampage" of some type—puts insults on several user (not user talk) pages, vandalizes several articles, etc.
4. a signed in user confesses to deliberate trolling

It did not go particularly well during the trial period. Immediately, User:Gdansk was the target of one Quickpoll, initiated with the message:

User has been involved with Polish and German related articles, engaging in near-vandalism for months. Recommend a 24-hour ban. —Hephaestos|§

After a unanimous 12–0 vote in favor of the proposal, User:Gdansk was blocked from editing for twenty-four hours.

In a community that prided itself on assuming good faith and thoughtful consensus, Quickpolls made an unusual public spectacle of these cases, creating a virtual village mob. Add to that the belief within wiki culture that VotingIsEvil, and it was clear this brand of instant justice was not getting widespread approval.

Besides, all the proposed disciplinary measures being voted on were mostly something an administrator could do on his or her own, without needing a chorus of support from Quickpoll voters. With no one enthusiastic to carry on the experiment beyond a month, the trial period expired in June 2004. Another method would have to resolve edit wars.

There was one thing from the Quickpolls experiment that had some popular support. The three revert rule, which prevented someone from constantly flipping back the edits of another, would come back in another way.

By August of that year, the community was growing so weary of contentious edit wars that the three revert rule (3RR) was proposed as a stand-alone policy to act as an "electric fence":

An editor must not perform more than three reverts, in whole or in part, on a single page within a 24-hour period.

Violating this would allow an individual administrator to block the problem user for twenty-four hours on sight. The proposal had the backing of Jimmy Wales himself:

I am personally endorsing and promoting this proposal, because I think that revert warring has become an absurd drain on us, and it has not worked for it to be a mere guideline of politeness, nor has it proved effective for the [arbitration committee] to consider every single case of this. Violation of the 3RR is widely considered to be a problem in the community, even by those who are the worst violators.[46]

Wales's endorsement carried lots of weight in the community. On November 28, 2004, the three revert rule passed a community poll, 159 to 28, in favor. And the acronym-happy community quickly adopted the new nickname for it: 3RR.

Some saw this as a betrayal of Wikipedia's original values of not having strict punitive rules and processes. Wikipedia had started out with the assumption that ultimately human beings should be reasoned with and not punished with a "three strikes" type policy.

"Setting this up allows too much power in the hands of admins who have their own agenda to enforce. In the case of a war between a contributor and an admin it gives the admin a 'big stick' with which to enforce his/her viewpoint," wrote one User:KeyStroke.

User:VeryVerily worried that once hard numbers were established, people could "game" the system. "A vandal need only make their edit four times. People can create sockpuppets, and in my experience have done so. Bad users can gang up on good."

Sock puppets are multiple fake accounts created by one user to impersonate many different users. While not inherently bad, if used to gain an advantage in matters related to voting or reverting, they can pose a massive disruption. It is among the worst problems in Wikipedia, and quite hard to track down.

Nevertheless, edit warring was so widely recognized as a growing problem, most Wikipedians welcomed the ability to stop an edit war in its tracks, even if it meant shutting a user out for twenty-four hours. Jimmy's input was important—if the founder was endorsing such a measure, it was probably something worth passing.

When 3RR was established as official policy, it would have implications for the Gdansk case. With "infinite war" no longer a possibility, the folks involved with the debate could not depend on exhaustively reverting to make their point. The involved parties would have to sit down at the table and figure out a long-term resolution, lest they be blocked every few days from editing for violating 3RR.

So Gdansk was ready to be a landmark case, setting a precedent for all other Polish-German articles. The community was looking in earnest to find out how this would play out.

In February 2005, User:Chris 73, an ethnic German editor living in Japan, traipsed into the debate, by reverting the Gdansk-oriented edits by User:Emax. After a few exchanges, he expressed his frustration:

My problem with Emax is that he seems to be unable to compromise. . . . We either have the option to have factual[ly] incorrect articles or to have edit wars.

Tired of the bickering, Chris 73 decided to solve the problem once and for all. He spent the next twenty-four hours crafting a vote proposal meticulously specifying every single time period that had been debated and disputed in Gdansk/Danzig's history. Being bold, he put up an excruciatingly detailed poll of ten different criteria, declaring:

> This page is a vote to decide the usage of the name of Gdansk/Danzig. This is a source of edit wars on dozens of articles mentioning the city on Wikipedia. There is a lengthy discussion on Talk:Gdansk and its archives, listing nearly every argument imaginable. Numerous previous attempts to reach a consensus have been unsuccessful, hence requiring a vote to end dozens of disputes and edit wars. Due to the complexity of the problem, there are six periods to vote for, plus three additional clauses.

Reading like an official ballot that would make any bureaucratic international standards committee proud, Chris 73's proposal listed all the alternatives:

1. VOTE: Period before 1308
2. VOTE: Period from 1308 to 1454
3. VOTE: Period from 1454 to 1466
4. VOTE: Period from 1466 to 1793
5. VOTE: Period from 1793 to 1945
6. VOTE: Period after 1945
7. VOTE: Bibliographies
8. VOTE: Cross-Naming Gdansk/Danzig
9. VOTE: Cross-Naming General
10. VOTE: Enforcement

Each of the ten items allowed voters to fill in their preference—Gdansk or Danzig. Many of these spawned vigorous debate, most of it rehashed from previous fights. But at least they were being aired in the same forum and they were held to something they were unaccustomed to—a time limit. Wikipedia's usual "eventualism" was going to be trumped by a hard deadline and a systematic breakdown of the conflict into tinier, more manageable issues.

In two weeks of voting, 80 people cast 657 votes. After exchanging more than 8,000 words of debate, a decision was reached.

And finally, when the results were tallied and the resolutions emerged, there was much rejoicing by Wikipedians. After nearly two years of bickering, the community finally had hard guidelines that would become the law on anything related to German-Polish issues related to the city. Word went out throughout Wikipedia:

> For Gdansk, use the name *Danzig* between 1308 and 1945
>> For Gdansk, use the name *Gdansk* before 1308 and after 1945
>> In biographies of clearly German persons, the name should be used in the form *Danzig (Gdansk)* and later *Danzig* exclusively
>> In biographies of clearly Polish persons, the name should be used in the form *Gdansk (Danzig)* and later *Gdansk* exclusively.
>> For Gdansk and other locations that share a history between Germany and Poland, the first reference of one name in an article should also include a reference to other names, e.g. *Danzig (now Gdansk, Poland)* or *Gdansk (Danzig)*. An English language reference that primarily uses this name should be provided on the talk page if a dispute arises.

As a result, a common paragraph could be finalized in the Gdansk article without fear of reverting, to what we see today:

> Once the city became a part of the Kingdom of Prussia in 1792 following the partitions of Poland it became more frequently populated by new German settlers. It remained in the hands of the German Empire until 1919. The German name Danzig was used by the German population until the end of World War II although among Poles it was known by its Polish name. The city's Latin name may be given as any of Gedania, Gedanum, or Dantiscum; the variety of Latin names reflects the influence of the Polish, Kashubian, and German names.
>> Former English versions of its name include Dantzig (borrowed from Dutch), Dantsic, and Dantzic.[47]

Thus ended the famous Gdansk/Danzig war in Wikipedia.

As heartening as this outcome was, it was incredibly inefficient. It took years of bickering, bad feelings, and countless wasted hours to arrive at something historians had figured out a long time ago. So while this showcased a community able to resolve a problem, it would likely drive away academics and scholars unaccustomed to Wikipedia's contentious work process.

This point has not gone unnoticed. Even those who join Wikipedia as enthusiastic contributors quickly see the unsavory agonistic side of the community.

Prominent Internet historian Jason Scott lamented this working aspect of Wikipedia during a public speech, highlighting the ominous side of a culture where "anyone can edit." Scott is no Luddite. As a veteran of electronic bulletin board systems and online culture, his criticism had resonance even among people who are fans of Wikipedia:

> Jimbo [Wales] holds this up as the great aspect of Wikipedia, is that everybody gets to get their hands in it and that we're all working together, but they don't realize, we kill each other! We kill each other every day! Over Nintendo games, over shit! Over the fact that someone parked in the wrong space. Wikipedia holds up the dark mirror of what humanity is, to itself.

The full range of Wikipedia criticisms is addressed in later chapters, but the point Scott makes highlights a hidden side of the Wikipedia process.

Most people encounter Wikipedia's articles as a useful, if not always reliable, end product. But because Wikipedia encourages confrontation and challenge as a necessary part of converging on the truth, there are many user casualties along the way for those who decide to try to edit.

At least this is the case with the English Wikipedia. With the role of English as a world language, the site gets an inordinately larger number of visitors than any other language version. That's why the Gdansk/Danzig conflict had passionate ethnic Polish, ethnic German, and other editors from around the world arguing vehemently.

Not only does English Wikipedia serve as the universal mixing bowl, bound together by language, it also has the highest profile in Google searches. That makes the stakes even higher for someone to want to "win" an edit war, so that user's viewpoint reaches the most people on the Internet.

It is as if the biblical Tower of Babel has been reassembled at Wikipedia.org, with the top of the Google rankings as the ultimate goal.

Though what is more intriguing about Wikipedia is not the English version most people see via Google, but the smaller language editions that reflect entirely different cultural norms. These are not simply direct translations or clones of English Wikipedia. They have robust grassroot cultures that surprise even seasoned Wikipedians.

Whether it's issues of American/British English, Chinese dialects, Native

American languages, German standards for article inclusion, the identity of Japanese editors, or the merits of a controversial "Montenegrin" language, there is no shortage of colorful differences across the languages of Wikipedia. When you look at the emergence of these community cultures, it's fascinating to see how they came about.

Chapter 6

WIKIPEDIA GOES INTERNATIONAL

"A different language is a different vision of life."
—*Federico Fellini*

"Language is not an abstract construction of the learned, or of dictionary makers, but is something arising out of the work, needs, ties, joys, affections, tastes, of long generations of humanity, and has its bases broad and low, close to the ground."
—*Noah Webster*

n the Bible, God seemed to want to make a point about the world's languages. It was put right up front and center, in Genesis 11:1-9 (English Standard Version):

1. Now the whole earth had one language and the same words.
2. And as people migrated from the east, they found a plain in the land of Shinar and settled there.
3. And they said to one another, "Come, let us make bricks, and burn them thoroughly." And they had brick for stone, and bitumen for mortar.

4. Then they said, "Come, let us build ourselves a city and a tower with its top in the heavens, and let us make a name for ourselves, lest we be dispersed over the face of the whole earth."

5. And the Lord came down to see the city and the tower, which the children of man had built.

6. And the Lord said, "Behold, they are one people, and they have all one language, and this is only the beginning of what they will do. And nothing that they propose to do will now be impossible for them.

7. "Come, let us go down and there confuse their language, so that they may not understand one another's speech."

8. So the Lord dispersed them from there over the face of all the earth, and they left off building the city.

9. Therefore its name was called Babel, because there the Lord confused the language of all the earth. And from there the Lord dispersed them over the face of all the earth.

Whether or not one believes this as literal truth, the Internet is perhaps "un-dispersing" humanity's languages by reconstituting them under one virtual roof at Wikipedia.

Marshall McLuhan once noted this aspect, saying, "Language as the technology of human extension, whose powers of division and separation we know so well, may have been the 'Tower of Babel' by which men sought to scale the highest heavens. Today computers hold out the promise of a means of instant translation."[48]

Most Wikipedia stories in the press tend to cover the English edition, but choose almost any other language and the story gets even more interesting and the effects more profound. We may compare the merits of Wikipedia against established print encyclopedias, but for many languages of the world, Wikipedia is the only encyclopedia in that native tongue. This is something many Wikipedia critics often fail to grasp.

Hiding in plain view on the side of the screen for any Wikipedia page is the area of Interwiki links. It's a list of other languages in which the current article has a version. By placing a short language code at the end of a given article, a link is created to the same topic in another language edition. For example, the page for [[Internet]] has listed among its Interwiki links:

[[ar:إنترنت]]
[[eo:Interreto]]
[[he:אינטרנט]]
[[sr:Интернет]]
[[ur:شبک]]
[[zh:互联网]]

languages

- Deutsch
- Español
- Français
- Bahasa Indonesia
- Nederlands
- 日本語
- Русский
- 粤語
- 中文

As we will see, different language versions sometimes mean a direct translation of another language, but Wikipedia users were encouraged to go their own way and interpret the subject in light of community and cultural norms.

To Split or Not to Split

Some of the more interesting debates are not about languages that are different but about languages that are close together.

George Bernard Shaw once quipped, "England and America are two countries separated by a common language." And because English Wikipedia was first, it didn't have the chance to go through a debate over whether there should be a British English Wikipedia or an American English Wikipedia. They started and lived in the same space. A détente was reached by agreeing to use British spellings and terms for primarily British topics, and American spellings and terms for American topics. No doubt, American spellings tend to dominate by default just because of sheer numbers.

[[London]] can talk about how it's "organised" and [[New York City]] how it's "organized."

When it's ambiguous, you have some amusing conflicts.

This was the case with [[potato chip]], when different factions each claimed the potato chip/crisp as their own American/British creation.

They came to a compromise on the first sentence, with "A potato chip or crisp is a thin slice of potato . . . ," making both sides happy. But when it came to saying whether chips were "flavored" or "flavoured," an edit war ensued.

Their solution? They made it "seasoned."

Portuguese is another language with distinct flavors that often gets scrutinized for splitting into a distinct Brazilian Portuguese edition. So far, the Wikipedians have resisted the move.

The case is quite different for Malay spoken in Malaysia and its close cousin the Indonesian language. These two *bahasa* are nearly the same, save for some vocabulary differences and honorifics. It is then too bad they have completely different Wikipedias, started at different times with different communities. Indonesian was started half a year later than Malay, but now sports about three times as many articles and active editors. Because these groups are largely drawn on national boundaries, merging is not likely to happen soon.

Spanish Wikipedia Fork

To advertise or not to advertise. It's easy to forget that in the early days of Wikipedia, it was not the nonprofit project we know today. Started as a staging ground for articles to be fed into Nupedia.com, Wikipedia was still part of Bomis's commerical ventures.

In February 2002 Larry Sanger was laid off because Bomis was not generating the income it had before, but he stayed on in volunteer mode on the chance that the paid position could be revived. In the meantime, Spanish Wikipedia was growing quickly.

Today, February 7th, Spanish Wikipedia met the challenge. We reached our first 1.000 useful articles.

Cheers

Edgar Enyedy
Spanish Wikipedia[49]

It's hard to imagine, just five days after this message was sent, the mood would be completely different.

Now that he was a volunteer, Sanger made a post to the group about his future plans, how he was staying but looking for a full-time job. One small mention in the middle of his mail, though, stood out, at least to Edgar:

Bomis might well start selling ads on Wikipedia sometime within the next few months, and revenue from those ads might make it possible for me to come back to my old job. That would be great. I've liked this job very much, and I'm willing to do some work to help make it pay for itself.[50]

It did not go over well.

I've read the above and I'm still astonished. Nobody is going to make even a simple buck placing ads on my work, which is clearly intended for community, moreover, I release my work in terms of free, both word senses, and I want to remain that way. Nobody is going to use my efforts to pay wages or maintain servers.

And I'm not the only one who feels this way.

I've left the project.

You can see the Spanish Wikipedia development in the last two days and then you may think it over.

Good luck with your wikiPAIDia

Edgar Enyedy
Spanish Wikipedia[51]

There was a flurry of messages over the next few days from Wales and Sanger, declaring that no immediate plans for ads were in the works, and that there was a misunderstanding. But Enyedy still saw even the possibility of advertising to be problematic, and initiated a "fork," or a wholesale copying of Wikipedia's content, so it could be edited on another site entirely. This was one of the aspects of "free" content, and because of its free license everything in Wikipedia was free to copy. But for Wikipedia, it was not just a movement of open content, it risked drawing away community members too. Sanger made a final plea, beseeching them to stop:

> Therefore, I urge you, please, to do what you can to stop this fork. Moreover, if those behind the fork will not relent, in spite of the arguments against them, I urge you please to put your efforts behind Wikipedia, where they will be much more beneficially used. The Spanish Wikipedia is part of a growing network of free, community-built and (soon-to-be) nonprofit-managed encyclopedias. It really does deserve your full, undivided support.
>
> Thank you for your time and attention!
>
> Best regards,
> Lawrence M. Sanger, Ph.D. ([Wikipedia home page])
> Co-founder and chief organizer, Wikipedia
> Editor-in-chief, Nupedia

By February 26, however, the Spanish Fork was created under the name Enciclopedia Libre, and hosted at the University of Seville. Enyedy convinced most of the volunteers to go with him, leaving Spanish Wikipedia rather inactive for all of 2002. Enciclopedia Libre generated well over 10,000 articles by the end of that year, and for a long time it seemed that Spanish Wikipeda would be the unfortunate runt left from the Spanish Fork.

However, by June 2003, likely because of Wikipedia's general popularity, newcomers started to work on Spanish Wikipedia who were not familiar with the bad history, and the articles started to grow. Spanish Wikipedia would reach more than 10,000 articles by the end of 2003, and in the fall of 2004, Enciclopedia Libre would be passed by Spanish Wikipedia.

It took more than a year for Spanish Wikipedia to get back on its feet again, which is why the question of forking and advertising is still a sensitive topic in the community. Advertising is the third-rail topic in the community—touch it only if you're not afraid to get a massive shock.

Making It Multilingual

When Wikipedia was launched in 2001, there was already a desire for more languages. Even back in its first month, some contributions were filed in languages other than English, though the community didn't really know what to do with them.

At first Wikipedia was an all-English project, even if its participants came from around the world. Germans were especially well represented, in both the editing and the development side, a result of the online Internet hacker and open source software culture being particularly strong in Germany and other European nations.

User:Bryce posted to the mailing list on January 27, 2001, about the fact he stumbled across non-English entries:

> The Photo Electric effect article is in German. How do we feel about multilingualism? What is the policy—to accept alternate languages/translations, or to only accept English articles? I know this opens a can of worms, but . . .

The question of multiple languages was not pressing at the start. But even in the first few months the founders knew they were onto something big. English Wikipedia went from 500 to 1,000 articles in just the third month, far faster than expected. On March 15, Wales took the initiative to create the French, German, and Spanish "domains" of wikipedia.com (as it was a dot-com back then), being obvious first steps outside of English, given the predominance of those languages. But he already saw a problem on the horizon.

Wales's wife, Christine, was of Japanese heritage, so he was particularly familiar with the basic intricacies of the Japanese language and was interested in going beyond European-language support in Wikipedia. Storing and displaying European language text was relatively straightforward. But when it came to Asian languages with glyphs and symbols numbering in the tens of thousands, the task was much harder and would require more complex solutions.

The German Wikipedia started out as the first separate language edition on March 16 of that year, and French took off a week later.

The community was keen at the time to treat the language editions distinctly.

A common misconception in the world is of an Interwiki-linked Wikipedia where hopping from language to language for a given article necessarily brings up the same translated content. A decision was made early on to allow for different language communities to decide on their own flavor of neutral point of view, and also to allow the language culture to come through. Sometimes articles in German Wikipedia were translations of English ones, sometimes vice versa, but sometimes articles on the same subject were quite different.

Consider the article [[Dog]] for example. In English, the main picture is one of a yellow Labrador. Simply using the same picture for other languages wouldn't make sense if they don't have Labrador dogs in those countries. As a result, that photo is a very localized item in the [[Dog]] articles. In Japanese the article shows a Shiba Inu; in German, a German shepherd; and in Swedish, a Norwegian elkhound. In Asian languages, the article may talk more about dogs in the lunar calendar zodiac, something you would not necessarily find in the Swahili or Finnish Wikipedia.

After a few months of attracting grassroots communities in non-English versions, it was apparent Wikipedia had momentum and that it could scale to many other languages.

But there was a problem: The UseModWiki software that Wikipedia first used was pretty basic, and did not support anything more complex than Latin-based languages. Wales knew this was going to trip up the project long-term:

> One problem is going to be technical support of these languages, since if there are "fancy letter" problems, I will not know much how to deal with them. Japanese is pretty much *all* "fancy letters," but I assume that Linux/Apache/Perl will just magically support it? Or will they be forced to use non-fancy ASCII urls?

Clifford Adams, the author of the UseModWiki software, was keenly engaged with the community via the mailing list. Wikipedia was the most ambitious user of his software, and he was anxious to keep it useful:

> Finally, I'm now working on a translation interface for the wiki interface. All the wiki messages will go through a translation function. The translation messages will be in a separate file for each language (which could be appended to the main wiki script for efficiency). At first the translation

will be a sitewide option, but later I may add the ability to allow users to
change their language individually. . . .

—Cliff
(Your slightly overwhelmed UseModWiki author)

After working at a methodical pace of development, Adams suddenly saw a
huge spike in "feature requests," which in the open source software world is a
way for the public to request new capabilities.

As the Internet became more global since the 1990s, more and more people
have run into this problem. Western script was the norm in the early days of the
Internet, since it started as an American military project.

Most systems in Europe and the United States used a standard system of
encoding letters, numbers, and symbols for Web pages that went by the cryptic
name of the "standard," ISO 8559-1.

Users of computers in the West use the Latin alphabet, and with some special diacritic marks, like the umlaut, accent grave, tilde, and the like can fit all
their symbols into one computer byte of information, representing 256 different
unique characters. For most Western languages it works out well. That's enough
symbols for all the lowercase letters, uppercase letters, numbers, punctuation
marks, fancy accented letters, and some other special characters. As long as
you're dealing with popular European languages, it worked out fine.

But what Wales was talking about with "fancy letters" gets complicated. Chinese, Japanese, and Korean (CJK) languages are much more demanding. CJK
languages are notoriously tricky because they each use thousands of unique
symbols for their written script. Chinese is perhaps the most demanding. It requires more than 4,000 characters for general use. And if you want complete
coverage of characters used in common texts, you're looking at more than
40,000 characters. This does not even factor in "ancient" classical Chinese
characters that are rarely used today but may be used in an encyclopedia. Wikipedia strives to be the "sum of all human knowledge," after all. Some estimate
that a complete coverage of Chinese characters past and present would require
some 90,000 symbols, or even more than 100,000!

Wikipedia was about to become an important proving ground for multilingual
collaboration across the global Internet. No other public project had ever had to
tackle this many languages, users, and computing platforms at once.

Fortunately, there was a solution that had been developed around that time. The ISO 8859-1 standard was pretty old, having been created in the mid-1980s by the European Computer Manufacturers Association. Recognizing that the Internet was becoming more international, and that a standard was needed to encompass all the languages of the world, a more robust system was created in 1991 called Unicode. It was designed to be extendable and was formed by a committee of experts around the world, in order to solve the vast majority of "internationalization" problems. (Computer folks, being quirky and lazy, got so tired of typing out that long word that they came up with a clever abbreviation—i18n.)

Unicode was a savior because it provided a map of all the possible symbols used in the world's languages and a standard way of mapping them together. In fact, even today it continues to evolve and add features from other languages. Unicode did not dictate exactly how the characters would be encoded on a computer, it was simply a master table of every possible character/symbol.

With the map of all the symbols of the world's languages, it invited people to propose different ways to encode and store the characters efficiently on computers, because folks might have different needs depending on different requirements.

So how would an encoder help fix Wikipedia's problem?

Encoding Language

An obvious and easy solution is to just make the container encoding each symbol bigger. Instead of one byte representing one symbol, use two bytes (sixteen bits), which would support more than 32,000 different symbols. While that's still not quite large enough for CJK, it's getting there.

Following this line of thinking, one of the encodings approved for Unicode used this philosophy of "bigger is better" to store symbols. Dubbed UTF-32, it used a full four bytes (thirty-two bits) for representing each symbol. The good news was that it encoded billions of different possible symbols! Certainly that provided enough space for all the languages of the world, and likely some extraterrestrial languages not yet discovered.

It was a solution, but a very inefficient one. Each character is a fixed size of four bytes, so even if you're using simple English text like "See spot run," you're using up four times as much space as the old ISO 8859-1. It's like using a cargo container to transport a single bicycle.

A Colossal Waste of Space

If Wikipedia converted to this system, it would bloat everything. Four times as much storage, four times as much information transferred to readers, and potentially four times the bandwidth used. Computer science types, Wikipedia developers included, like efficient and elegant solutions. Unicode's UTF-32 was not the right one.

Ken Thompson was a legend in the computer industry as the creator of UNIX, the inspiration for Linux, and he happened to have the solution. He was working at AT&T Bell Laboratories on the next big thing, a computer operating system called Plan 9, when he came across the Unicode problem in the summer of 1992.

Someone had proposed an encoding system that would use Unicode for "backward compatibility" with ISO 8859-1. This was good news, because it meant that standard text documents encoded the old way with ISO 8859-1 would work fine with Unicode, allowing it to represent symbols of non-Latin languages. But the problem was, the encoding worked because it was of variable length. Sometimes a character would use one byte, sometimes two, three, or four bytes. It depended on what that character was. For example, an article about Chinese naval explorer Zheng He of 1421, would likely have English, Chinese, and Arabic names for the historic Chinese-Muslim sailor.

But a system that uses variable length for storage provides some problems. Computers like things to be predictable—they like to know how much storage space is necessary, how to find the next symbol, and how to move around quickly within a document. But if a given symbol can be anywhere from one to four bytes long, that makes it pretty unpleasant for computer programmers to deal with.

Great ideas in technology often happen in obscure places. Wikipedia was imagined in a Mexican restaurant in San Diego. The solution to the encoding issue came to light in a diner in New Jersey (home territory of Bell Labs). Thompson pondered this problem and eventually sketched the solution on a paper place mat.

He knew that the approach of using a variable length, multibyte system was the right way to go. It's like using an accordion file to hold papers—it's space-efficient for small things, but can expand to hold bigger things if necessary.

As he and his friend Rob Pike pondered the problem over a meal, they worked off the "variable length" idea but made a small but crucial adjustment to make it more computer-friendly: They cleverly arranged the bytes and changed the encoding so that computer programs could easily tell by looking at any given byte whether that particular byte was the beginning, middle, or end of a Unicode character. This would make it much easier for folks to integrate Unicode into their computer programs. A program could then traipse around computer memory much faster than it could cautiously reading each byte one by one from the beginning through the end of a document.

It was Wednesday, September 2, 1992, when Ken started thinking about it, and by working furiously he had a working version by Monday. Thompson presented the solution to the standards group, who immediately took to it, officially naming it UTF-8.

When it was made public in 1993, it immediately became a popular way to get sites internationalized. It could be "dropped in" quickly to running systems, was space efficient, and could expand as needed to encode more complex characters.

For Wikipedia, it was the ultimate solution because it could be inserted into the already running computer servers without a major overhaul.

Before UTF-8 was used as the encoding to store articles, Wikipedia had to use an unwieldy "hack" to store Unicode by simply embedding the numerical codes in the document. For example, the characters for the Chinese Xia Dynasty (夏朝) were stored as the cryptic codes 夏朝 corresponding to the standard Unicode values in Hypertext Markup Language that Web pages use. The same type of numerical-style encoding was used for languages with special scripts, such as Korean, Japanese, Arabic, and others.

While it displayed fine in a user's Web browser, this was obviously not a good situation. Normal people don't think in numbers, and when users went to edit the document, they would be faced with arcane codes instead of accurate characters.

UTF-8 was so clearly the solution for Wikipedia. As it grew to include more languages, UTF-8 became the standard encoding for any new edition that was created. There were virtually no downsides in using it, since it was backward compatible with ISO 8859-1.

For English Wikipedia, it was a bit more complicated. Being the earliest edition, it was started in ISO 8859-1 mode, and moving everything over to UTF-8 would take time. That's where individual editors and software robots would come in to help slowly and methodically to work their way through to convert each page at a time.

Japanese Wikipedia

As we look across the different Wikipedia editions, we tend to think the main variation is the written language, but many of the editions have drastically different community norms based on existing online Net cultures. This is seen quite starkly in the Japanese Wikipedia, which is a rather unique strain.

Wikipedians accustomed to the acerbic debate, edit wars, and community spirit of English Wikipedia will find a different dynamic in the Japanese community. Much of this is due to the Japanese Internet culture, which has more anonymous users than you find in other Internet communities. One of the largest influences on online Japanese behavior is the site 2channel (known as 2ch for short), which is famous for its anonymous chitter chatter. 2ch's popularization of "perfect anonymity," where users never identify themselves, is often cited as a reason why many Japanese Wikipedia editors never bother to register with usernames. In an interview with 2ch founder Hiroyuki Nishimura, his reasoning sounds downright "Wikipedian" in rationale:

> If there is a user ID attached to a user, a discussion tends to become a criticizing game. On the other hand, under the anonymous system, even though your opinion/information is criticized, you don't know with whom to be upset. Also with a user ID, those who participate in the site for a long time tend to have authority, and it becomes difficult for a user to disagree with them. Under a perfectly anonymous system, you can say, "it's boring," if it is actually boring. All information is treated equally; only an accurate argument will work.[52]

Anecdotally, Japanese editors in Wikipedia are less likely to engage in the cantankerous edit wars that one sees in English. The more formal and polite culture makes nasty drawn-out arguments like Gdansk/Danzig much less common, and less socially acceptable. Users are typically much less "bold" than their Western counterparts and will often edit alternative versions on the side or in talk pages, rather than blithely altering existing publicly displayed articles.

Because of the lower incidence of registered users, a big downside in Japanese Wikipedia has been much less interaction when it comes to engaging the international community of Wikipedia users and the nonprofit Wikimedia Foundation that coordinates all the projects.

At the first Wikipedia convention, Wikimania Frankfurt in 2005, there were only two registered Japanese participants, even though Japanese Wikipedia was one of the largest editions. Smaller editions, such as French, Polish, Dutch, and even the much smaller Chinese version, each had more representatives than the Japanese Wikipedia. Japanese Wikipedia remained something of a mysterious outlier to the community of global volunteers. A main motivation of global Wikipedians at Wikimania was to meet one another, and particularly the legendary founder Jimmy Wales they'd heard so much about. When Takashi Ota, one of the two Japanese Wikipedians who attended, and who edited anonymously, was told he must meet Jimmy Wales, he famously quipped, "Who's Jimmy Wales?"

The Japanese language is one of the tougher languages in the world to learn because it effectively has three different writing systems, used simultaneously and mixed in varying proportions. It consists of two syllabic scripts, katakana and hiragana, as well as kanji, which is based on modified logographic Chinese characters.

One would think that with the choice of different writing systems, it would prove more confusing for users to choose which script to use for which situation, adding an extra obstacle in Japanese Wikipedia. Surprisingly, the fact is the community sees very few edit wars about anything dealing with the writing systems.

One Japanese Wikipedian, User:Aphaia, attributes this to the fact that Japanese culture is relatively homogenous, making for fewer disputes, both in usage and in behavior. As the large majority of Japanese speakers in the world live in Japan, with the same newspapers, television shows, and books, this has some resonance. If Japanese Wikipedians simply followed the established norms from the mainstream media, that would explain the lack of variation, or rather the general agreement of people on using proven written conventions. Aphaia thinks that there are other implications of this culture:

> A friend of mine in Germany once said to me "Ihr Japaner sind furchtbar hoflich" [you Japanese are terribly polite]. This characteristic affects Japanese Wikipedia community. In my opinion it may be partly why the project, even suffering shortage of sysops [as ratio user/admin, half of the other major Wikipedias], is running day by day. "Being polite" is a strong pressure on the community as well as "You must listen to the other and reply." However this politeness is sometimes turning into stickiness to the written rules and thus, bureaucracy.

This is perhaps why Japanese Wikipedia, which started out strong, has lagged somewhat in recent years in terms of growth. What used to be the third largest Wikipedia in 2005 is now the fifth, having been passed by French and Polish. A graph of the top language editions shows, however, that the Japanese have a remarkable trait. They have no telltale Rambot-like spikes from bulk additions by a software robot. They are simply a dedicated crew of largely anonymous individuals, working by hand, one article at a time.

German Wikipedia

As the second language edition ever created, German Wikipedia has played a special role in the development of Wikipedia global culture. Germany already had a very strong hacker culture, and it seemed that the Wikipedia community blossomed aided by users familiar with the open source concept. Something peculiar to the German culture is the concept of the *verein,* which is literally a "union" but is a sort of voluntary association or interest group. The *verein* idea is quite strong in Germany, the joke being that there is a compulsion to make a *verein* for anything with more than three people. The Germans formed a *verein* for Wikipedians rather early on and had face-to-face meet-ups and social functions, benefiting from the relatively compact geographic region of Germans in Europe.

So it was no surprise that it was the Germans who first organized the global face-to-face conference for all Wikimedia projects in 2005, when Wikimania was held in Frankfurt, Germany, predominantly organized and run by the German community.

The German knack for organization also comes through online in the German Wikipedia culture. They have become famous for their strict standard for inclusion and have a very different type of editing culture than other editions. Whereas English Wikipedia embraces new articles on a range of pop culture topics and current events, German has a much higher bar. Wikipedian Nina Gerlach attributes it to, early on, "influential, thoughtful Wikipedians who rationally argued for quality and not quantity."

While the norm in many Wikipedias is to encourage the creation of incomplete stub articles as starting points, the Germans see it differently. To them, having no article at all is better than a very bad article. Where having administrator status was seen as "not a big deal" by Wales, and sysops were deliberately held back from having too much authority, this was not the case on the German Wikipedia. Administrators in the German edition voted among themselves on matters important to the community, and they were not afraid to have closed discussions among sysops. Compared to the freewheeling English community culture that often bent over backward to assume the best "good faith" in problematic users as long as possible, the Germans certainly viewed things in more no-nonsense practical terms.

As a result, German Wikipedia started to see a "flattening" of their growth even before English Wikipedia did. Sometime in mid-2006 their rate of adding articles shifted from accelerating growth to becoming simply constant growth.[53] In fact, in 2007, the rate at which new users were signing up to edit the German edition actually began to steadily decline into 2008. But with this deceleration came a maturity that has provided many opportunities.

Perhaps because of the emphasis on quality and the formal incorporation of a Wikimedia Deutschland organization, the Germans have been able to engage with respected institutions such as the Ministry of Agriculture, the Academia of Science and Literature, the University of Mainz, the National Library, and other entities, on a scale not found in other language editions.

As 2008 was starting, another new feature was being pioneered by the Germans called "flagged revisions." Reminiscent of the original Interpedia's concept of "seals" to certify content as meeting some type of quality standard, the idea of "sighted" or "validated" versions of articles had been discussed for many years as a solution to Wikipedia's problem of articles in flux and how to determine trust in a particular version. By allowing users to flag an article with an indication that they had checked an article for spelling, factual accuracy, or some other criteria, Wikipedia could start recommending to readers the actual overall quality of an article. The Wikipedia page on Sighted versions described it this way:

> This proposal is for the introduction of a system whereby users who are not logged in may be presented with a different version of an article than users who are. Articles are validated that they are presentable and free from vandalism. The approved versions are known as Sighted versions.[54]

For ordinary users, an article that was flagged as "Sighted" could be displayed to the public, instead of the most recent one, which might be in some state of flux. This was potentially a huge shift to increase the credibility of Wikipedia and to refute those who deemed it lacking in reliability.

While the software implementation had been done a year beforehand in 2007, the flagged revisions project sat on the sidelines. English Wikipedia had more than 2 million articles and its leadership was famously dispersed and chaotic. Adding such a sweeping change would have been incredibly disruptive not only technically, but culturally as well. No one was willing to pull the trigger on imposing such a dramatic change.

The German Wikipedia, on the other hand, had all the advantages to be the pioneer—it was smaller in size, more focused as a group, and had a strong leadership based around their own well-funded chapter in Wikimedia Deutschland. They were able to pay developers to help implement the change, and to deploy it on de.wikipedia.org.

In May 2008, German Wikipedia turned on the flagged revisions feature and encouraged experienced users to comb the articles to check and flag articles as "Sighted" if they contained no vandalism and were of presentable quality. While being sighted did not mean an article was fact-checked or vouched for as being 100 percent accurate, it was a big step forward. They took to it quickly. By the end of the month, they had "sighted" 280,000 of the 750,000 articles,[55] something quite amazing for a new feature and a community of 1,200 core editors.[56]

Chinese Wikipedia

In contrast to the linguistic and cultural unity of the Germans, Chinese Wikipedia has a combination of community and technical issues that show just how different these language groups can be.

If anything was going to challenge Wikipedia's community with a problem with both size and breadth, it was Chinese. Consider the written language problem: It takes somewhere in the neighborhood of 100,000 unique glyphs to represent the total written works of the Chinese language. Add to that a far-flung diaspora of Chinese speakers with different writing methods and political backgrounds, and you have a spectrum of problems to choose from.

Even the naming of what constitutes "Chinese" is not without controversy. Chinese is made up of many different dialects, from Cantonese in the south of China, to Fujianese up the southeast coast and Taiwan, to Shanghainese on the central coast. There is still much debate about the distinction between dialects and languages within the Sinitic languages, but there are usually between seven and fourteen subgroups identified.

The most widely used and accepted version of "Chinese" is usually referred to as Mandarin, or *hua yu* (as in Singapore and Malaysia), or *putonghua* (in the People's Republic of China), meaning "ordinary speak."[57] This is the variation based on the Beijing dialect of Chinese and is the most widely spoken version of Chinese in the world.

While there are many different dialects, there is one saving grace: The written Chinese language is based on visual logographic characters that represent meaning, and not phonetic pronunciation. People who cannot speak intelligibly to one another in the same dialect can communicate in writing, because they use the same writing system of vernacular Chinese. This is quite a surprise for those from the West, where there is an exact correlation between spoken pronunciation and written text.

It would seem that different dialects could unite under one writing system. In fact, there is a schism because of two different writing systems for Chinese—simplified and traditional.

The Chinese had established themselves for centuries outside of China around Southeast Asia, with significant communities in Vietnam and Indonesia.

Starting in the eighteenth and nineteenth centuries, the Chinese began to immigrate in wider numbers, especially to British colonies such as Singapore and Malaysia, to seek work in labor and trade. This started to create significant Chinese diaspora enclaves. But even with this widespread community, they all used the traditional Chinese characters in writing.

In 1949, after World War II, the Communists won control of mainland China, and the Nationalist government of Chiang Kai-shek fled to the island of Taiwan, located just off the southeast coast of the mainland's province of Fujian.

The Communist government of China, in an aim to revamp the language toward making it easier to teach the masses, employed a system of "simplified Chinese," which replaced many commonly used Chinese words with more abbreviated versions. Taiwan and Hong Kong never used this system and kept with "traditional Chinese." The Chinese in Singapore and Malaysia stuck to what was commercially practical (that is, what made the most business sense) and went with the simplified Chinese of China.

Fast-forward many decades to the Internet era, and the start of Wikipedia, and you can imagine the problems Chinese Wikipedia faced. Not only were there ideological differences between the editors from the Mainland, Hong Kong, and Taiwan, but also from the larger overseas communities of Chinese in Malaysia, Singapore, the United States, Canada, Great Britain, and other locales.

Not only did you need to build consensus on point of view, but also on writing systems.

Wikipedia's Chinese edition started in October 2002, and for lack of any coordinated policy, had a mix of some articles in traditional and some in simplified, mainly depending on who started the article first.

People's Republic of China users wanted to use simplified Chinese for writing, and were joined by Chinese users in Singapore and Malaysia. Editors from Taiwan, Hong Kong, and older Chinese communities in the United States, Canada, and others stuck with traditional.

As Chinese Wikipedia grew, it was clear that the haphazard intermingling of simplified and traditional writing was not workable. Also, unlike the Americans and Brits, there was much more political bad blood between Taiwanese and Chinese users. Taiwan was regarded as a "renegade province" of China by the Beijing government, with limitations on direct travel.

Chinese Wikipedia was ambling along, but the writing system was a cause for dispute. In 2004, still early in Wikipedia's history, growth was flat. With a team of two dozen core editors, they were seeing anywhere from twenty-five to fifty new articles per day, when other Wikipedia editions were growing much faster. Catalan and Russian, with much smaller numbers of speakers, were producing at the same rate. Swedish was adding roughly one hundred articles a day.

Chinese Wikipedia had become a hodgepodge of simplified and traditional writings, with no consistency or predictability. Readers wanted to see the entire Chinese Wikipedia in the writing system they preferred. It was a schizophrenic way to present the sum of all human knowledge to Chinese readers.

There was a solution that everyone knew would fix everything, but which no one thought was practical: create a software system that automatically mapped from one system to another. An article could be written in either of the two systems, and the reader could choose whether it would be displayed in simplified or traditional. Simple, right?

The reason why people didn't think it was readily possible was that it's not an exact one-to-one mapping from traditional to simplified characters and back. Most folks felt that it took a lot of reader knowledge to do the mapping correctly and that a pure machine mapping was not feasible.

To be sure, there were commercial systems from Microsoft and other software companies that could successfully do this. But most felt that programming of this by volunteers posed a very hard problem and was impractical for the amateur community of Wikipedia. All the known systems to do this were commercial and proprietary, and the task just seemed too hard to do.

One intrepid Wikipedia user, nicknamed ZhengZhu, didn't think so. He was an overseas Chinese Ph.D. student at the University of Massachusetts at Amherst when he stumbled across Wikipedia and was drawn to the project. While the community lamented the situation of mixed systems, ZhengZhu was confident a solution could be whipped up rather easily. He kept telling the community that it wasn't that hard, and that he would do it himself if he had the time. Chinese Wikipedians were skeptical.

So it was to great surprise that in September 2004, ZhengZhu emerged with a message saying, "I have started to implement this idea. I am running a test site to see how far this can go." After a month of development (and a few months of testing), to the Chinese community's delight, it worked.

After ZhengZhu's system went live, users suddenly found that on each page of Chinese Wikipedia, there was a button they could click to choose to display the text in simplified or traditional text. And by and large, it worked.

ZhengZhu's solution was simple, using a very clever hybrid of computer programming and the human-powered wiki.

He was smart enough to create a program to do most mapping automatically, but also provided a way to harness users' knowledge that could be incorporated into the wiki markup itself. That is, automate as much as possible, but allow human intervention to perfect it.

Even those skeptical about automatic mapping of traditional to simplified Chinese (and vice versa) agreed with ZhengZhu that much of it could be done by machine.

For example, the traditional Chinese character for "room" is notoriously complicated to write, while in simplified, the character takes four strokes. That's quite a savings in ink for someone writing it by hand. One always maps directly to the other, so it's very easy for a simple computer program to do this en masse, all the time.

Traditional vs. simplified forms
of the word "room."

But there are many cases where several different traditional characters map onto one simplified one. Going back the other direction (one-to-many) is not so simple.

This is the case with the Chinese word pronounced "gan," which has a mapping of several traditional characters to a single simplified character.

乾 DRY

干 EXPERIENCE

幹 (TREE) TRUNK

ZhengZhu's system could account for this type of many-to-one problem simply by allowing users to put into the text markup the manual mapping of these terms if an automatic mapping didn't do it correctly.

One particularly interesting problem the automatic mapping solved was names. For many Western proper names like Leonardo da Vinci or the country of Guinea, Chinese try to use a close phonetic match for the sound in English. But this varies widely based on locale.

In the case of Guinea, you have the unusual case of many different variants, roughly pronounced "ji nei ya."

CHINA (PRC) SIMPLIFIED 几内亚

TAIWAN TRADITIONAL 幾內亞

HONG KONG TRADITIONAL 畿內亞

The system ZhengZhu created was powerful enough to handle all of these (and more) by having a mapping table that included each and every variation. This mapping table was simply a page in Wikipedia that anyone could edit. It was like a dictionary of mappings that anyone could modify as new articles were written or new proper names emerged.

No conversion	Simplified	Traditional			
不转换	简体	繁體	大陆简体	港澳繁體	马新简体	台灣正體
			Mainland China	Hong Kong/ Macu	Malaysia/ Singapore	Taiwan

In the end, the Chinese Wikipedia adopted four different variants, reflecting the main centers of modern Chinese language use: Mainland China (cn), Taiwan (tw), Hong Kong/Macau (hk), and Malaysia/Singapore (sg). Each of these used its own mapping table that administrators could change on request. On the Chinese Wikipedia they actually provided six options, the four variants and two generic "simplified" and "traditional" buttons.

This was a breakthrough accomplishment for two reasons. One, it turned on its head the idea that mapping between simplified and traditional Chinese required

solving a tough artificial intelligence (AI) problem completely by a computer algorithm. Instead, ZhengZhu and the wiki community channeled lots of smart human
beings as volunteers into the solution. Why not create software to harness human
smarts as opposed to embedding that tough problem into the software? The read/
write web was not just for writing text articles. It allowed ordinary non-techie users
to insert their knowledge into the mapping database to effect change throughout
the site, even affecting articles not yet written. It shifted the burden of solving
from one of computer science to one of harnessing knowledge of the masses. That
is perhaps the central story of Wikipedia.

Secondly, this provided the spark to create a growth spurt in Chinese Wikipedia that has made it blossom. The month that the system was launched, the
site had 15,000 articles; one year later it would have roughly 45,000. Nearly
every other statistic grew rapidly after ZhengZhu's system was put in place.
They would be signing up nearly two hundred people a month in the middle of
2005.

ZhengZhu's system was good because it was simple. And typical of good
programming, he designed it as a general tool that was not Chinese-specific. It
could be used for any language with similar issues of having multiple writing
systems. So while he didn't know it at the time, he happened to create the solution to help two other Wikipedias that needed exactly the same thing.

Serbian Wikipedia and
Kazakh Wikipedia

The Balkan states of former Yugoslavia went through dramatic changes in the
1990s, ranging from a war in the area to the creation of many different independent nations. As a result, the question of language, ethnicity, and nationality in
the region is rather charged.

Serbian Wikipedia, for example, had a problem—it could be written in either
Cyrillic or Latin script. The article for [[Earth]] in Serbian could be either [[Земља]]
or [[Zemlja]].[58]

Cyrillic: Земља је једна од осам планета у Сунчевом систему. Трећа је
планета по удаљености од Сунца и највећа терестричка планета у Сунчевом

систему. Планета Земља има један природни сателит, Месец. За сада је једина позната планета на којој има живота.

Latin: Zemlja je jedna od osam planeta u Sunčevom sistemu. Treća je planeta po udaljenosti od Sunca i najveća terestrička planeta u Sunčevom sistemu. Planeta Zemlja ima jedan prirodni satelit, Mesec. Za sada je jedina poznata planeta na kojoj ima života.

ZhengZhu's software, though, was made to be generic. All you had to do was tell it how to map X->Y and Y->X. After some smart folks made the mappings between Cyrillic and Latin, the community's language problem was solved. At the top of Serbian Wikipedia users see two tab buttons, one for each variant.

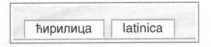

Sadly, most people have been introduced to Kazakhstan by the fictitious Borat character and his use of a fake Kazakh language (actor Sacha Baron Cohen actually used Hebrew). The Kazakh real language is perhaps one of the most interesting ones needing the mapping feature. Sandwiched in the triangle between Russia, China, and the Middle East, the Kazakhs require not two but three different writing systems—Cyrillic, Latin, and Arabic, the latter written right to left no less.[59]

جەر (عالامشار)

قازاقشا ۋىكىپەدياسىنىڭ ماعلۇماتى

باسقا ماعنالار ٷشىن، جەر (ايرىق) دەگەن بەتتى قاراڭىز.

جەر — كٷن جۇيەسىندەگى كٷننەن ٴارى قاراي
ساناعاندا ٷشىنشى عالامشار.

جەر مەن كٷن اراسىنداعى ورتاشا قاشىقتىق — ١٤٩،
١٠٦×٥٨ كم. بۇل قاشىقتىق قالىپتى «استرونومىيالىق
بىرلىك» بوپ تابىلادى.

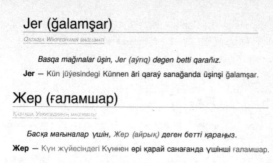

Jer (ğalamşar)

Qazaqşa Wikipediyaniñ maǵlümatı

Basqa mağınalar üşin, Jer (ayrıq) degen betti qarañız.

Jer — Kün jüýesindegi Künnen äri qaraý sanağanda üşinşi ğalamşar.

Жер (ғаламшар)

Қазақша Уикипедияның мағлұматы

Басқа мағыналар үшін, Жер (айрық) деген бетті қараңыз.

Жер — Күн жүйесіндегі Күннен әрі қарай санағанда үшінші ғаламшар.

| кирил | latın | توت |

While the Cyrillic alphabet still dominates, a nod to when Kazakhstan was part of the Soviet Union, there have been recent movements from the government to adopt the Latin alphabet instead. There are more than 1 million Kazakh speakers in China who use a script that is based on the Arabic alphabet. Fortunately, in kk.wikipedia.org, there are three tabs at the top of the screen, which allow the reader to quickly switch among these systems. While the Kazakh Wikipedia is resource-poor, with fewer than fifty active editors having produced fewer than three thousand articles, the tough problem of multiple scripts has been solved, courtesy of the cross-mapping system.

ZhengZhu's software is a classic example of what makes a good tool—it was used in applications not even imagined by its creator.

African Languages

As Wikipedia fills out most of its Western and Asian languages, African languages have become a new focus of a number of Wikipedians. Florence Devouard, chairwoman of the Wikimedia Foundation, attended the Digital World Africa 2006 Conference in Abuja, Nigeria, to help evangelize the role of Wikimedia projects on the continent.[60] In 2007, Jimmy Wales started an initiative to bring Wikipedia-based education to South Africa in conjunction with another free culture NGO, iCommons:

> Wikipedias in the South African languages are still fairly small. For example, the Afrikaans Wikipedia, which is the largest South African language Wikipedia, has slightly under 7,000 articles. Wikipedias in languages like Sesotho, Zulu, and Swati contain fewer than 100 entries each. Strength-

ening and growing the South African language Wikipedias will help pre-
serve those languages, and the cultural knowledge of their speakers, for
future generations.[61]

Though a noble goal, it's not clear whether these efforts are sustainable in
the long run. Prominent Wikipedian Danny Wool was less optimistic about such
online efforts for language preservation: "Encyclopedias record culture, they
don't create culture."

Wikipedia's reliance on having a critical mass of users to create the swarm
effect makes it difficult to imagine substantial efforts for languages of fewer than
a million speakers. Not only are the numbers small, but editors need access to
the technology of the Internet, as Wikipedia is only edited practically online while
connected live in cyberspace. There is nothing lonelier than being the only person on a wiki.

Nevertheless, one of those kick-start seed communities in Africa was started
by Kasper Souren, working for the NGO Geekcorps to spread Internet literacy to
developing nations. Souren, from the Netherlands, while on mission in Mali,
helped establish Wikipedia in the Bambara language, only spoken by 6 million
people in the country. Souren wrote in his report to an open source conference
about his experiences:

> The Wikipedias in Bambara, Peul and Wolof were started in the beginning
> of 2005.
>
> The interface of the Bambara and Peul Wikipedias was partly trans-
> lated and some articles had been written as part of a side project of a
> Geekcorps Mali volunteer, in which people were given one dollar for
> every article placed on-line (with total expenses less than $100). After
> 2005 there was only sparse activity, and in December 2007 there are
> respectively 142 and 28 articles.
>
> Not much happened to the version in Wolof until 2006, when many tiny
> articles with no real content were added to the Wolof Wikipedia. Then in
> April 2007 a Senegalese student living in Italy starting adding a lot of text
> in Wolof, and in November the Wikipedia reached 500 articles.[62]

The Wolof language of Senegal, Gambia, and Mauritania suddenly got its sole
grassroots volunteer: Ibou, a student studying overseas with access to the modern tools of the Internet. As of June 2008, Wolof had 543 articles, for a language with fewer than 4 million speakers.

The Numbers Game

In mid-2008, Wikipedia as a whole boasted more than 10 million articles in more than 253 languages.[63] However, these oft-cited impressive numbers should be taken with caution. While Wikipedia has empowered those in the top 100 languages in the world, the next 100 languages in Wikipedia face an uphill climb. At the top of the next 100 list are Yiddish, Kapampangan (dialect in the Philippines), Nahuatl (Mexican Aztecan language), Tatar (Central Asia), Sanskrit (classical language in India), Limburgish (regional language of the Netherlands), Armenian, and Alemannic (Upper German dialect). Each has fewer than 5,000 articles and, aside from automated bot addition of articles, exhibits anemic growth.

In the end, Wikipedia's faith in eventualism has its limits. Simply counting the number of editions and articles sounds impressive on paper, but the reality is quite different. Most of the 253 languages will fail to achieve the critical mass to produce anything comprehensive given Wikipedia's current model.

On the bright side, there are indeed languages for which there are numerous speakers that have tremendous potential. This includes dozens of languages spoken in India, a country of more than 1 billion people. The Wikipedia community compiled a list in 2007[64] of Wikipedia articles in relation to the population of speakers for that particular language. The top ten languages most underrepresented include those from Asia—seven from South Asia (five from India), two Sinitic dialects, and one from Afghanistan.

Rank	Language	Code	Articles (Jul07)	Speakers	Ratio (per million)
1	Punjabi	pa	233	88,000,000	3
2	Gujarati	gu	342	46,000,000	7
3	Sinhalese	si	194	15,000,000	13
4	Pashto	ps	999	50,000,000	20
5	Hindi	hi	12,371	330,000,000	37
6	Nepali	ne	1,461	40,000,000	37
7	Malagasy	mg	231	6,000,000	39
8	Min Nan	zh-min-nan	2,641	46,000,000	57
9	Urdu	ur	6,061	104,000,000	58
10	Cantonese	zh-yue	4,337	66,000,000	66

Of the larger Asian Wikipedias, the ones that are smaller than their speaking population would suggest include Bengali, Javanese, Tamil, and Tagalog, each with at least 70 million speakers yet each having fewer than 20,000 articles apiece. In fact, for Bengali the situation is even more pronounced: It claims more than 200 million speakers worldwide.

Clearly, South Asia and Southeast Asia have lots of potential—they have the numbers of people to throw at the problem, and with economic development and better education, in time the critical mass may come.

The total list of Wikipedia's languages by size, March 2008:

Rank	Language	Total articles	Article growth (year)
1	English	2,259,431	596,012
2	German	715,830	166,177
3	French	629,004	175,803
4	Polish	475,566	121,172
5	Japanese	472,691	138,454
6	Italian	418,969	153,238
7	Dutch	413,325	134,425
8	Portuguese	363,323	121,027
9	Spanish	337,860	130,694
10	Swedish	276,212	63,682
11	Russian	237,856	98,787
12	Chinese	167,206	53,447
13	Norwegian	155,133	53,918
14	Finnish	153,079	50,381
15	Catalan	106,127	51,728
16	Romanian	103,864	48,374
17	Turkish	102,488	54,709
18	Ukrainian	95,406	41,246
19	Esperanto	95,048	27,739
20	Czech	90,102	28,905
21	Hungarian	87,657	35,881
22	Slovak	87,120	22,002
23	Danish	81,547	23,182

Rank	Language	Total articles	Article growth (year)
24	Indonesian	77,818	26,248
25	Hebrew	72,489	19,207
26	Lithuanian	61,761	21,751
27	Serbian	60,047	17,352
28	Slovenian	59,801	17,827
29	Arabic	55,131	29,698
30	Korean	54,933	20,888
31	Bulgarian	53,294	17,133
32	Estonian	46,383	15,037
33	Croatian	41,077	12,975
34	Newar / Nepal Bhasa	41,011	31,819
35	Telugu	39,104	12,559
36	Cebuano	33,650	1,136
37	Galician	33,072	10,943
38	Thai	32,564	13,114
39	Farsi	32,382	14,029
40	Greek	32,372	13,009
41	Vietnamese	31,309	15,763
42	Norwegian (Nynorsk)	30,712	10,133
43	Malaysian	26,934	8,934
44	Simple English	26,119	11,584
45	Basque	24,344	7,551
46	Bishnupriya Manipuri	23,272	10,977
47	Bosnian	22,731	8,902
48	Icelandic	20,367	6,778
49	Georgian	20,361	6,387
50	Luxembourgish	20,323	6,940
51	Albanian	19,135	5,484
52	Breton	18,880	6,493
53	Latin	18,705	6,985
54	Azeri	17,547	12,728
55	Bengali	17,013	1,782
56	Hindi	16,574	8,748
57	Marathi	16,239	8,295

(continued)

Rank	Language	Total articles	Article growth (year)
58	Filipino	15,912	10,275
59	Macedonian	15,697	6,657
60	Serbo-Croatian	15,537	6,489
61	Ido	15,327	734
62	Welsh	14,537	7,126
63	Piedmontese	14,242	10,354
64	Sundanese	13,626	5,090
65	Latvian	13,572	5,249
66	Tamil	13,012	5,737
67	Neapolitan	12,715	326
68	Javanese	12,114	5,433
69	Haitian	11,818	4,774
70	Low Saxon	11,739	6,938
71	Sicilian	11,726	3,165
72	Occitan	11,589	4,431
73	Asturian	10,966	3,032
74	Kurdish	10,906	2,753
75	Walloon	9,880	1,353
76	Belarusian	9,788	3,204
77	Afrikaans	9,335	2,838
78	Tajik	8,722	3,033
79	Old Belarusian	8,683	8,683
80	Aragonese	8,323	2,876
81	Tarantino	7,587	7,560
82	Venetian	7,386	3,606
83	Ripuarian	7,354	1,351
84	Cantonese	7,334	5,074
85	Chuvash	7,208	1,930
86	Frisian	7,128	2,749
87	Urdu	7,026	2,228
88	Yoruba	6,727	5,663
89	Swahili	6,686	3,451
90	Uzbek	6,522	1,107
91	Maori	6,392	5,815

Rank	Language	Total articles	Article growth (year)
92	Quechua	6,333	4,277
93	Irish	6,208	1,535
94	Samogitian	5,920	4,757
95	Malayalam	5,771	3,597
96	Corsican	5,639	311
97	Kannada	5,242	832
98	Scottish	4,959	670
99	Upper Sorbian	4,878	4,195
100	Yiddish	4,877	1,446
101	Kapampangan	4,683	2,310
102	Nahuatl	4,336	3,275
103	Tatar	4,044	139
104	Interlingua	4,032	575
105	Sanskrit	3,878	1,853
106	Limburgish	3,827	995
107	Armenian	3,694	971
108	Alemannic	3,512	639
109	Aromanian	3,464	3,209
110	Lombard	3,403	-11,499
111	Banyumasan	3,127	2,030
112	Amharic	3,059	183
113	Pangasinan	3,034	2,819
114	Minnan	2,981	636
115	Norman	2,969	762
116	Faroese	2,918	748
117	West Flemish	2,697	1,366
118	Northern Sami	2,665	1,461
119	Wu	2,654	2,397
120	Dutch Low Saxon	2,641	534
121	Waray-Waray	2,585	547
122	Nepali	2,528	2,074
123	Friulian	2,510	723
124	Rumansh	2,415	2,087
125	Bhojpuri	2,408	2,287

(continued)

Rank	Language	Total articles	Article growth (year)
126	Ligurian	2,400	853
127	Novial	2,368	490
128	Divehi	2,353	2,087
129	Pali	2,316	2,200
130	Ilocano	2,286	119
131	Scots	2,267	458
132	Zazaki	2,239	1,173
133	Ossetian	2,033	377
134	Arpitan / Franco-Provençal	1,985	64
135	Kazakh	1,972	1,420
136	Classical Chinese	1,966	1,103
137	Maltese	1,917	453
138	Ladino	1,706	621
139	Pennsylvania German	1,685	272
140	Cashubian	1,663	600
141	Cornish	1,534	234
142	Võro	1,496	458
143	Bavarian	1,401	827
144	Tongan	1,372	575
145	Hawaiian	1,247	1,201
146	Pashtu	1,221	341
147	Mongolian	1,211	754
148	Anglo-Saxon	1,079	309
149	Turkmen	1,052	226
150	Lingala	1,019	570
151	Tok Pisin	806	512
152	Khmer	792	678
153	Interlingue	672	374
154	Crimean Tatar	650	650
155	Lojban	628	116
156	Wolof	548	321
157	Emilian-Romagnol	543	352
158	Zealandic	542	481
159	Oriya	542	531

Rank	Language	Total articles	Article growth (year)
160	Igbo	538	524
161	Aymara	518	483
162	Malagasy	504	283
163	Tahitian	501	24
164	Congo	499	312
165	Kyrgiz	493	195
166	Zamboanga Chavacano	484	316
167	Gilaki	480	294
168	Sinhala	478	309
169	Aramaic	456	63
170	Gujarati	451	163
171	Sardinian	448	246
172	Manx	415	256
173	Moldovan	401	0
174	Kabyle	388	388
175	Kashmiri	373	25
176	Somali	363	223
177	Guarani	358	324
178	Mazandarani	334	326
179	Old Church Slavonic	322	222
180	Udmurt	315	74
181	Tetum	312	116
182	Sindhi	302	161
183	Chechen	300	278
184	Panjabi	287	223
185	Bashkir	280	112
186	Vlax Romani	274	67
187	Nauruan	264	28
188	Inuktitut	261	104
189	Lao	251	126
190	Tibetan	232	35
191	Gothic	231	118
192	Saterland Frisian	204	204
193	Cherokee	201	10

(continued)

Rank	Language	Total articles	Article growth (year)
194	Oromo	187	177
195	Hakka	186	186
196	Central Bicolano	185	185
197	Uighur	183	-928
198	Samoan	182	59
199	Ewe	180	168
200	Tigrinya	178	148
201	Assamese	177	143
202	Min Dong	167	80
203	Avar	158	8
204	Bambara	151	21
205	Lower Sorbian	145	145
206	Zulu	140	55
207	Navajo	132	73
208	Norfolk	126	112
209	Burmese	126	52
210	Papiamentu	123	69
211	Cree	118	5
212	Venda	111	81
213	Kinyarwanda	105	69
214	Xhosa	101	70
215	Siswati	100	89
216	Greenlandic	89	41
217	Klingon	83	21
218	Iñupiaq	78	61
219	Tsonga	71	67
220	Dzongkha	71	57
221	Buginese	64	51
222	Bislama	62	35
223	Komi	59	26
224	Kalmyk	54	31
225	Sotho	52	14
226	Setswana	51	32
227	Chamorro	51	36

Rank	Language	Total articles	Article growth (year)
228	Akan	47	24
229	Buryat (Russia)	44	28
230	Twi	43	27
231	Chichewa	43	32
232	Abkhazian	42	-11
233	Fijian	40	13
234	Lak	35	29
235	Zhuang	33	14
236	Fulfulde	31	17
237	Tumbuka	28	8
238	Shona	28	11
239	Hausa	27	7
240	Sangro	23	13
241	Luganda	22	10
242	Gikuyu	19	6
243	Yi	19	6
244	Kirundi	17	5
245	Cheyenne	16	10
246	Choctaw	15	13
247	Afar	15	5
248	Marshallese	12	0
249	Ndonga	7	4
250	Kuanyama	6	2
251	Hiri Motu	4	-7
252	Muskogee	3	-10
253	Kanuri	2	-1
254	Tokipona	0	-239
255	Herero	0	-6

TROLLS, VANDALS, AND SOCK PUPPETS, OH MY

"The best victory is when the opponent surrenders of its own accord before there are any actual hostilities. . . . It is best to win without fighting."

—*Sun Tzu*

"The trouble with fighting for human freedom is that one spends most of one's time defending scoundrels."

—*H. L. Mencken*

When Wikipedia works, it exceeds nearly all expectations. Because on the face of it, an encyclopedia that anyone can edit should fall into chaos and produce nothing but a pile of incomprehensible junk. But as we've seen, successful communities have the critical mass of people to keep watch and make sure quality is ever increasing, and they've crafted the tools to help.

But Wikipedia hasn't been able to keep out all the problems, and perhaps the worst problems are folks who don't quite fall into the category of outright vandals but straddle the line between being boldly productive and being disruptive.

The Internet has a name for such troublemakers: trolls. "Trolling" consists of dragging issues through the community so as to incite a reaction or disruption. As such, Internet trolls delight in sowing discord, to "inspire flaming rhetoric."[65] They have been the recurring nuisances of online communities since even before the Internet. Bulletin board systems had trolls, Usenet had trolls, and modern-day blogs and online forums often find them as well. People who have nothing to bring to the community are easy to deal with. Clear troublemakers with no contribution to make can quickly be blocked from the community.

Borderline trolls, however, provide the most troublesome cases, and Wikipedia is full of those who are undoubtedly intelligent, incredibly studious, and may adhere to almost all the community principles, but interact with others in such a nasty manner that they wind up driving others away, and disrupting entire swaths of users.

For Larry Sanger, this was one of the main reasons he became disillusioned with the project he helped to create.

Wikipedia's original policies of 2001 were geared to be inclusive, and the community ethics provided a lot of latitude to people with troll-like tendencies. The encyclopedia was a small project that solicited newcomers with the radical openness of a wiki. As a result, the indulgent policies, such as "assume good faith," meant members bent over backward to see the good side of someone, even if faced with mounting evidence to the contrary.

In Wikipedia legend, perhaps there were no more famous trolls than Wik and Lir, two users who were prolific editors but always pushed the envelope on acceptable behavior, created multiple accounts, and went on rampages to disrupt Wikipedia. Each of them led administrators to chase down bogus and reckless additions, to the point of earning permanent bans from the community.

What were some ways to troll and cause trouble? Create an article about something extremely controversial and offensive, but otherwise adhere to every rule of Wikipedia and use the system against itself. This was the case with creating an article that had an intentionally offensive name, the Gay Niggers Association of America. GNAA was a name that caused immediate alarm in anyone with a semblance of good taste. It was a phenomenon for many years in the online tech communities, as legions of trolls attempted to have an article in Wikipedia about the mischievous group. It's not clear a defined group ever existed as

GNAA. Supposed GNAA "members" were simply troublemakers online who unified under a common moniker in an effort to disrupt Wikipedia for amusement.

In the early days, when Larry Sanger was editor in chief of Nupedia, and in the employ of Bomis, he was the head of the community of academics. What he said was the final word. When Wikipedia launched as a much more open adjunct to Nupedia, it got more complex. If Wikipedia was viewed as a staging ground for Nupedia, which it was at its inception in 2001, then it was less important to have firm authority on the wiki. After all, the articles would be feeding into greater oversight at Nupedia. But as it became clear that Wikipedia was coming into its own, and overshadowing Nupedia, the attitude started to change. Larry was a believer at the beginning in Wikipedia's lack of hard rules, but he started to see problems as 2001 wore on. To Sanger, Wikipedia was taking on the flavor of other more chaotic Internet communities, veering away from being an academically credible publication. By the end of 2001, he started to put his foot down a bit harder than before, in an attempt to provide more direction.

This was not always to people's liking. One of the first folks who made noise about it was a user named The Cunctator. Despite sounding uncomfortably close to an obscenity, the name is Latin for "the procrastinator." (As with many Wikipedians, The Cunctator's addiction to the project was at the expense of other responsibilities.) As Wikipedia attracted more denizens from other established online communities, the "anarchistic" tendencies became more prominent. The Cunctator was leading the charge.

Marshall Poe of the *Atlantic,* when writing about the conflict between The Cunctator (or, simply, Cunc) and Sanger, perhaps best described the term troll as "users like Cunc who baited others for sport."

Wikipedia has a community guideline: "Don't disrupt Wikipedia to make a point." If you're not happy with how dates are handled, don't change all the dates from BCE to BC. Don't keep nominating the same article over and over for deletion.

But "disrupt" is essentially what trolls do, and it's not always easy to tell the difference between a borderline troll who stays just one step behind the line of transgression and ones who deserve to be ejected. The Cunctator continually instigated conflict with Sanger, eventually wearing him down to the point where Sanger made a plea to the community.

Sanger also had his own quirks. He was extremely pedantic and exacting, and that tended to be perceived as control that the grassroots community did not like. Instead of earning the respect and authority needed to help guide the process and attract folks, he demanded it. Explicitly. In November 2001 he wrote:

> I need to be granted fairly broad authority by the community—by you, dear reader—if I am going to do my job effectively. Until fairly recently, I was granted such authority by Wikipedians. I was indeed not infrequently called to justify decisions I made, but not constantly and nearly always respectfully and helpfully. This place in the community did not make me an all-powerful editor who must be obeyed on pain of ousting; but it did make me a leader. That's what I want, again. This is my job.

The note hit absolutely the wrong chord with the Wikipedia crowd. It wasn't in the sprit of the hacker ethos to demand authority by fiat.

How did The Cunctator react? He penned an essay that he put on the wiki, so everyone could see it. It was his gripe sheet about the state of Wikipedia, and he didn't hold back. His satirical essay was called "How to Destroy Wikipedia."[66]

* 1   Be in Charge and Be a Dick
* 2   Delete Entries
* 3   On your Own, Totally Redesign the Wikipedia Software, and
      Implement it Without Testing
      o 3.1 Or, Act Like Microsoft
* 4   Make big plans on the Mailing List
* 5   Set up a Cabal

It caused quite a stir, calling out not just Sanger but Wales by name, as the ones responsible for a behind-the-scenes "cabal." This would become a recurring theme in Wikipedia, to the point where an acronym was created to repeatedly address the claim: TINC (there is no cabal).

The Cunctator would later say "How to Destroy Wikipedia" was, simply, "a semi-parodic act of hyperbolic dissent" that he would later retract. But his essay is now legend, as it threw the gauntlet down about whether Wikipedia was going to further Nupedia's model of received authority or take on the distinctly more "anarchic" culture of the open source software world.

In his famous essay "The Cathedral and the Bazaar," software hacker Eric

Raymond detailed and heralded the working process that produced the wildly popular open source project Linux. It quickly became a must-read for the Internet age. Even those not into software knew that the upstart Linux operating system, written by a distributed set of volunteers around the world, was posing a serious challenge to corporate-developed software like Microsoft's. "The Cathedral and the Bazaar" was a description of that dynamic, and the essay directly influenced online communities and future thinking about effective, so-called crowdsourcing.

Problem was, it was directly counter to Sanger's belief in a strong authority.

Raymond felt that Linus Torvalds's letting go of top-down authority ultimately gave him the moral authority to do more things within the Linux project, with more people, without using a heavy hand:

> Linus, by successfully positioning himself as the gatekeeper of a project in which the development is mostly done by others, and nurturing interest in the project until it became self-sustaining, has shown an acute grasp of Kropotkin's "principle of shared understanding." This quasi-economic view of the Linux world enables us to see how that understanding is applied.
>
> We may view Linus's method as a way to create an efficient market in "egoboo"—to connect the selfishness of individual hackers as firmly as possible to difficult ends that can only be achieved by sustained cooperation. . . .
>
> I think the future of open-source software will increasingly belong to people who know how to play Linus's game, people who leave behind the cathedral and embrace the bazaar.[67]

It is not easy for conventional project managers to cede this control to the crowd. Going the anarchic route means noisy borderline trolls become the continual background radiation of open communities, always a few clicks away from disrupting the community.

Most wiki communities by now have seen that harnessing the benefits of openness and radical inclusion means trolls are an unavoidable by-product. The idealists say you can redirect them to useful endeavors in the community. Pessimists simply screen them out, tolerate them, or choose to leave altogether in frustration.

For Sanger, trolling was not something he was willing to suffer. He had no patience in having his authority or expertise challenged at every turn by users for whom he had no respect.

In Sanger's extensive memoir written for the Slashdot tech Web site—with exhaustively detailed writing being his hallmark—he reflected on this part of the Wikipedia history as the point where things could have been turned for the better. As part of documenting his experience with more than 16,000 words, he wrote about community management:

> As difficult users began to have more of a "run of the place," in late 2001 and 2002, opprobrium was in fact meted out only piecemeal and inconsistently. It seemed that participation in the community was becoming increasingly a struggle over principles, rather than a shared effort toward shared goals. Any attempt to enforce what should have been set policy—neutrality, no original research, and no wholesale deletion without explanation—was frequently if not usually met with resistance. It was difficult to claim the moral high ground in a dispute, because the basic project principles were constantly coming under attack. Consequently, Wikipedia's environment was not cooperative but instead competitive, and the competition often concerned what sort of community Wikipedia should be: radically anarchical and uncontrolled, or instead more single-mindedly devoted to building an encyclopedia. Sadly, few among those who would love to work on Wikipedia could thrive in such a protean environment.

On December 1, 2001, employees from Bomis, including Sanger, Wales, and Shell, made a weekend trip from San Diego to Las Vegas together. Sanger was getting married and they made it a quasi-company affair. It would be one of the last times they would all spend together, because by mid-December, Wales had to break the bad news to Sanger.

"I was informed that I should probably start looking for another job, because Bomis was having to lay off most of its workers," he recalls.

It was near the bottom of the dot-com industry slump, and there was not enough money to pay Sanger, even though the Wikipedia project was a success. As Sanger moved out, Wales stepped to the fore.

In contrast to demanding authority, Wales's approach with the community was much softer. He understood the open source culture more than Sanger and was willing to commit. Wales has described himself as "notoriously nonconfrontational," making his personal style much more like the role Raymond described in his essay.

That's one reason that despite the disruption and consternation The Cuncta-tor kicked up, Wales still considers him one of the most significant influences on his thinking about how to govern Wikipedia. Wales had a front-row seat when Cunc and Sanger clashed on the wiki and mailing lists, and he saw what did and did not work with his crowd of volunteers.

Sanger was officially laid off at the beginning of February but stayed around as a volunteer in case things picked up. But on March 1, 2002, he announced his formal resignation on friendly terms, if not without a bit of doubt about the future of the project:

Wikipedians, don't take my departure as an excuse to leave yourself. My departure should not be taken as a reflection on Wikipedia, or you. It still might succeed brilliantly. It's very important that you continue to edit each other's work, that you encourage in each other good habits, that you welcome new contributors, and that you praise good work when you see it.

Wales became the primary face of Wikipedia from then on, and by adopting a Linus Torvalds style, he was able to work in ways with the community that kept the balance between frenzy and order. He largely stepped in only when be-seeched, or when he saw difficult cases that needed some form of final say.

For the next two years he played this role of a humble constitutional monarch in the community, using the powers only as necessary. It can be argued that this was crucial to the success of Wikipedia: the delicate balance between a com-munity in control of the site and an individual with power and authority in reserve to defuse extreme situations.

The risk in such a system, of course, is that those in the power seat may abuse their authority. A fickle grassroots community can quite quickly find a God-King distasteful. The veterans of online communities at MeatballWiki defined a GodKing as "a site owner or administrator who uses their special authority more than absolutely necessary," something Wales certainly tried to steer clear of, being mindful of his experience with the Spanish Fork.

Researcher Andrea Ciffolilli, who wrote about Wikipedia's model in Sep-tember 2003, instead used the term "phantom authority" to describe the "self-selective recruitment and retention of members in virtual communities."[68] It seemed an apt description of what had emerged.

As an homage to Wales's sticking with a low-key style, the community adopted the saying "The GodKing drives a Hyundai,"[69] making fun of his humble Korean-made car, a brand known more for frugality than flash.

Vandals and Sock Puppets

Along the spectrum of online troublemakers, trolls at least are identifiable individuals in the community. Wikipedia vandals, on the other hand, have no redeeming qualities and provide a steady stream of nuisance edits.

But not all vandals are equal. Since the beginning of Wikipedia, there has always been, and there will always be, the innocent "Does this work?" test vandal, who cannot believe a Web site would actually allow anyone to change any page on it. It's the equivalent of kicking the tires, tapping the microphone, or scribbling a pen on a paper pad. For these users, there is no malice. In fact, Wikipedia has traditionally used undoing new users' test edits as a chance to surprise them immediately with a welcome message, in the hope of turning them into useful contributors. It's the community's way of saying, "Yes, your test works, and you can't imagine how fast we work around here. Aren't you impressed?"

Then you have your pranksters, troublemakers, and long-term vandals.

On the front lines of fighting vandalism in any Wikipedia edition is the "Recent Changes patrol." The Recent Changes page in any wiki is a reverse chronological log of every edit, page deletion, or move in the system. Watching the edits for malicious behavior is one of the activities volunteers pitch in to do as RC patrollers.

Some liken RC patrolling to Whack-A-Mole, a popular arcade game where you take a hammer and try to hit plastic rodents as they pop up out of their holes. There is no shortage of vandalism on Wikipedia, and the job of a patroller is to locate and revert erroneous or useless edits. Some of the edits are an easy call. The most common forms of vandalism involve putting "poop" or common obscenities on a Wikipedia article. Those are relatively easy to recognize and fix. More obscure and harder to determine are the subtle vandals, who might change a date from 1971 to 1972.

In the first few years of Wikipedia, monitoring the Recent Changes list was enough to catch most vandalism. Even an edit every ten seconds or so can be checked by hand while watching the list. Since 2005, however, in the English Wikipedia it's been like drinking from a firehose. With editing rates of more than two hundred edits a minute (more than three each second), it's simply impossible to check activity straight off of Recent Changes. So the community has gotten more sophisticated and created more tools to help.

While User:Ram-man used software robots to create articles, innovative programmers have adopted the same type of bot code to filter out Recent Changes, looking for miscreants and telltale signs of vandalism.

Some techniques include highlighting anonymous editors (who are more likely to be vandals) or identifying sophomoric chunks of text that are known to recur, like "poop" or "Josh is gay." Bot authors have also been clever enough to create customizable white lists and black lists for users and words, not unlike an email program that can flag good mail and bad mail to prevent spam. The result, after running the bots for months on end, and having trusted RC patrol users to tweak the white and black lists, is that the antivandalism bots do quite a good job at identifying bad behavior. At the very least, it's just enough to keep the patrollers one leg up on the vandals.

Wikipedia user Tawker, a young Canadian programmer, was one who pitched in to defend Wikipedia from vandals. Like many volunteer hackers before him, he took existing software robot code and customized it to help repel the onslaught of vandals that were overrunning the site in 2006. His bot did even more, though, by actually automatically undoing the vandalism, creating a hands-free solution to vandal fighting. Bots don't always get everything right, so Tawker built in some manual overrides and some human oversight to monitor operation. But the bots have helped tremendously by catching well over 50 percent of the obvious vandalism, freeing up RC patrollers for the harder cases.

One particularly humorous, if tedious, strain of daily vandalism comes from students editing Wikipedia from schools. All too often, students sitting bored at school in their computer lab will simply goof around and play with Wikipedia. This typically consists of pranksters creating a salacious article about their teacher, [[Mr. Davenport]], or listing their friends on the article [[Gay]]. RC patrollers find the same type of vandalism day in and day out, that the lack of originality is quite surprising. The remedy for unabated vandalism from the same source is to block the Internet address that it comes from for anywhere from one minute to the "indefinite."

But there's a catch.

This is especially problematic with schools, as most of them funnel all their Web traffic through one particular network access point for the entire school. So, in essence, the sins of one student can trigger a block for all traffic from that school or, in the worst case, the entire school district. The end result is that a Wikipedia administrator can lock out an entire set of hundreds of schools, and tens of thousands of students, with one click of the mouse. It has happened, and still continues to happen, and it's a balancing act to make sure these blocks don't last longer than they need to.

If administrators are doing a good job, they're keeping vandalism at bay, reverting edits to restore pages, and blocking troublesome users. But what if people insist on getting onto Wikipedia despite being blocked?

Users coming back under the guise of another user are particularly frustrating and hard to deal with in Wikipedia, and it happens often. As a side effect of open editing and assuming good faith, the problem of "sock puppets" comes up.

A traditional sock puppet, according to Wikipedia, is a "puppet made from a sock (or similar garment) which is placed over the hand of a puppeteer. When a sock puppeteer fits their hand into the closed end of the sock, the sock puppet can be made to 'talk' with the opening and closing of the hand."

The more ominous meaning is found in the article [[Sock puppet (Internet)]]:

> A sock puppet, also commonly known as an alt, is an online identity used for purposes of deception within an Internet community. In its earliest usage, a sock puppet was a false identity through which a member of an Internet community speaks while pretending not to, like a puppeteer manipulating a hand puppet

Sock puppets are extra accounts created by users as alternative identities. Sometimes there may be legitimate uses for them, such as if you're embarrassed to edit an article about [[Teletubbies]] under your own name. In general, sock puppets are heavily discouraged, because they can be used abusively to stack votes or to create false consensus, sowing mistrust in the community.

One of the most obnoxious and legendary vandals was Willy on Wheels (WoW), who created hundreds, if not thousands, of sock puppet accounts with some variation of Willy and Wheels in the name. As such, WoW was not so much a problematic sock puppet creator as he was a determined vandal. Whoever was behind WoW's accounts used a software bot to move pages, create accounts, and generally vandalize pages within Wikipedia at speeds that were hard to keep up with.

Tawker's bots handled many of these types of vandalism sprees. In trying to explain the psychosis behind such people, he said, "[Vandals] derive pleasure knowing they've been able to annoy other people. Once you make it not fun for them anymore, they stop."

Where sock puppets become a problem is the case of banned users. Wikipedia has had its share of long-term problem users who have been banned for periods of months to a year to "forever" based on their disruptive behavior. But many of these banned users simply create another user and persona, and wind up slowly wreaking havoc again. Trying to prove that a new user is simply a previous user in a new sock puppet is quite hard for the ordinary user and even administrators.

But deep in the bowels of Wikipedia, the system records the Internet address of each and every user who visits the site. So if a banned user and a sock puppet are using the same Internet address, that information is in Wikipedia's logs somewhere. It just needs to be retrieved by the right people.

Because this information is rather sensitive (an IP address gives away physical location and sometimes corporate or school affiliation), accessing it is not a privilege that many people are given. "Extremely trusted" users who are committed to not abusing the power are given this "checkuser" privilege in Wikipedia, which allows them to quickly ascertain the Internet address a user is coming from. The technique is used in the rare cases when there is an urgent need to check whether an account is a sock puppet.

Jimbo Doesn't Scale

Trolls, vandals, and sock puppets have provided a stream of problem cases for the community, and for the first few years, Wales always played the part of benevolent dictator whose final say was taken as gospel. As problem cases came up, Wikipedians, like a village mob going to the town sheriff, would approach Wales with the problem at hand. Wales would review the merits of the case and, more often than not, go with the consensus recommendation, or try to mediate between the two sides.

Wales as final arbiter was not going to scale into 2004. As Wikipedia became more popular he had to deal with the media and the press attention, keeping him too busy to deal with the increasing volume of day-to-day disputes. In the past he personally handled cases like Wik and Lir, trying to negotiate and curb their behavior through heavy personal email correspondence and coaching. When Wikipedia was smaller, and had a few problem cases a month, this was possible. But now it was no longer something he could do with the same care or time commitment. However, with no other individuals in the community with any acknowledged moral authority, he had no way to offload those responsibilities either.

So in November, Wales asked for volunteers from the community to help establish a "Wikiquette committee" that would assist in helping with these problem cases. He was ready to hand over this responsibility, or headache, to community members. After getting about two dozen volunteers, he announced on the mailing list:

Everyone who volunteered was appointed to something, and two who didn't volunteer I appointed anyway. (Obviously, they can decline if they must.)

The solution was to make two sets of dispute resolution bodies—a mediation committee and an arbitration committee. Mediation was a way to try to settle differences amicably with the aid of mediators, and arbitration was left as the last resort, a binding decision by a council of respected Wikipedians.

As Wales announced the membership of the two committees, he really wasn't sure how arbitration would work, so he tapped members of the new arbitration committee (ArbCom) to propose a system to him.

Mark Pellegrini, aka User:Raul654, was one of the first arbitrators. He was passionate about serving because he saw firsthand how dysfunctional dispute resolution had become. He saw how the community tried to sit down to reason with and rehabilitate acerbic users who were clearly miscreants. To him it was too soft an approach, and to Wales this was exactly the type of person he wanted on a diverse committee to decide these things.

Raul654 was well known in the community as the large, cheery, and bombastic computer science graduate student who never shied away from cleaning up messes around Wikipedia. He had taken on obnoxious users in the past and wanted a more systematic way to deal with them.

In 2004, he was on the case of a prickly user named Plautus Satire, who had vandalized the articles on [[Albert Einstein]], [[Hubble Space Telescope]], and [[Black Hole]] with nonsensical claims. In the Einstein article, he insisted on pushing the idea that the scientist was a fraud:

> **Einstein performed no experiments and claimed his ideas came to him in dreams. His poor grasp of mathematics, as evidenced by his failure to pass admissions examinations to engineering schools, prevented him from doing mathematical analyses of the hypotheses he presented, and his method of pure deductive reasoning has been roundly dismissed as unscientific, unproductive and prone to deviate far and wide from reality.[70]**

Raul654 was not amused. "I literally went through every one of his edits and he had . . . two that were indisputably good, and the rest were conspiracy theory gibberish."

While Wikipedians typically try to bend over backward to see some good side of the site's users, that's not Raul654's way. He professes he's "more of a hanging judge." It took six weeks to kick Plautus Satire off the site, and the Arbitration Committee made it their second-ever case to ban him for a period of one year. As a council of "last resort" ArbCom's decision would be binding, and Wales liked the process they initiated.

Eventually, it was found that the mediation part of the process was rarely successful, and ArbCom wound up taking more of the load. From its inception in 2004 to August 2006, ArbCom handled more than 200 cases, making it a rather busy crew. "One every five days," declared Pellegrini.

One of the first arbitrators, a young London resident, James Forrester, User:JamesF, mused about the history:

> **Mediation and arbitration . . . at the time they were two forces one and the same, which were going to work together, the mediation to be the carrot and arbitration to be the stick. As it turns out sticks work far too well for us, and carrots . . . aren't too tasty.[71]**

CRISIS OF COMMUNITY

"Think like a wise man but communicate in the language of the people."

—*William Butler Yeats*

"He who cannot agree with his enemies is controlled by them."

—*Chinese proverb*

A lexa.com is a peculiar site. It has found a niche in providing "Web site rankings" to give a sense of a site's popularity. Nearly everyone in the industry knows that the way it measures Web site popularity is nearly a decade out of date and deeply flawed. Yet for the lack of anything better, everyone uses the "Alexa ranking" as a benchmark for success.

Halfway through 2003, Alexa indicated that Wikipedia had equaled the traffic rank of Britannica.com, marking that it had "arrived." Around the same time, Bomis signed over the Wikipedia project assets to the newly formed Wikimedia Foundation, which was established in St. Petersburg, Florida, where Wales had moved. Bomis knew from the Spanish Fork incident that there was no real commercial chance of monetizing anything without upsetting the community. A spinoff to a nonprofit was the best thing to do.

Wales set up the foundation with members of Bomis as the initial board of trustees: Tim Shell and Michael Davis. An election would be held for the other seats from the community. That's when two particularly active members, Angela Beesley and Florence Devouard, were elected. While this was a big first step, there was grumbling in the community that the foundation board was mostly appointed. Many of the same voices that wanted Wikipedia to be free of Sanger's authority in the early days in fact wanted community members to make up the board of trustees.

Creating the ArbCom in 2004 was another step forward, but there were signs that other parts of the community "consensus" were not scaling with the growth. As Wikipedia became more popular, it was less of a village where you knew everyone on the street, and more of a faceless impersonal metropolis that was unfortunately driving the adoption of hard, cold, binding policies, something frowned upon in classic wiki culture.

Another casualty of Wikipedia's popularity and high traffic was the number of folks who got burned out. For outsiders it's hard to imagine how an online volunteer position from which people can come and go freely can cause burnout and stress, but this was the case with the passionate community that Wikipedia fostered.

At first Wikipedia was a curious project in a small corner of the Internet, but as the traffic and ranking on Google got higher, it became more and more important and in the public eye. Also, as more people participated, there were more who thought of themselves as stakeholders and felt a type of investment in articles and edits. And as more unwashed masses came to "help" edit, earlier contributors felt that articles were sliding backward and their work was being ruined.

It became so endemic that people started putting "stress meters" on their user pages to indicate what state they were in. Most had color bar warnings like the DEFCON warnings; some used a thermometer to show their stress level: "Just fine" to "A bit tense" to "Pretty stressed" to "I quit/I need a vacation."

In the extreme cases of folks absolutely burned out, frustrated, or simply dropping out of the community, there was the Missing Wikipedians page. Started by user Stevertigo in August 2003, it was a document dedicated to those who came and went: "Wikipedians who were once an integral part of our community, and who have decided to either leave forever, join a cult, have tired of vandalism, found a job, or have some otherwise lame or legitimate excuse for leaving."

Perhaps one of the most high-profile departures was the case of User:RickK. Few people knew who exactly RickK was in real life, as he chose not to reveal his real name, but his presence in Wikipedia was well known. During a time of rapid rise in popularity, he was a fixture on the front lines of vandal fighting.

RickK arrived in June 2003, after having watched the community in action but never contributing. With a modest message on his user page he made his debut as an editor: "My name is Rick, and I live in Southern California. . . . Now I've gotten brave enough to step up and use my name to create things."

Sitting at his computer in the bedroom with the TV on in the background, he browsed through Wikipedia, contributing to various articles he found interesting. He quickly got assimilated into the community, meeting other users at the virtual Village Pump, cleaning up typos, and voting on deleting articles. As a technical writer by profession, RickK had found the ultimate diversion. "I've always been interested in writing, editing and research, and so felt that Wikipedia was a way of doing that 'for fun.'"

Within a few weeks he had more than 500 edits to his name, and attracted attention in the community with his editing prowess. So much so that he was nominated within a month by veteran user Hephaestos to be an administrator. Never mind that RickK didn't even know exactly what an administrator did. It was a small and trusting community back in 2003, and was quite willing to give administrator (or sysop) privileges to anyone who acted responsibly. Wikipedia was a relatively small site on the Internet, and it was easy to figure out whom to trust with the virtual "mop and bucket." With six community members giving the thumbs-up, and none dissenting, RickK was made a sysop in July, just weeks after joining.

If we look to 2007, the climate for making administrators is a completely different scene. Nominees for administrator on English Wikipedia run the gauntlet, first requiring more than 1,000 edits and at least three months of experience just to get consideration. (Many community members consider the bar even higher.) A candidate can then expect a fusillade of questions, ranging from copyright policy, to libel, to how to react in hypothetical situations. Anyone from the community can pose questions, and as a result, the inquisition becomes a pile of pet peeves and litmus tests by a small band of gatekeepers. Hardly what Wales originally deemed "not a big deal."

Though the Wikipedia policy page says, "There are no official prerequisites for adminship, other than having an account and having a basic level of trust from other editors," everyone knows in today's Wikipedia it's not true.

"Request for Adminship is becoming a rapidly elite crowd threatened by any newcomers and change. People get the nods down instead of getting the benefit of the doubt anymore," says veteran User:Tawker.

Nominees can expect voters to dig into their edit histories and bring up past debates, reverts, votes, and comments, with just a single lapse capable of tripping up a nomination. It's hard to imagine today's brutal process and RickK's six "support" votes, one of which simply read, "The force is strong with this one," as coming from the same roots.

With his new sysop powers, and an obsession for correcting edits like a kid popping Bubble Wrap, RickK reverted useless edits and banned vandals by the dozen, repeating this for hours on end.

RickK was prolific, and a fixture in the ad hoc vandal fighting brigade that would watch the Recent Changes for erroneous edits and miscreants. At his peak, he averaged more than 2,000 edits a month, oftentimes spending hours in a row keeping Wikipedia pristine. "Vandal fighting just sort of came out of the editor mindframe. Correcting errors, fixing things others messed up. I don't know why I became so dedicated to it, I still don't," he says.

There seemed hardly a day when RickK was not working, but his style was not always to everyone's liking. He was known for his speedy but also his prickly comments: "Further racist vandalism will cause you to be blocked from editing," "Delete troll who refers to himself in the third person."

He didn't know it then, but after two years as a Wikipedian, June 20, 2005, would be RickK's last day editing Wikipedia.

In the normal process of fighting vandalism, he ran across the case of a suspected copyright violation by a user named CoolCat, someone who was known to have copied and pasted text without authorization before. RickK reverted CoolCat's edits, but other users thought CoolCat should be given the benefit of the doubt, and in turn reverted RickK's edits. Outnumbered but determined, RickK insisted on removing the copyright violation, as he viewed it as putting Wikipedia in legal jeopardy. When RickK reverted for the fourth time, other administrators considered him in violation of the three revert rule, something normally only applied to malcontents, not fellow administrators. 3RR did not require a block, it only authorized an administrator to apply one at his or her discretion. Another admin, User:Silsor, deemed it appropriate and put a twenty-four-hour block on RickK.

Even though he was unblocked twelve minutes later by another user, Gamaliel, who thought it was a misunderstanding, RickK was insulted. He posted a farewell message on his user page.

> **There is a fatal flaw in the system. Vandals, trolls and malactors are given respect, whereas those who are here to actually create an encyclopedia, and to do meaningful work, are slapped in the face and not given the support needed to do the work they need to do.**
>
> **There is no reason to continue here.**

Wikipedians streamed to RickK's talk page, begging him to stay. But he would not go back on his decision. He could not stand being treated like the troublemakers he worked so hard to repel, even if it was repealed in twelve minutes.

"I had always sworn that if I was ever blocked from editing, that I would leave. I had been feeling more and more frustrated at the [Assume Good Faith] crap that was being offered to newbies and repeat vandals, and repeated assumptions of bad faith against those of us like myself who were actually trying to make it a good encyclopedia. Not having a single voice of support just finished it for me," RickK recalls.

When he'd finally had enough, he signed off in a tradition all too familiar to Wikipedians. He removed all information on his user page, deleting all personal and community information, and left a bitter poison pen message.

RickK would never come back. But people remembered his two years of work with nostalgia. He would rack up more than 36,000 edits, on 19,777 different pages in Wikipedia, a clear sign he was contributing across a wide swath of articles. So missed was RickK that the community even renamed one of its awards in honor of his legacy.

Wikipedians adopted a convention of recognizing each other's efforts, derived from the original MeatballWiki community. There, they believed that building an online community was similar to the traditional "barn raising" efforts of German-American farming communities in the 1800s. All able-bodied members of an Amish community, for example, were expected to volunteer to help construct and erect a wooden barn structure for their neighbors. When the barn was completed, they would place an iron "barnstar" on it as a decorative element. MeatballWiki members used this as inspiration for recognizing good work:

"Here at Meatball, one of our most central values is BarnRaising. We believe in building things collaboratively and collectively . . . To win an award, someone just has to write it on your name-page. To give an award, you just have to decide someone deserves one, and then give it to them. Don't hesitate, just give one in the typical wiki fashion. And, hey, if you want to give it to people from other communities, go right ahead. Meatball doesn't have a monopoly on good people, even if it does look like it some days." In Wikipedia, what started out as a generic barnstar to convey a message of "good job," became more complex, with barnstars given for good copyediting, photography, translation work, or excellence in any number of subject areas. The new barnstar description read:

> The RickK Anti-Vandalism Barnstar (formerly the Anti-Vandalism Barnstar) may be awarded to those who show great contributions to protecting and reverting attacks of vandalism on Wikipedia. . . .
> This award was renamed on July 24, 2005, in appreciation of the efforts of former Wikipedian RickK in fighting vandalism.

What does this tell us about Wikipedia's modern community? Unfortunately, the case of RickK has become much too familiar.

The Missing Wikipedians page provides a way to see some of the casualties. Many exercise the right to vanish, an online community practice of allowing one to withdraw fully and quietly.

RickK's departure was a shock to many. In a project that kept going higher on the charts, and garnering more and more press exposure, it was jarring to see veterans departing out of frustration. Would Wikipedia always be able to lose good contributors and replenish them from the ranks of new visitors?

Criticisms

Perhaps because of Wikipedia's dash out of nowhere and passing Britannica in traffic, Robert McHenry felt he needed to speak up. The former Britannica editor in chief had seen Wikipedia's popularity rise, and on a post called "The Faith-Based Encyclopedia" he publicly mused about how one could trust Wikipedia's working process and articles:

> Then comes the crucial and entirely faith-based step:
> 3. Some unspecified quasi-Darwinian process will assure that those writings and editings by contributors of greatest expertise will survive;

articles will eventually reach a steady state that corresponds to the highest degree of accuracy.

Does someone actually believe this? Evidently so. Why? It's very hard to say. . . .

The user who visits Wikipedia to learn about some subject, to confirm some matter of fact, is rather in the position of a visitor to a public restroom. It may be obviously dirty, so that he knows to exercise great care, or it may seem fairly clean, so that he may be lulled into a false sense of security. What he certainly does not know is who has used the facilities before him.[72]

Jason Scott, mentioned previously as a critic of the phenomenon of edit warring, observed firsthand the problems that could occur when amateurs didn't get it right. He had an anecdote from his experience with the article about New York politician [[Carmine DeSapio]]:

Carmine DeSapio was the last head of Tammany Hall, which is the political machine that controlled New York City for a hundred years. He was the only non-Irish head, he basically got into a lot of trouble, and that was the end of Tammany Hall.

Now, almost all the information on Carmine DeSapio is from Wikipedia. If you go and type this man's name in, you'll get a hundred matches. All of them are variations of the Wikipedia article. The Wikipedia article was typed in by a retiree from Iowa, off of the New York Times obituary from Carmine DeSapio's death, which happens to be locked down under registration so it doesn't get out as much. He transcribed it wrong! In doing so he got the name of his daughter wrong, he got his age wrong, he got a number of other important facts wrong, all of which are duplicated now throughout the web.[73]

A month later, on the last day of 2004, Larry Sanger chimed in with his warning for Wikipedia on Kuro5hin, a tech blog, with an article, "Why Wikipedia Must Jettison Its Anti-Elitism." He recalled his frustration with the chorus of folks who challenged his authority in ways he found unsavory:

Far too much credence and respect accorded to people who in other Internet contexts would be labelled "trolls." There is a certain mindset associated with unmoderated Usenet groups and mailing lists that infects the collectively-managed Wikipedia project: if you react strongly to trolling, that reflects poorly on you, not (necessarily) on the troll. If you attempt to take trolls to task or demand that something be done about constant disruption by trollish behavior, the other listmembers will cry "censorship," attack you, and even come to the defense of the troll. This drama has played out thousands of times over the years on unmoderated Internet groups, and since about the fall of 2001 on the unmoderated Wikipedia.

. . . As a community, Wikipedia lacks the habit or tradition of respect for expertise. As a community, far from being elitist (which would, in this context, mean excluding the unwashed masses), it is anti-elitist (which, in this context, means that expertise is not accorded any special respect, and snubs and disrespect of expertise are tolerated). This is one of my failures: a policy that I attempted to institute in Wikipedia's first year, but for which I did not muster adequate support, was the policy of respecting and deferring politely to experts. (Those who were there will, I hope, remember that I tried very hard.)

Sanger is convinced here, and in his Slashdot memoir, that he could have changed one aspect of policy to "deferring politely to experts." But it's hard to say if that would have worked. How does one define and identify an expert? A new policy would attract a different crowd, a different growth curve, a different set of articles. Would Wikipedia be nearly as popular or recognized as it is today?

Sanger's new project might shed some light on this. He has poured his efforts into replicating exactly this part of the dynamic in a new project, Citizendium, which he considers the "citizen's compendium of everything." When it was launched in March 2007, the press release announced Citizendium's "attempt to unseat Wikipedia as the go-to destination for general information online." Of particular note in Citizendium was the required use of real names, no anonymous editing, and two tiers of users—editors and authors. Editors are imbued with more authority, as they are considered the experts, with higher degrees or academic pedigrees. At just about one year of operation, it had just over 4,000 articles. Not a bad start for the project starting from scratch.

The Seigenthaler Incident

For Wikipedia, 2005 was a year about numbers. In March, the English-language edition hit 500,000 articles, and by September, Dutch public educational company Kennisnet had donated eleven servers in Amsterdam, and Yahoo! Korea had donated twenty-three servers to help balance Wikipedia's traffic overseas. Things were looking bright, until a November 29 editorial in *USA Today* gave Wikipedia a full smackdown.

Penned by John Seigenthaler, a noted veteran journalist, it detailed in slow motion his discovery that the Wikipedia article about him was not only factually incorrect, but accused him of being part of murder. In "A False Wikipedia 'Biography,'" Seigenthaler started right with the bad news, quoting from Wikipedia:

> "John Seigenthaler Sr. was the assistant to Attorney General Robert Kennedy in the early 1960's. For a brief time, he was thought to have been directly involved in the Kennedy assassinations of both John, and his brother, Bobby. Nothing was ever proven." . . .
>
> I have no idea whose sick mind conceived the false, malicious "biography" that appeared under my name for 132 days on Wikipedia, the popular, online, free encyclopedia whose authors are unknown and virtually untraceable.

Seigenthaler detailed his attempt to track down the anonymous editor's IP address at the Internet address in the edit history. But the U.S. Internet provider BellSouth would not assist him.

The editorial illustrated on a very public level what Wikipedia was and was not on the hook for. Fortunately, the U.S. law Section 230 of the Communications Decency Act protects Wikipedia from having to be liable for the content in Wikipedia. As a forum and provider of the virtual space, and not the editorial content, it is protected. Seigenthaler wrote:

> Section 230 of the Communications Decency Act, passed in 1996, specifically states that "no provider or user of an interactive computer service shall be treated as the publisher or speaker." That legalese means that, unlike print and broadcast companies, online service providers cannot be sued for disseminating defamatory attacks on citizens posted by others.

While Wikipedia was in the clear legally, it was the worst public relations black eye so far. The not-so-secret thing was, most informed users knew Wikipedia was full of these little biography bombs. For damage control, Wales appeared on CNN the next week to discuss the incident with Seigenthaler. But by then, the case was buzzing around the media, and Wikipedia clearly had to find a way to prevent a repeat.

Unfortunately, Wikipedia likely suffered from a perfect-storm scenario with Seigenthaler: He was just famous enough to have an entry, but not famous enough for many editors to have checked his article.

The controversy directly informed at least two new policies that continue to this day. One was that the ability to create new articles was shut off for anonymous IP users. Two, a Biography of Living Persons (BLP) Policy was crafted. The new guideline declared, "Unsourced or poorly sourced contentious material—whether negative, positive, or just questionable—about living persons should be removed immediately and without discussion from Wikipedia articles."

With these policy changes, Wikipedia escaped the PR disaster and changed its practices for the better. As the project got larger and more public, it was hard to get wholesale changes done from within, as the old nimble and smaller Wikipedia of 2001 had done. It was usually external crises like Seigenthaler that got people to react and change, as with BLP. But the case would have an unexpected twist in the weeks to come.

Daniel Brandt, an outspoken privacy critic of both Google's and Wikipedia's influence on the Internet, was watching the Seigenthaler episode from the sidelines. It would be charitable to say he's had "differences" with the Wikipedia community. As creator of Google Watch and Wikipedia Watch, Brandt has been a staunch advocate of "accountability" for the Internet's two big influencers. He's tried to keep Google accountable for the questionable use of long-lived HTTP cookies to track users.

Brandt has tried to bring to attention copyright violations in Wikipedia, and pushed for more accountability for the identity of users on the site. The article about him in Wikipedia, [[Daniel Brandt]], is an epic in itself. Never happy with the existence or the quality of the biographical article, he made it a battleground for his cause. Through extreme persistence and tactics at Wikipedia Watch, he has the rare distinction of having been able to convince Wikipedians to delete it, and keep personal details about himself out of Wikipedia.

So if there was ever a case that set off Brandt's rage (besides his own entry),

it was Seigenthaler's—the veteran journalist harmed by the work of an anonymous editor, who had no way to track the editor down. Brandt grabbed the of-
fending IP address off Wikipedia. It was listed right there in the edit history when
the article was modified on May 26, 2005.

Standard checks of the address came up empty, other than it being located
somewhere in Nashville, Tennessee. In an interview with CNET, Brandt related
how he tracked down the exact business, and eventually, the exact person:

> All I had was the IP address and the date and timestamp, and the various
> databases said it was a BellSouth DSL account in Nashville. I started
> playing with the search engines and using different tools to try to see if I
> could find out more about that IP address. They wouldn't respond to trace
> router pings, which means that they were blocked at a firewall, probably
> at BellSouth.
>
> But very strangely, there was a server on the IP address. You almost
> never see that, since at most companies, your browsers and your servers
> are on different IP addresses. Only a very small company that didn't
> know what it was doing would have that kind of arrangement. I put in the
> IP address directly, and then it comes back and said, "Welcome to Rush
> Delivery." It didn't occur to me for about 30 minutes that maybe that was
> the name of a business in Nashville. Sure enough they had a one-page
> Web site. So the next day I sent them a fax.
>
> The next night, I got the idea of sending a phony e-mail, I mean an
> e-mail under a phony name, phony account. When they responded, sure
> enough, the originating IP address matched the one that was in Seigen-
> thaler's column.
>
> I called Seigenthaler and I said I have proof that the IP address [was
> the same]. We still didn't know Brian's name at that point, but the very
> next day some guy named Brian Chase walks into Seigenthaler's offices
> at Vanderbilt University and delivers the confessional letter.[74]

Chase said it was a prank gone wrong and apologized to Seigenthaler, who
decided not to sue or take any action. When Chase resigned his job over this incident, Seigenthaler even interceded on his behalf and asked Rush Delivery to
hire Chase back.

Brandt had been a thorn in the side of the inner circle of Wikipedians for
years, banging the drum about his own personal saga for accountability and privacy. But suddenly Brandt's cause could not just be written off as one person's

mad crusade. These concerns were now magnified on the global stage with the plight of Seigenthaler. Suddenly all Brandt's theoretical complaints about Wikipedia's editing methods and accountability of editors had urgency and gravitas.

It wouldn't be the last time Brandt would be part of a Wikipedia controversy.

The Seigenthaler incident caused some soul searching in the community, and brought about a big policy change. After the dust had settled, the English Wikipedia prevented anonymous users from creating new articles in Wikipedia, thereby preventing "drive-by" page creation. This would, in theory, up the quality of new content. It was controversial at the time. Some users complained that it was anti-wiki, that the encyclopedia that "anyone can edit" would be missing out on converting users into editors. In the end, Wales's social capital won out, and page creation was turned off for anonymous users.

Another measure put in place was a feature called semi-protection. Wikipedia already had a way to protect a page completely, so that no one but administrators could edit it. This was used largely to stop vandalism to popular pages. However, as a blunt tool to prevent editing, it also stopped an article in its tracks from evolving and improving. What they needed was to have an article editable, but not by inexperienced users or drive-by vandals. That's where the concept of "semi-protection" came about. After the Seigenthaler incident, this plan was put into place. Semi-protection could be applied to any article, so that unregistered users or newly registered users (less than four days old and having made fewer than ten edits) would not be able to edit such articles. The new policy was focused on vandalism, specifically:

> Semi-protection is only applied if the page in question is facing a serious vandalism problem. It is not an appropriate solution to editorial disputes of any kind since it may restrict some editors and not others.[75]

It would be hard to imagine these changes happening without an external crisis, to prod the community to action.

The Essjay Controversy

Perhaps Wikipedia's most embarrassing episode came in early 2007, when one of their prolific editors became embroiled in a crisis that shook the faith of both Wikipedia insiders and outside users.

The origins of the crisis date back to February 2005, when an account with the name Essjay was created and edited the article [[Imprimatur]] to clarify a Latin phrase in Catholicism: "Nihil obstat is a separate distinction granted by a Roman Catholic censor; imprimatur can be granted by any bishop." While he didn't describe much about himself at the time, in May he become much more active and introduced himself on his User:Essjay page:

> For various reasons, I prefer to maintain my anonymity here at Wikipedia, however, I do offer the following information about myself:
> I teach both undergraduate and graduate courses in Theology at a private university in the eastern United States. My research interests include Roman Catholic Doctrine, particularly canon law; Catholic Liturgy; and issues of Homosexuality and Christianity.
> I possess the following academic degrees:
>
> • B.A. in Religious Studies
> • M.A. in Religion
> • Ph.D. in Theology
> • J.C.D. (Doctorate in Canon Law)

Even though there was no way to confirm any of the credentials Essjay listed, one of Wikipedia's core mantras was to assume good faith. Wikipedians generally took things at face value. Staying pseudonymous was not unusual in Wikipedia, given the possibility of real-life harassment when being bold in editing contentious topics. Generally, the community respected these boundaries by using username "handles" and not demanding anything more about one's personal life than one was willing to reveal.

By July 2005, Essjay had become an active and respected member of the Wikipedia community by editing numerous Catholicism-related topics and engaging in discussion about the state of Wikipedia's religion articles. As the volume and quality of his contributions grew, he was nominated to be an administrator just five months after joining. He saw overwhelming support, with sixty-eight votes for promotion and only one vote against. Essjay's involvement with the community deepened as he edited more subject areas, fought vandals, joined the mediation committee, and became a primary contact for the IRC network that Wikipedians used for real-time chat. In the process, he racked up thousands of edits across Wikipedia and the other Wikimedia project sites. A year later he gained enough trust to receive the keys to the castle: "bureaucrat" status (the ability to promote other administrators), and the very rare "checkuser" privilege for inspecting the private Internet address information of any Wikipedian. Only a dozen or so experienced users had this power. The affable and respected Essjay was in an elite class of Wikipedians.

It should be no surprise that his story was attractive to outsiders, with Essjay appearing as an intellectual superhero and "caped crusader." As an accomplished professor, he contributed his doctorate expertise pseudonymously while working with ordinary Wikipedians to spread free knowledge. How could anyone not find that inspiring?

When Pulitzer Prize–winning reporter Stacy Schiff wrote a detailed feature story for the *New Yorker* magazine (July 2006) about Wikipedia, she described how its online denizens were "devoted . . . to a higher good." In her story "The Know It All," Essjay was prominently profiled as one of Wikipedia's heroes as he patrolled topics ranging from Justin Timberlake to Israel and Palestine. Schiff reported, from information gathered from his user page and through live phone interviews, that he was a "tenured professor of religion at a private university" and held a "Ph.D. in theology and a degree in canon law."

The problem? It was all false.

The story ran in the *New Yorker* and none were the wiser. Even Wikipedians in the English-language community believed Essjay's story of being a professor who had to use a pseudonym to avoid problems with his school.

It was six months later that the shock came.

In early 2007, Essjay accepted a job with Wikia, the for-profit company formed by Wikimedia Foundation board members Jimmy Wales and Angela Beesley. Facing the reality of having to work in person with colleagues, Essjay came clean and said he was in fact not a "tenured professor" but Ryan Jordan, a twenty-four-year-old from Louisville, Kentucky, with a background as a paralegal and perhaps no college degree at all. He posted a new, "real" biography with still seemingly too much experience to fit into two dozen years of existence.

The *New Yorker* found out, and had to publish an embarrassing editor's note:

Essjay was recommended to Ms. Schiff as a source by a member of Wikipedia's management team because of his respected position within the Wikipedia community. He was willing to describe his work as a Wikipedia administrator but would not identify himself other than by confirming the

biographical details that appeared on his user page. At the time of publication, neither we nor Wikipedia knew Essjay's real name. Essjay's entire
Wikipedia life was conducted with only a user name; anonymity is common for Wikipedia administrators and contributors, and he says that he
feared personal retribution from those he had ruled against online. Essjay now says that his real name is Ryan Jordan, that he is twenty-four and
holds no advanced degrees, and that he has never taught. He was recently hired by Wikia—a for-profit company affiliated with Wikipedia—as
a "community manager"; he continues to hold his Wikipedia positions. He
did not answer a message we sent to him; Jimmy Wales, the co-founder
of Wikia and of Wikipedia, said of Essjay's invented persona, "I regard it
as a pseudonym and I don't really have a problem with it."

Wales, traveling in India at the time and likely working off imperfect information, defended Essjay in public and to the press.

Shortly after, Essjay was elevated by Wales to the ranks of serving on the
Arbitration Committee, the highest level of service for deciding on community
matters. Wales stated later, "Essjay has always been, and still is, a fantastic
editor and trusted member of the community. . . . He has been thoughtful and
contrite about the entire matter, and I consider it settled."[76]

Meanwhile, Wikipedians erupted in debate on the mailing lists, the user talk
pages of Essjay and Wales, as well as the Community Noticeboard. The blogo-
sphere was raging, with Larry Sanger coming back to Wikipedia to challenge
Wales on this:

Jimmy, to call yourself a tenured professor, when you aren't one, is not a
"pseudonym." It's identity fraud. And the full question is not why you appointed Essjay to ArbCom, but: why did you ignore the obvious moral implications of the fact that he had fraudulently pretended to be a
professor—ignoring those implications even to the point of giving him a
job and appointing him to ArbCom—until now?[77]

Best-selling author of *Freakonomics* Stephen J. Dubner brought up his
concern. "This is hardly a felony, but it does make you wonder about what
else happens at Wikipedia that Jimmy Wales doesn't have a problem with," he
wrote.

Wikipedians, usually quick to circle the wagons to protect their own from media distortions, didn't come to Essjay's rescue. On the contrary, most seemed offended by Essjay and started to dig into his detailed history of editing. Meanwhile, Essjay remained coy, refusing to make statements of clarification until pressed to do so a few days later. Ultimately, he claimed the "professor" was a defensive persona to evade online stalkers and trolls. It's not an uncommon problem in Wikipedia, but it didn't quite smell right to the community.

After more community pressure, Essjay finally posted a message called "My Response," but was hardly contrite. The message only raised more ire in those who sensed he felt no remorse for deceiving a reporter and his fellow Wikipedians:

> I *am* sorry if anyone in the Wikipedia community has been hurt by my decision to use disinformation to protect myself. . . . I have no intention of going anywhere, because to do so would be to let the vandals, trolls, and stalkers win.

Essjay had his supporters. Even skeptics appreciated his widely recognized good work in the community. But their trust had been violated. Scores of fellow users didn't buy his cover story, and many started using Wikipedia's years-deep database to comb through his past behavior, made possible because of Wikipedia's belief in transparency.

What people turned up was disturbing.

Users dug up numerous accounts of Essjay using the "professor persona" and false credentials to gain the upper hand in article and policy debates.

His fourth-ever edit as User:Essjay was April 11, 2005, when he was already using false credentials to end debate on the article [[Imprimatur]]:

> This is a text I often require for my students, and I would hang my own Ph.D. on it's [sic] credibility.[78]

Later in 2005, Essjay bragged to the community how he had addressed fellow professors with a form letter stating his credentials to defend Wikipedia in the academic arena:

> I've contacted a few professors after other Wikipedians have pointed out that the instructor made the "Wikipedia is not a reliable source" argument to students who were, in fact, Wikipeidans [sic]. I have a copy of my form response at User:Essjay/Letter. When I was head of my department,

I certainly would have taken knowledge of such conduct into consideration, and I think similarly minded department heads/deans would as
well.[79]

The letter, which may or may not have ever been sent, stated:

I am also a tenured professor of theology; feel free to have a look at my
Wikipedia userpage (linked below) to gain an idea of my background and
credentials.

It was clear the argument that his identity was simply a defensive online persona no longer held any water. He used his fake credentials for social capital
within the community, parading a fictional persona and fishing for accolades.

It was no longer just an external embarrassment, it was an internal crisis of
confidence. During this time, he still had access to the most powerful tools concerning privacy and trust—checkuser and oversight, both of which provided access to private and deleted information in Wikipedia's databases.

As the story got more implausible, the community seethed. Debate raged as
ad hoc straw polls were taken as to what to do about Essjay. Wales's early support was crucial to keep Essjay's standing intact, but as the pressure built, Jimbo
changed his mind. "I have asked EssJay to resign his positions of trust within the
community," he later said.[80]

Shortly afterward, Essjay signed off for good, posting a farewell message, but
never coming clean on the whole deception.

The *New Yorker* tried to defend its actions. In a statement to *The New York
Times* they said, "We were comfortable with the material we got from Essjay
because of Wikipedia's confirmation of his work and their endorsement of him.
In retrospect, we should have let our readers know that we had been unable to
corroborate Essjay's identity beyond what he told us."

It was a big strike against the vaunted fact-checking operation of the *New
Yorker*. The Wikimedia Foundation's employee Danny Wool disagreed with the
New Yorker's statement, and was keen to emphasize that the nonprofit founda-
tion never endorsed the authenticity of Essjay, ever.

The crisis occurred on many levels. The community felt embarrassed that a
member would lie while representing Wikipedia's volunteer editing corps. Editors
also felt betrayed by Essjay claiming false credentials. It was simply puzzling why

Essjay had to lie when nearly all of his edits were clearly good, constructive contributions and did not hinge upon his fake pedigrees.

Interestingly, Daniel Brandt, a vocal critic of Wikipedia who broke open the John Seigenthaler libel case, figured into this episode as well. The Signpost, an independent community newspaper within Wikipedia, reported that Brandt noticed a hole in Essjay's (nee Ryan Jordan's) cover story:

> As an explanation for the fake persona, Jordan pointed to the problem of people trying to harass and stalk Wikipedia editors. This concern implicitly included the work of people like Wikipedia critic Daniel Brandt, although the persona predates Brandt's Wikipedia-related activity by several months. . . .
>
> For his part, Brandt helped bring the discrepancy to the attention of The New Yorker.[81]

The Essjay controversy took place over many days, almost unfolding in slow motion. This gave enough time for seasoned editors to do their own crime scene investigation of Essjay's edit history, to great dismay. Unlike the crises of the past, which were used as learning experiences and a chance to improve community policy, this one had no such benefit. People just had to shake their heads. There were no good lessons to take away, just disappointment and regret that perhaps "assume good faith" was the biggest casualty.

WIKIPEDIA MAKES WAVES

"First they ignore you, then they laugh at you, then they fight you, then you win."

—*Gandhi*

"Emulation is the sincerest form of flattery."

—*Unknown*

O n the evening of July 31, 2006, viewers of Comedy Central witnessed a great experiment in the gonzo nature of Web 2.0. Stephen Colbert, impersonating his trademark fictional bombastic conservative news host on his show *The Colbert Report,* presented his regular segment "The Wørd." That night he chose to unveil the target of his satire: a newly minted term, "Wikiality."

The comedian prankster declared to his viewers what Wikiality meant:

I love Wikipedia. . . . Any user can change any entry and if enough other users agree with them, it becomes true. . . .

We're going to stampede across the web like that giant horde of elephants in Africa.

> Find the page on elephants in Wikipedia and create an entry that
> says the number of elephants has tripled in the last six months. . . .
> Together we can create a reality that we all agree on—the reality we
> just agreed on.[82]

Colbert's show airs at 11:30 P.M. Eastern Standard Time in the United States,
and not surprisingly there were plenty of Internet-savvy viewers watching TV and
sitting in front of their computers. At 11:39 P.M., Wikipedians started noticing a
flurry of activity at the article [[Elephant]]. User:EvilBrak was able to get this edit
into the article: "THE NUMBER OF ELEPHANTS HAS TRIPLED IN THE LAST
SIX MONTHS!" at 11:40 P.M. before being reverted within one minute. The article was then protected and locked down, but over the next few days, each attempt to open up the article to editing saw an influx of pranksters following
Colbert's orders. Fortunately, it was easy for Wikipedia's administrators to undo
the vandalism, and lock up the article and wait out the enthusiasm. Ever since,
it has been a running joke by Colbert to periodically ask his viewers to overrun a
Wikipedia article to vandalize it. Originally annoyed by such shenanigans, many
Wikipedians now consider it a sign of prankish affection.

The Wikipedia phenomenon had hit late night TV, even being the target of
comedy. Even though Colbert chided Wikipedia's practices, he was actually a fan
of the site. He wasn't the only one. As Wikipedia's influence in Google rose, it
was no longer just a crazy idea to be mocked. Academics were studying it, and
companies were examining what they could learn. Even the U.S. government created a project in 2006 called Intellipedia, linking sixteen agencies of the U.S.
intelligence community. Modeled on Wikipedia's success, in 2008 it had 37,000
users and 200,000 pages.[83]

It was suddenly hip to evoke Wikipedia's name and model as something to
try. The site's success even saw the return of Wikipedia's original "chief instigator," Larry Sanger, back to the world of encyclopedia creation.

JewWatch

One of the earliest examples of Wikipedia's influence on the Internet occurred in
April 2004, quite early in Wikipedia's history, when Steven Weinstock, a New York
real estate investor, performed a simple Google search on the word "jew."[84]

At the top of the search results was the site JewWatch.com, a site containing anti-Semitic content, referring to Jewish Mind Control Mechanisms and Jewish Communist Rulers, one after the other. He was shocked, and was sure Google had made some kind of mistake allowing this site to be at the top of the search results. Unfortunately they hadn't. Google's entire search livelihood rests in its PageRank algorithm, a method of evaluating who is linking to whom on the Internet, and determining what should come up first in search results. It just so happened that there was a network of interlinked sites with a preponderance of the word "jew" on it. And that network happened to be made up of mostly anti-Semitic Web sites. Google certainly wasn't happy that JewWatch came up first either, but they were not about to alter their search results by hand.

Google created a special page specifically to point this out to the public, saying that their algorithm was agnostic about content, and that sometimes this might go against one's tastes, but that Google would not tweak the outcome. Titled "An explanation of our search results," it read:

> If you recently used Google to search for the word "Jew," you may have seen results that were very disturbing. We assure you that the views expressed by the sites in your results are not in any way endorsed by Google. We'd like to explain why you're seeing these results when you conduct this search.
>
> A site's ranking in Google's search results relies heavily on computer algorithms using thousands of factors to calculate a page's relevance to a given query. Sometimes subtleties of language cause anomalies to appear that cannot be predicted. A search for "Jew" brings up one such unexpected result.[85]

People upset at Google's results were not going to let it stand. A movement quickly formed to use a grassroots technique to counteract this: the Google-Bomb. It was a way to artificially influence the results of Google's PageRank by encouraging people to put the word "jew" on their Web sites and link to something else, in effect diluting the network effect of JewWatch.

The problem was, what should people link to? Asking sites to point to a "pro-Jewish" site could possibly create a problem in the other direction, promoting causes and stances not everyone might agree with. The GoogleBomb activists instead decided that linking to the Wikipedia article [[Jew]] would have the widest appeal. Because of Wikipedia's neutral-point-of-view policy, this was widely considered fair and egalitarian, providing the ideal alternative destination for a search of "jew." Daniel Sieradski,[86] editor of the Jew School Web site, headed an effort encouraging people to add links to the Wikipedia article http://en.wikipedia .org/wiki/Jew from their blogs and Web pages. It was so effective that the next week, the [[Jew]] article supplanted the JewWatch.com Web site at the top of the list. The two shuffled positions for the next few weeks, possibly the result of some "counter-GoogleBombing." However, since the end of 2004, the Wikipedia entry has been firmly in the number one slot without interruption. Wikipedia was filling a unique role on the Internet, and it was a big vote of trust in its model.

UK Censors Wikipedia

The headline for December 8, 2008 said it all: "Wikipedia Censored In U.K. Over Nude Girl"[87]. In one simple action and without any warning, one of Wikipedia's most sensitive content disputes would be played out in the public theater.

It was December 6, a relatively quiet Saturday, when reports started filling Wikipedia's troubleshooting channels—the IRC chat room, the Administrators' Noticeboard and its trouble ticket system—that people who tried to edit Wikipedia from within the United Kingdom found themselves suddenly and inexplicably barred from the site. Because the problem was so widespread, English Wikipedia's administrators scrambled to figure out how an entire country could have been hobbled all at once.

Unbeknownst to them, it involved a little-known organization called the Internet Watch Foundation (IWF). Described as an "independent self-regulatory body," it serves as a clearing house, investigating and maintaining a "blacklist" of sites exhibiting potentially illegal or indecent material. With financial support from EU and UK Internet service providers, it responds to consumers and browsing tipsters, by adding or removing contentious sites from its rolls. To protect their customers the companies funding the IWF use the resulting list as a basis for their own blocking. On its Web site, the IWF declares itself:

The UK Hotline for reporting illegal content specifically:
Child sexual abuse content hosted worldwide and criminally obscene and incitement to racial hatred content hosted in the UK

Just below the message is a large virtual red button, which reads: "CLICK HERE REPORT ILLEGAL CONTENT". On December 4 someone had done just that, pointing out Wikipedia page [[Virgin Killer]] as problematic.

A heavy metal album by the 1970s band Scorpions, *Virgin Killer* was noted for being the group's first international success. But it was also infamous for its cover art. Featuring a full-body photograph of a nude prepubescent girl staring to the camera, with a strategic cracked-glass effect covering her genitalia, it was so controversial that the US version used an image of the band's five members instead.

However, in the English Wikipedia the article on the album included a picture of the original cover, complete with the nude girl. The image, though copyrighted, was included in Wikipedia by asserting "fair use", a doctrine that allows copying for the purposes of criticism, comment or scholarship[88]. So, while not always tasteful, the practice of including historically significant images for commentary was nonetheless widespread and legal—or so it appeared.

Long before the IWF was tipped off about *Virgin Killer,* the Wikipedia community had already wrestled with the image's status as possible child pornography. But in Wikipedia, built on the backs of instinctively libertarian free culture types, there was an almost collective reflex to defy anything that smacked of censorship. The community even adopted a shorthand for this, [[WP:NOTCENSORED]], that could be thrown down as a trump card during any discussion that sought to raise the "appropriateness" of content. Clicking on this all-cap term brings you to the policy page, which states[89]:

> **Wikipedia may contain content that some readers consider objectionable or offensive, even exceedingly so . . . Discussion of potentially objectionable content should not focus on its offensiveness, but on whether it is appropriate to include in a given article. Beyond that, "being objectionable" is generally not sufficient grounds for removal of content.**

This is certainly not part of your ordinary encyclopedia "style guide". Beneath the verbose official policy runs a distinct crusading undertone, lionizing the role of defiant instigator as virtuous and heroic, even if it presses right up against the boundaries of good taste.

Even so, in November 2007 a number of attempts were made to delete the album's image from Wikipedia, albeit without success. In May 2008, after a long debate on the "Images and Media for Deletion" page, an administrator concluded there was a consensus and deleted the image. After some controversy over whether the proper process had been followed, three days later this ruling was overturned during "Deletion Review", and the image restored, demonstrating just how contentious it had become, even before the IWF controversy. Indeed in that same month the conservative U.S. news Web site WorldNetDaily complained about the *Virgin Killer* image under the headline, "FBI investigates Wikipedophilia", but nothing came of it[90].

This all changed when [[Virgin Killer]] was placed on the IWF list on December 5, 2008. Most of the Internet service providers in the UK took their cue from the IWF and dutifully implemented their own blocking system to keep residential broadband customers from accessing the blacklisted site.

Blocking the *Virgin Killer* image would not have been terribly controversial on its own. After all, it was simply one image among thousands. When loading the page in question, one of the Internet providers, Demon, returned this error to its customers:

Access Denied (403)
We have blocked this page because, according to the Internet Watch Foundation (IWF), it contains indecent images of children or pointers to them; you could be breaking UK law if you viewed the page.[91]

The real problem arose when the blocking had an unintended and surprising side effect, one that crippled Wikipedia editors throughout the UK.

To block a site, most of the ISPs in the UK use a method called a "transparent proxy" to handle requests to questionable sites. In practice this meant that any Web page requests that contained "en.wikipedia.org" were funneled through this proxy system, and that was where the problems began.

Thousands, if not millions, of unwitting Wikipedia surfers around the country were suddenly thrown into the same system. Since they all seemed to be coming from the same Internet IP address the innocent readers and accomplished editors of Wikipedia found themselves grouped in with the malcontents and vandals looking to do harm to the articles. Wikipedia administrators, as part of their normal vandal-fighting procedures, then blocked the apparent source of the troublemakers. But unbeknownst to them, all the traffic was coming from the same proxy server, meaning they had inadvertantly blocked all ordinary and anonymous editors as well. Because UK users didn't know a proxy was being used (hence, the transparent part) it wasn't clear to Web surfers why this problem was occurring.

This became a huge headache, literally overnight, as Wikipedia administrator User:Daniel described it to *The Sydney Morning Herald* [92]:

> "We can't determine who's who from Britain, and so that's causing trouble with people vandalising [Wikipedia] from Britain and we can't work out who it is and can't block just them. We have to block a lot of people to do it," he said.
>
> As a result, Wikipedia, which contains 2.6 million articles all written by its users, has instituted a blanket ban on anonymous edits from the six ISPs[93], which account for 95 per cent of British residential internet users.

With Wikipedia one of the top ten most visited sites in the UK, this new restriction became painfully obvious within a day. Internet mailing lists and discussion groups buzzed about the problems. The IWF responded publicly by saying:

> A Wikipedia web page was reported through the IWF's online reporting mechanism in December 2008. As with all child sexual abuse reports received by our Hotline analysts, the image was assessed according to the UK Sentencing Guidelines Council . . . The content was considered to be a potentially illegal indecent image of a child under the age of 18, but hosted outside the UK.

Interestingly, the *Virgin Killer* page was considered a relatively minor offender. IWF spokesperson Sarah Robertson disclosed it rated "1 on a scale of 1 to 5, where 1 is the least offensive."[94] It was considered "erotic posing with no sexual activity."

To most in the Wikipedia sphere, and many beyond, the judgment appeared inconsistent and arbitrary. One of Wikipedia's high profile UK editors David Gerard pointed out the IWF's block wasn't even executed correctly—it wound up blocking the text of the article on en.wikipedia.org, while not actually blocking the image, which was hosted on another server, upload.wikimedia.org. The Wikimedia Foundation's legal counsel noted that the image could be found easily elsewhere online, uncensored. "We believe it's worth noting that the image is currently visible on Amazon,[95] where the album can be freely purchased by UK residents. It is available on thousands of websites that are accessible to the UK public," pointed out Mike Godwin. Curiously, not long after that statement, the image was abruptly removed from Amazon. It may have made things consistent, but it didn't solve the problem of UK residents losing the ability to edit.

While the IWF usually operated quietly and without comment behind the scenes, this was not one of those times. It soon became clear that both they and the ISPs were on the losing side in a public relations battle. In fact, because of the controversy and the attendant media coverage, more people than ever were actively seeking out and perusing the album cover. Wikipedia's Signpost noted, [[Virgin Killer]] was the most viewed article on en.wiki for most of the week, and traffic increased over 200-fold to over 371,900 hits at its peak."[96] This unintended consequence of censorship, the creation of more publicity, was not a new phenomenon and even had a name "the Streisand effect", which had its origins in a 2003 case in which Barbra Streisand sued to have an aerial photograph of her house removed from a public collection of images. Coverage of the case wound up giving the picture, and the location of her home, far more airtime than would ever have been the case otherwise.

As a result of the fallout the IWF backpedaled. In less than a week, they issued a statement announcing the block would be lifted due to "contextual issues":

Following representations from Wikipedia, IWF invoked its Appeals Procedure and has given careful consideration to the issues involved in this case. The procedure is now complete and has confirmed that the image in question is potentially in breach of the Protection of Children Act 1978. However, the IWF Board has today (9 December 2008) considered these findings and the contextual issues involved in this specific case and, in light of the length of time the image has existed and its wide availability, the decision has been taken to remove this webpage from our list . . . IWF's overriding objective is to minimise the availability of indecent images of children on the internet, however, on this occasion our efforts have had the opposite effect. We regret the unintended consequences for Wikipedia and its users. Wikipedia have been informed of the outcome of this procedure and IWF Board's subsequent decision.

It was the most gracious, face-saving way to get out of a rapidly worsening situation. It was also unprecedented. Hitherto the IWF had never reversed a decision due to appeal; indeed their spokesperson, Robertson was "not aware of it ever being used before."[97]

What lessons had been learned?
Contrary to the media hysteria that sometimes surrounds the subject, it's

relatively easy to identify and filter pornographic sites that propagate illegal and lascivious content. In this respect the Internet Watch Foundation actually does a rather effective job, geared as it is towards filtering "child sex abuse websites, run by organised criminals."[98] But the old adage about pornography ("You know it when you see it") isn't as obvious with Wikipedia articles, especially those maintained with its customary neutral and clinical style. Pages and images depicting explicit sexual content (or in this case, controversial album covers) are presented for reasons of instruction and education, rather than prurient interest, and it was exactly this "contextual issue" for which the IWF realized the appeal was valid.

To be sure, there are other controversies akin to *Virgin Killer* in Wikipedia, just waiting to be exposed to the public. But in the end this furore shows Wikipedia's crowd of editors have been startlingly good at striking the fine balance between pushing forward their mission to inform and butting up against common standards of taste and decency. Rather than adhere to any single strict policy that gives an answer to what is legal or not, the community dynamics instead allow conversations to triangulate on accepted norms. After eight years of existence, the Wikipedia community has emerged with a pretty good idea of where the line rests—even if Jimmy Wales doesn't always agree.

In the aftermath of the controversy, he pondered on the mailing list:

> So then the question becomes: does this image fit the definition under (especially) US law, or the law of any particularly relevant countries (UK)? That is a question of judgment of fact that I do not think has been looked at sufficiently. I am not an expert, but I can tell you that—as for me—I am not downloading or looking at the image at all, I don't want it anywhere near my computer.[99]

Microsoft Encarta's Experiment

After seeing Wikipedia's popularity soar, Microsoft Encarta, in one of the surprising moves of 2005, announced a system for soliciting user contributions. Editorial director Gary Alt announced on the Encarta blog in March 2005: "We're about to roll out a new set of tools that will make it far easier for you to suggest revisions in En-carta. By the time of our next post, we should have the new tools up and running, and we'll be looking to you to help us help you."[100]

It seemed clearly a reaction to the threat of Wikipedia, and many news out-lets heralded it as Microsoft adding wiki-like features to its venerable encyclope-dia. But a closer examination of the feedback system showed this was far from what was happening. In the fine print of the newly branded Encarta Feedback system, it stated that contributors submitting content to Microsoft also gave the company rights to user submissions under traditional copyright. In addition, there would be no confirmation that a submission was received, no recognition for the person, and no compensation for the effort. The policy sounded esoteri-cally wiki-like but in reality had very little in common with Wikipedia at all—it was not timely, open, social, or free.

The announcement and half-hearted implementation was not a surprise to those who follow Microsoft. They are famous for their "embrace and extend" strat-egy, by borrowing successful methods from competitors to reap the same benefits. (Critics of Microsoft often say "extinguish" is step three.) In this case, Microsoft's announcement had the potential to benefit from Wikipedia's slipstream.

At least Wikipedia's free content could not be bought or shut down by any-one. It was with some fanfare that Microsoft announced on its Encarta blog and picked up on Slashdot:

> Encarta is not just a pell-mell conglomeration of information and random bits of trivia (some would argue that that would pretty much describe the Internet itself, but that's a different discussion).
>
> So you won't find Encarta articles on each of Ashlee Simpson's teeth—indeed, you won't find an article on Ashlee Simpson at all. Nor will you find an article about Barney, Homer's best pal on The Simp-sons. Not that I don't love The Simpsons (I'm not going to comment on Ashlee or her teeth), but that's not what we do.[101]

In the end, the wiki-like experiment didn't get much traction. It was never integrated into the pages at Encarta in any visible way like Wikipedia's "Edit" button. There was also no way for people to discuss and build off one another's work. Microsoft's plan was to engage their local academic institution for help.

The Encarta Feedback FAQ gave this explanation:

> Graduate students at the University of Washington Information School are fact-checking all proposed changes to Encarta. They are trained in research and passionate about corroborating facts. Stay tuned for possible plans to expand our pool of researchers to the Encarta community.

If you have never heard of the Encarta Feedback function, it's with good reason. It never developed much beyond the public announcement. The Encarta staff produced a six-month report with a sample of the types of feedback they were getting, but the last mention of Encarta Feedback was on their blog on September 28, 2005. Today most links to this feature are defunct, without a trace of this wiki-like experiment on Encarta's pages.

Wikitorials

Something that got more attention was the *Los Angeles Times* experiment with something called Wikitorials. Opinion editor Michael Kinsley, a legend in the news industry, admired what he saw in Wikipedia and thought it would be interesting to experiment with the wiki method for publicly editing an editorial column.

Editorial page editor Andrés Martinez announced,

> We'll have some editorials where you can go online and edit an editorial to your satisfaction. . . . We are going to do that with selected editorials initially. We don't know how this is going to turn out. It's all about finding new ways to allow readers to interact with us in the age of the Web.

Kinsley was prophetic when he declared, "It may be a complete mess but it's going to be interesting to try."

What happened to Wikitorials has gone down as a case study in how not to launch a wiki, or what happens when there is too much faith in its mythical magic. On June 17, 2005, Wikitorials started out with a fairly complete editorial called "War and Consequences," and invited people to come help collaborate on editing it. The editorial started with the contentious issue of the military conflict in Iraq:

> As the war in Iraq grinds on and the number of U.S. troops remains stubbornly fixed at 140,000, murmurs of dissatisfaction at home become louder and more widespread. Republican members of Congress have joined Democrats in questioning how much longer the troops will have to stay.

At 1064 words, it covered strategies, personalities, statistics, and recommendations about U.S. conduct in the region. The *Los Angeles Times* was bold in choosing a topic of this size and scope. The editorial ended:

> Bush should be honest with the American people and the Iraqis. That requires setting realistic goals and holding people responsible for them.
> Click here to Wiki this morning's editorial about Iraq.

With an issue that deeply divided Americans about what to do next, there would certainly be no lack of opinions. What happened next was best described by the Wikipedia editor Michael Snow in a story for the Wikipedia Signpost newsletter:

> The wikitorial wiki used MediaWiki software, although creating an account was required in order to edit. Among those participating were Jimbo Wales and Wikinews administrator Ilya Haykinson. When the original wikitorial was moved to an inappropriate title, this was reverted and the offender blocked within five minutes. Wales then tried to launch a counterpoint page to provide an outlet for opposing views; however, this mostly drew sarcastic additions from those sympathetic to the original editorial's stance.
>
> Other than the one block, however, the LA Times staff seemed to merely be observing developments and made little effort to get involved in guiding or developing the process. The plan as outlined by Michael Kinsley, the editor of the newspaper's editorial page, was to "filter it very lightly." This minimal level of supervision apparently left the wiki unprepared for the effect of being featured on Slashdot, as happened Saturday.
>
> The effect of Slashdot items that link to wiki pages is fairly familiar on Wikipedia. A flurry of new edits is a certainty, quite a bit of which will be vandalism, and the article must be reverted frequently and often protected from editing. Similarly, the wikitorials project was hit with

several vandalism attacks within a few hours of appearing on Slashdot, and the wikitorials were taken down on Sunday. The statement left behind read: "Unfortunately, we have had to remove this feature, at least temporarily, because a few readers were flooding the site with inappropriate material."[102]

What the *LA Times* did not realize was that it takes a legion of dedicated users and administrators in the background of Wikipedia to keep things vandal-free. Kinsley's simple launch of the feature without this in mind was like building a theme park without sanitation workers or security guards.

There was bound to be trouble. And it was about as bad as one could imagine, with some of the Internet's most famous shock images making unexpected appearances on the *LA Times* wiki site. That was simply too much for a mainstream media organization to handle, and it was shut down faster than you could say "undo."

Ross Mayfield, head of the commercial wiki company Socialtext, posted an open letter from the community as advice for Mr. Kinsley:

Devoted users take care of their wikis. If you had left the Wikitorial up, users could have grown to love and appreciate the community you were creating. Given guidance and time, vandalism disappears, as if by magic, but actually by the work of a handful of devoted users who care about what happens to the common resource they help create.[103]

It's an intriguing proposal. Could a mainstream newspaper attract a set of core admins to help sustain a site like Wikitorials? More interestingly, would they be willing to hand over the reins of "adminship" to folks on the Net they didn't know so well? It's hard to imagine they would.

The shock of the experience was likely too much for any news organization to even dare dip a toe back into the wiki pool. And since then, no real major media outlet has done anything as high profile with wikis.

Nature Study

Wikipedia was already highly regarded, anecdotally, but it got a glowing evaluation from the prestigious *Nature* magazine in December 2005, when it concluded that Wikipedia "comes close" to Britannica in the quality of its science articles. "Our reviewers identified an average of four errors in each Wikipedia article, and three in each Britannica article."[104]

The news came as a bit of a surprise. Many folks felt Wikipedia did better than they'd have thought, and Britannica did, well, worse than they expected. The result of the study was hotly debated between *Nature* and Britannica, but to most Wikipedians it was a vindication. They knew that Wikipedia was a minefield of errors, but to be in such close proximity in quality to a traditionally edited encyclopedia, while using such a grassroots process, was the external validation they had been waiting for.

Britannica wasn't pleased with the methodology, and posted a rebuttal with this criticism: "Almost everything about the journal's investigation, from the criteria for identifying inaccuracies to the discrepancy between the article text and its headline, was wrong and misleading."[105] *Nature* and Britannica exchanged barbs and rebuttals, but in the end, the overall result seemed clear.

"The Nature article showed that we are on the right track with our current methods. We just need better ways to prevent the display of obvious vandalism at any time," wrote longtime Wikipedian Daniel Mayer on the mailing list.

Britannica Goes Free and Collaborative

In early 2008, Britannica announced changes that clearly showed it was not sitting still. As Wikipedia had completely overshadowed Britannica online in terms of traffic and attention, Britannica adopted a new hybrid approach that would embrace contributions by users while banking on Britannica's expert-driven content. President Jorge Cauz wrote in June 2008:

It should not be a surprise then that among the main objectives of our new site are to make it very easy for our contributors, other scholars, and regular readers to engage with our content by suggesting improvements to our editors; and to provide the editing tools they need to create and share their own content at the site.[106]

Britannica had already launched a project called WebShare in April 2008, which was described as "A special program for web publishers, including bloggers, webmasters, and anyone who writes for the Internet. You get complimentary access to the Encyclopaedia Britannica online and, if you like, an easy way to give your readers background on the topics you write about with links to complete Britannica articles."[107] This was a rather radical move, obviously trying to vie with Wikipedia's emergence as one of the most linked-to resources on the Internet.

But the latest initiative was something quite astonishing, as Britannica was now inviting users to be part of the team of content creators:

> To elicit their participation in our new online community of scholars, we will provide our contributors with a reward system and a rich online home that will enable them to promote themselves, their work, and their services. . . . Encyclopaedia Britannica will allow those visitors to suggest changes and additions to that content.[108]

The area that is the most intriguing is Britannica's multimedia content, which has always been superior to that of Wikipedia. Over the years, having produced a multimedia CD-ROM and online encyclopedia, Britannica has acquired video and negotiated rights to copyrighted content that Wikipedia simply cannot host because of its "free content" policy.

> Readers and users will also be invited into an online community where they can work and publish at Britannica's site under their own names. Interested users will be able to prepare articles, essays, and multimedia presentations on subjects in which they're interested. Britannica will help them with research and publishing tools and by allowing them to easily use text and non-text material from Encyclopaedia Britannica in their work.

Under the heading of "listening to experts," Britannica's Cauz was emphatic about the difference between Wikipedia and Britannica:

> But there are significant differences between our approach and what is popularly termed "Web 2.0." . . . We believe that the creation and documentation of knowledge is a collaborative process but not a democratic one, and this has at least three consequences.[109]

Cauz listed the same types of concerns that Daniel Brandt and Larry Sanger had about Wikipedia: owning the responsibility for what is published, recognizing the voices and powers of experts, and addressing subjects with objectivity.

Digital Universe and Citizendium

Finally, we get reacquainted with Larry Sanger in his life post-Wikipedia. After Sanger left the Wikipedia project in 2002, he returned to Ohio State University, where he obtained his Ph.D. and taught philosophy. In his spare time, he was also known to fiddle around and teach Irish traditional music as well.

In 2005, he went back to his encyclopedic roots, as the Digital Universe Foundation was starting a new knowledge-based venture to create a number of projects, including the Digital Universe Encyclopedia and Encyclopedia of Earth. Sanger and his wife moved out to Santa Cruz, California, to be near the headquarters and the eccentric head of the Digital Universe effort, Joe Firmage.

Firmage was somewhat of a legendary character. During the 1990s, he was a founder and CEO of USWeb, one of the ephemeral powerhouses of the dot-com era. Like many other high-flying "interactive firms" at the time, it merged and merged again until nothing discernible from the original remained. But Firmage did make out well financially, to the point where he could create his own foundation.

Sanger was initially drawn to the idea of a well-funded project dedicated to a knowledge product. You couldn't blame him. Slick visual demonstrations of Digital Universe products had been floating around for years. With sophisticated graphics and professionally designed pages, the encyclopedia certainly looked like it was a formidable effort. But the pace at which it was going made the former Wikipedian feel like it was moving in slow motion. Sanger imagined being able to use some of Wikipedia's open content principles to help Digital Universe push forward, but he did not find much support.

In 2006 he started to contemplate other side projects. This culminated in September 2006, at the Wizards of OS conference, where he was invited to speak. He announced to the crowd the start of a project to be called Citizendium, which would be a fork of Wikipedia. He wanted to address some of the flaws he perceived in the Wikipedia model, most notably by eliminating anonymous editing, requiring the use of real names, and installing a layer of experts with extra authority. For the new project, the equivalent of administrators would be called constables, and unlike Wikipedia admins, they would be a rather big deal. Constables would be required to have a college degree and be at least twenty-five years old, according to Citizendium guidelines. There would also be chief subject editors who would have dominion over different fields.

Citizendium marked the reunion of Sanger with Ruth Ifcher, the chief copy editor of the original Nupedia project, as she took on the role of chief constable.

Sanger took a leave of absence from Digital Universe to work on Citizendium, and the Wikipedia crowd generally received it in a friendly yet lukewarm way. Some were enthusiastic that if the license for Citizendium was Gnu Free Documentation License (GFDL), like Wikipedia's, then it could be good for cross-pollination between the two. This was not meant to be, however, as Sanger decided to go with another license by Creative Commons, called Attribution ShareAlike 3.0. (It is possibile in the future that the new version of GFDL will be compatible with the Creative Commons license.)

The styles of Citizendium and Wikipedia have proven to be quite different. Citizendium has taken on a more narrative and less clinical style, but sometimes to comical effect. This is rather evident in comparing the two versions of the article on Dog.

Citizendium:

Domesticated from selected wolves thousands of years ago, the dog is often called "man's best friend." Throughout the world today, dogs are found associated with humans, although certainly not always as a part of

the household! Their status ranges all the way from being a form of food, to a full-time worker, to the privileged role of cherished companion. Perhaps more easily than any other species, dogs communicate with people.

Wikipedia:

The **dog** (Canis lupus familiaris) is a domestic subspecies of the wolf, a mammal of the Canidae family of the order Carnivora. The term encompasses both feral and pet varieties and is also sometimes used to describe wild canids of other subspecies or species. The domestic dog has been (and continues to be) one of the most widely-kept working and companion animals in human history, as well as being a food source in some cultures.

Sanger's project has had some hiccups, but it has gathered steady momentum. In October 2008, it had more than 8,000 articles, with over 800 as advanced, "developed" articles and around 80 "approved" articles. The challenge for Sanger is that growth is flat, with articles increasing only at a linear rate. While Citizendium is in no position to prove a foil to Wikipedia, it's an interesting alternative view of a volunteer encyclopedia effort and may show once and for all whether the core modifications Sanger desired for Wikipedia work in practice.

The Future

It is remarkable that a reference site created only in 2001, with a shoestring budget, has so solidly dominated the top of the Google rankings. People visit and come back to Wikipedia because it has proven useful, even if its quality has not been certified in any systematic way.

Wikipedia has been able to leapfrog existing encyclopedias by having a broader range of subjects, a deeper treatment for articles, and faster updates thanks to legions of volunteers filing information as fast as the news happens. But the emergent behavior that drives Wikipedia has a large problem area—coherence. Consistency and congruity across articles is the biggest weakness. The articles for Britney Spears, Madonna, Star Wars, Naruto, Pokemon, science fiction, and computer science are detailed, researched, and top quality. The nature of community expertise and interest has made that the case. Turn to articles about African, Asian, or Middle East history, and it's often slim pickings. Similarly, articles that should warrant short treatment often grow much longer than is likely warranted by their overall historical or academic significance. Editors are driven by their interest and passion, making the quality and length of articles across subject areas uneven.

Wikipedians have tried to correct this imbalance by driving more editors and efforts to neglected articles. There have been experiments with bounty systems, which pay individuals if they get articles to a certain level, but these have had little success. It is not clear that there is any ready solution to this problem. It may be a fundamental characteristic of wiki production that the problem of coherence will be hard to solve to anyone's satisfaction.

Wikipedia's impact on the world has been profound, but one also has to look at the cold, hard reality: It's become so big and influential that it is now a large technical operation with real-world demands on it and some real challenges to be faced going forward.

The Wikimedia Foundation has handled the oversight of finances and operations since Jimmy Wales founded it in June 2003. The Board of Trustees, which started as three appointees and two members elected from the community, now has the majority of its members coming from the ranks of Wikipedians. It's with mixed results. While it may be heartening to see a passionate band of volunteers give their time and energy to such noble endeavors, experience has become an issue, with few of the board members steeped in governance, finance, or fund-raising issues with respect to nonprofit organizations.

So far, the foundation has been using twice-a-year fund-raisers to solicit funds for Wikipedia's projects. The results are impressive given how little work is needed to fill the coffers. From the legions of visitors using PayPal or Money-Bookers donations, hundreds of thousands of dollars have been taken in each fund-raiser from visitors often donating no more than twenty dollars at a time. The budgets for the foundation have been modest so far at under $1 million a year until 2007, so the numbers pair up nicely.

Money raised by the foundation has been largely used to run the infrastructure of Wikipedia—the computer servers, the network connections, and affiliated maintenance costs. For an operation that rivals Yahoo, Microsoft, and Google in the traffic, it is a highly lean and efficient operation.

But 2008 will be a whole new domain. The foundation moved from St. Petersburg, Florida, to San Francisco, California, hired a new executive director, and set its sights on many more staff positions. The budget of $4.6 million is more than a fourfold increase over the previous year's. The usual method is pulling in roughly $1 million of revenue per fund-raiser, leaving quite a shortfall. It will require more aggressive fund-raising strategies if the foundation is to avoid living from "paycheck to paycheck," and having to seek funds each year simply to make the next budget. Currently there is no endowment fund or investment to sustain the project long-term.

Contrast this to what many consider a close cousin, the Mozilla Foundation, which was also established in 2003. As maintainers of the popular Firefox Web browser and other free software packages, Mozilla has a novel revenue model that rakes in tens of millions of dollars a year. The legend in Silicon Valley is that Mozilla has more money than they know what to do with. How does Mozilla make out so well? The numbers are impressive.

In October 2007, the Mozilla Foundation disclosed that their 2006 revenue was $66,840,850, with ninety full-time employees. Roughly 85 percent of this revenue came from Google, as it is the default option in the Firefox browser search bar. That and a Firefox-branded Google page as the standard home page means Mozilla gets lots of associated advertising and affiliate revenue. When users see the Google search listings resulting from the Firefox start page, any clicks on advertisements also generate revenue for the Mozilla Foundation. Each click on an ad may generate only pennies or even a few dollars. But given the increasing number of Firefox users and how many times one does a search each day, it adds up to a nice sum.

It's these types of numbers that make Jason Calacanis agitated. A high-energy tech entrepreneur best known as the founder of Weblogs Inc., he is an unabashed fan of Wikipedia. He's also a fast-talking guru on Internet advertising and revenue, and has been continually trying to prod Wales and Wikimedia's board to get on a similar type of revenue-generating program. Calacanis thinks there would be "$50,000 in the bank right now like Mozilla if they put up one advertisement on Wikipedia."[110]

As the bad blood regarding the Spanish Fork has shown, advertising or any on-site revenue-generating scheme on the backs of the community is bound to be a dangerous option, even if only for discussion. It's questionable whether the

Mozilla strategy can be directly mapped over to the Wikipedia experience, as the community and the encyclopedia are so intertwined.

The difference between Firefox and Wikipedia is the amount of community involvement. Firefox's community is largely made up of users of the browser, as only a small number of people write the Firefox software. By contrast, Wikipedia depends on legions of volunteer editors who feel invested in the product. If they perceive money is made off the sweat of their work, there is a much larger constituency to deal with regarding the use of the funds. And if the community walks, the project will wither and become stale. (Spanish Wikipedia living one year in the doldrums is a stark reminder of that.)

More important to consider is the lifetime horizon for the entire Wikimedia movement.

The euphoria of exponential growth is just now wearing off. Both English and German Wikipedia, the two bellwethers of influence, have entered into a period of slowing growth. It's only natural—the low-hanging fruit has been picked and both encyclopedias are entering into a maintenance mode, where current events and the long tail of minor topics will be the main areas for new content. The basic human knowledge articles about things like [[Earth]], [[Space]], [[Philosophy]] have all been written, and done quite well.

This is perhaps the biggest challenge for the project overall. One cannot have blind faith that Wikipedia will be ever increasing in size, quality, and community. There have been significant examples of articles backsliding from featured status into something less readable and reliable than before. The idea of "flagged revisions" of articles to note their quality was launched by the Germans in 2008, more than a year after it was slated to go live. There is some trepidation about introducing a new feature to a fickle community that may revolt if it is not done right the first time around. Wikipedia has also slowly morphed away from its freewheeling wiki roots as a general writing space. With protection, semi-protection, and flagged revisions, it has become a more regimented system, specifically for the task of writing structured encyclopedia articles on a large scale.

But the question for this community has always been: Are you here for the wiki-ness or the encyclopedia-ness? The "five pillars" of Wikipedia have as their very first item, "Wikipedia is an encyclopedia," something that people often have to be reminded of, and even pruned back to, when the community engages in too many frivolous MySpace-esque social networking activities.

But if Wikipedia is getting close to some level of being done, then the "community" and "wikiness" can be turned toward other useful endeavors. Wikisource, Wikibooks, and Wikiversity, for example, are other projects started within the WMF and inspired by Wikipedia. One of the more successful offshoots is Wikimedia Commons, a repository for photos and multimedia that can be shared across all Wikimedia projects. These will no doubt become more important, but it's not clear if they will garner the same passionate crowds as Wikipedia.

That's because Wikipedia was the remarkable beneficiary of some very special dynamics and uncanny timing.

By happening to launch at the bottom of the dot-com advertising market, it perhaps benefited from many out-of-work or lightly employed dot-com types. Wiki software had come onto the scene at just the right time, and the task of writing an encyclopedia was perhaps perfectly suited for the software. The wiki software was simple, and provided an easy entrée to this malleable community. People universally understood what an encyclopedia consisted of and looked like, and the task was easily modularized into writing articles relatively short in length.

On top of that, both existing dominant encyclopedias were behind paid firewalls, making the environment ripe for a new, free player. Combine the goal of "free content" with veterans of Slashdot, Linux, open source software, and an academic culture, and one can see the fertile ground that nurtured Wikipedia.

However, throughout this book, we've seen that the community is constantly evolving, exhausting old members and attracting a different breed of new volunteers. It is a very special time in the history of human knowledge and the history of Wikipedia. Will the community's veterans and the foundation be able to capitalize now, at the height of Wikipedia's potential, to sustain it in the future?

It stands at a crossroads. Will the community and the product hold together long-term? Will sustaining Wikipedia be financially viable? Have the steps been put in place to guarantee that it is around in one, five, or ten years from now?

Wikipedia followed Richard Stallman's philosophy of being free to distribute and modify, continuing the hacker ethos of sharing information to foster learning and furthering the content. A policy of openness allows anyone to edit and participate, and to see others' contributions, leading to an international, socially connected network that supports its neutral-point-of-view editing policy. And because it is timely, people now depend on Wikipedia as a historical running log of human endeavors.

With more information available at the fingertips of Internet users, this trustworthy distillation of information into knowledge has become Wikipedia's currency. It's not so much technical phenomenon as social phenomenon, which is why, despite its flaws, it has become an overwhelming success that continues to grow, as people discover the usefulness of the site and come back day after day.

To the Afterword

We are doing something quite unique here. We are letting the community write the next chapter. Literally.

The Afterword is a compendium of voices from a wiki specifically set up to allow the community to write Wikipedia's prognosis. We hope it will encapsulate the knowledge, the hopes, the humor, and the aspirations for what this community can, and will, do next. I hope it will provide an honest contemplation of what is ahead for an enterprise the development of which has been a tremendous joy to observe.

I have been a Wikipedian for five years, both participating in and chronicling the adventures of this global community of passionate scribes of human knowledge. It has been a fascinating ride. I can only hope that once in your lifetime you can be part of something this great that advances human achievement. I consider it a privilege to have met and interacted with the revolutionary set of individuals that make up the Wikipedia community.

''"What Is Next for Wikipedia?"''

Since launching in January 2001, Wikipedia has expanded from its single initial article in English to more than 10 million articles across 250 languages.[111] The number of editors has likewise grown from a handful to millions.

At first, the challenge was to create articles. To at least *have* any article about anything was an achievement back in 2002. Then the goal was to obtain a critical mass of usefulness. It happened at a phenomenal rate, even by Internet standards. As Wikipedia soared past Britannica and Encarta, then the *New York Times* and CNN, in terms of traffic, it was clear it had arrived and was growing at an astounding pace all through 2005.

One of the reasons Wikipedia has been among the Internet's most radical successes during the first decade of the twenty-first century is that it addressed several long-standing problems of printed encyclopedias:

- A good multivolume printed encyclopedia, costing more than $1,000, is beyond the financial means of many households, so ready access is limited by income.
- A truly comprehensive printed encyclopedia is economically unfeasible to produce. It simply takes too much physical space and expense.

- Keeping a printed encyclopedia of any size accurate and up-to-date is a difficult task.

With its legions of volunteers and a free content license, Wikipedia astonished even Internet veterans when it started to become mainstream in 2003. The encyclopedia was reliably doubling in size each year from 2004 to 2006, going from 188,000 articles to 895,000 articles. It was a golden time, as Wikipedia garnered accolades from users and became a widely used reference.

However, by 2007 there were signs that the astounding pace had leveled off, at least in the largest Wikipedia editions of English and German. The rate of article creation noticeably slowed. By the end of that year the previous five-year growth curve could no longer be described as exponential. To be sure, English Wikipedia was still a powerhouse, with more than 2 million articles at the start of 2008, but its growth trajectory was starting to sag.

Wikipedia had to deal with unique problems, since anybody could edit. With its popularity, spam and shameless self-promotion became a constant problem. These were challenges predecessors didn't have to face. Pasting a sales brochure into the Web pages of "Britannica" was impossible, yet this phenomenon was a continual battle for Wikipedia's patrollers in an open editing environment. More and more resources were dedicated to the task of reverting obvious commercial content or clandestine advertising.

Numbers are not the only story either. The lack of top-down editorial oversight resulted in uneven development of Wikipedia's articles, oftentimes with stark examples: The biography of Britney Spears takes up nearly twice the space as the one for Socrates. Whether Spears should be shorter or Socrates longer is an exercise left to the reader.

At the end of 2006, Jimmy Wales proposed that the community focus on quality versus quantity, that Wikipedia was sufficiently high-profile that embarrassing episodes concerning its reliability and credibility were taking a toll. It started with the Seigenthaler incident at the end of 2005, when a newspaper column in *USA Today* related the personal frustrations of a veteran journalist when his Wikipedia biography was vandalized. A potentially libelous statement added by an anonymous user was meant originally as a joke few would see, but suddenly turned into the biggest public crisis in Wikipedia's history.

It showed the challenge that had crept up with the increasing influence of the project. Maintaining articles about living people had serious consequences for the subject in an era when Wikipedia was showing up at the top of many Google searches. With over a quarter million of these biographies on the English Wikipedia, it was something that could not be left unaddressed.

This led to a new so-called BLP (biography of living persons) policy that set a much higher standard of quality for subjects who were alive, to avoid potential libel and harm. For the freewheeling community, it was a stark change.

BLP was a positive step toward quality, but did it come at a cost? Wikipedia after all was meant to be fast, using "radical inclusion" so "anyone can edit." Early mantras for the community were oriented around action without hesitation: "Be Bold" and "Ignore All Rules." Didn't find something to your satisfaction? SOFIXIT.

New policies enforced as part of the 2006 quality movement seemed to go against being bold: ensure each fact was verifiable and reliable sources were being cited; eliminate references to "bad sites" of information; protect high-traffic articles from editing by new users. It was a step toward quality, but would Wikipedia still really be the encyclopedia that "anyone can edit"?

Not only have the policies been of concern, but the ever increasing feature set of the wiki markup language has become more arcane and user-unfriendly. Even a new user who braves the community policies is likely to be scared off by the increasing complexity of the markup language.

To be sure, since its early days of CamelCase, Wikipedia has excelled tremendously through the addition of useful features. Templates give uniform looks to articles; infoboxes standardize the professional display of statistical information. The introduction of categories made the millions of articles in Wikipedia more navigable by putting them into browsable sets of topics. Make no mistake, the evolution of Wikipedia's software, MediaWiki, to support legions of editors in so many languages is an astonishing achievement.

But it hasn't come without caveats. Wiki markup was rather simple in the early days, providing not much more than bold, italic, links, headings, and bullets. However, today, hitting the "Edit" button often displays something nearly as complex as the messy Hypertext Markup Language code wiki sites were supposed to simplify in the first place.

The big problem is that wiki markup has no formal syntax. In computerese this means it's extremely hard, if not impossible, to write a compact, well-structured computer algorithm for decoding the wiki markup language. Instead, to interpret wiki markup and display it on the screen correctly involves a tangle of computer code, implementing a massive cascading series of conditional tests (so-called IF-THEN-ELSE statements).

The lack of a formal syntax may seem like a trivial gripe, but it has a serious consequence—Wikipedians are stuck "coding" wiki pages like a computer program, and likely will be for a long time. Without a formal syntax, it's not possible to implement the holy grail of page layout—"What you see is what you get" (WYSIWYG) editing. WYSIWYG was pioneered by word processors like Apple MacWrite or Microsoft Word, which let people graphically edit on the screen exactly what you would see in the end. Tables, charts, graphs, indexes, references, footnotes, and other features were suddenly easy to use in WYSIWYG.

In Wikipedia today, these have to be done with complex incantations of computer code. With the current wiki markup language, it's nearly impossible to create a WYSIWYG system without major redesigns and changes, which would cause huge problems with the millions of stored pages. Not only would the wiki syntax have to change, this transition would cause community bickering over having to implement such wholesale modifications. But without WYSIWYG editing, Wikipedia risks appealing only to those with strong constitutions for computer code, while staying inaccessible to newcomers accustomed to easy, on-screen editing.

Not everyone laments this. Some see the high bar to entry as a harsh natural selection process that ensures only conscientious members populate the community. But what if they're wrong, and in fact it simply keeps newcomers of all stripes away? What if the wiki markup problem is in fact too high a bar for entry, and a reason for community stagnation?

Facing Up

It's not clear whether the community has faced the fact that these recent changes have fundamentally altered its dynamic makeup.

With the slow morphing of policy to be more restrictive, and the challenge of editing more complex pages and simply scaling up from hundreds to millions of users, the Wikipedia community might be like the frog slowly boiling to death—unaware of the building crisis, because it is not aware how much its environment has slowly changed.

In the early days, when the core team of Wikipedians was measured in the dozens, it was easy to have a familiar conversation and form a consensus on direction. This was done on collegial mailing lists and friendly online chat rooms. But Wikipedia is no longer a small village of familiar townsfolk; it's a metropolis of faceless commuters.

What are the consequences of size? With the encyclopedia's influence and high profile came responsibility and the fear of doing harm in articles. With the centralized community that existed on the English Wikipedia in the early days not able to scale up with the growing community, forums for discussion have been divided and subdivided into highly specialized topics.

Cases where two highly active editors fail to encounter each other, nearly impossible in the early days, are now common and perhaps the unavoidable rule. Wikipedia is now fairly typical of human groups with broad shared activities—it is overlaid with localized communities formed around shared sub-interests. How these communities interact and how well they avoid claiming ownership over groups of articles (and what happens when they don't avoid it) are key factors in how the community goes forward.

Wikipedia's shift toward a partitioned community risks stifling some of its revolutionary features and inevitably changes the dynamic of the community, though this "tragedy of the commons" is not unique to Wikipedia. The problem of scaling up is one many online communities have had to deal with, from Usenet to DMOZ. But it's especially acute with a massive project where maintenance of articles (more than 2.5 million in the case of English Wikipedia) is paramount, and deterioration in quality shows quite quickly.

One Wikipedian, with the handle Durova, is pessimistic about the ability of Wikipedia to remain personable. She came up with a formulation that seems to track Wikipedia's evolution:

Durova's fourth law: small organizations run on relationships. Formal policies emerge when the organization becomes too large to operate on that basis. Policies continue to grow in both quantity and complexity in proportion to organizational growth until the policies no longer work, at which point the policies remain in place while the organization reverts to running on relationships.

The formation of the Arbitration Committee was an example of this reliance on institutional procedure, as Jimmy Wales no longer had time to personally sort things out himself as benevolent dictator.

Adminship

The problem of expanded policy and procedures dominating the community instead of the emergent "social" interaction of Wikipedia is striking when it comes to the selection and behavior of administrators. These admins or sysops are community members given access to the more privileged tools such as blocking other users and deleting articles. With the increasing volume of edits and more administrators on the prowl, the conception of "policy" has drifted from a folksy "description of how we do things" to a punitive "way one must do things because otherwise they will punish me."

In addition, attaining the status of an administrator is perhaps harder than ever. What used to be "no big deal" and jokingly referred to as a "janitor" has become a rather powerful role.

Administrators used to be expected to largely learn on the job. These days they are expected to be fully versed in policy, making the open process of questioning and challenging a candidate rather intense. Attempts have been made to draw bright lines around admins and to thoroughly vet candidates by researching previous edits and looking for anything resembling incivility. Others will toss in a pop quiz about copyright and the philosophy of American fair use law. Any inadequate defense of one's previous actions or current policy often means votes "against" the user.

Many feel that the grilling of potential administrators has gone too far, with common laments of "Request for Adminship is broken" and calls for reform.

In order to protect themselves from the imposition of policy and for support in the day-to-day running of the wiki, users naturally turned to other users with whom they have had amicable relations. These smaller networks have largely taken the place of the sitewide "community," which no longer offers the long-term relationships that it once did. Organized around article subject (e.g., WikiProject NASCAR), ideology (e.g., deletionism), location (e.g., Australian Wikipedians' notice board), administrative task (e.g., checking new pages), and sometimes just Wikipedians who like each other's style, they offer overlapping identities for Wikipedians from which they can seek support.

Where simple directives, such as "Ignore All Rules," might have worked in the early days, with the current size of the project clear guidance is needed for new users.

Divisive issues and contentious policies have taken their toll over the years at Wikipedia. Disillusioned editors don't always simply drift away. Many conflicts and critiques have migrated off the wiki to other forums dedicated to critiquing the influence of Wikipedia, such as http://WikipediaReview.Com Wikipedia Review and http://www.wikback.com/Wikback, and to externally produced audio commentary such as *Wikipedia Weekly* and *Not the Wikipedia Weekly*.

Experts

The English-language Wikipedia prides itself on being a collaboratively produced resource created by self-determined individuals. However, some, such as Wikipedia's early "chief instigator" and the founder of Citizendium, Larry Sanger, have criticized Wikipedia for being a primarily amateur-operated project and for not having any specialist roles for professional experts such as academics. In his memoir written for Slashdot, Sanger reflected on the guidelines he would have changed in Wikipedia if he started today:

> In knowledge-creation projects, and perhaps many other kinds of projects, make special roles for experts from the very beginning; do not attempt to add those roles later, as an afterthought.
> There are special requirements of nearly every serious community, however, best served by relevant experts; and so I think a prominent role for the relevant experts should be written into the charter.[112]

However, this marriage of professional and amateur cultures, united to produce a free encyclopedic reference work of high quality through collaboration, is a tough balance to strike. It's not clear that experts will have the constitution to deal with editing with the masses, Wikipedia-style.

Relationship with the Wikimedia Foundation

With English Wikipedia being the largest by far of all of the Wikimedia Foundation's projects, it draws the majority of the press, accolades, and donations for the Wikimedia Foundation. But size can be a problem. As it continues to grow, other projects and languages tend to fall under the English Wikipedia's shadow.

What was once a modest "five-figure" budget for maintaining inexpensive but efficiently used technology aims to be more than $4 million in 2008. With a new San Francisco office and a dozen paid staff members, and more to come, the foundation is in the midst of a cultural shift. If the Wikimedia Foundation continues to grow, as some have predicted, it will start to need more and more resources to fund its development. Several different ways of dealing with this have been proposed, from limiting the number of articles, to carrying banner ads at the top of every page. The prospect of advertising has been one of the most sensitive issues in the community, ever since the departure of Spanish Wikipedians in February 2002 when the mere mention of ads caused a miniature revolt. As a result, Wikipedia's revenue stream has historically been modest, coming from the sale of updates or "feeds," of content changes to search engines. The bulk of its funds comes from grants and donations, which have been steady in the last few years. However, the foundation is living hand-to-mouth. With no endowment, the organization has no funds for long-term survivability, and this is something it needs to address now that it has a professional fund-raising staff in San Francisco.

The role of this new built-up paid executive staff itself is of concern. This is something identified in open source projects as jalt—the jealousy altruism factor, of whether people get paid differently for participating. The disparity will be an ongoing problem, as some developers and project leaders receive monetary compensation for work previously handled by volunteers. Will this tamper with the community dynamics, where volunteers are increasingly on the sidelines when it comes to governance and direction?

Perhaps the biggest challenge of the foundation's pursuit of more sources of income is that it has not effectively made its argument that additional funding is needed. That is not to say that the Wikimedia projects do not need additional funding, but that beyond a vaguely defined goal of "more outreach"—especially in developing countries—the foundation has not expressed in much detail which needs they want to address. Unless the foundation improves its relationship with the community of editors, the strong base of support it currently enjoys may erode rather quickly.

Legal Status

People have described Wikipedia as being full of libelous content, sitting as a big legal threat on the horizon. There are scores of articles with unsourced statements written by anonymous individuals. Will there be a big lawsuit that will put community members in jeopardy?

Editors are legally responsible for their edits, and the Wikimedia Foundation, being protected as a common carrier in the United States under the Section 230 safe harbor provisions of the Telecommunications Act, is not responsible for content on the site. It is likely an editor will be on the receiving end of a civil action sooner or later. There has already been at least one criminal case.[113] However, if one makes an edit to another section of the article, is one then responsible for the previous edits to which one added a change? These are issues that have yet to be tested in a court of law.

Stability of Articles

While the English-language Wikipedia has shown it can produce high-quality content, it does not successfully maintain this accuracy continuously. In order to address this situation, which deters many academics, teachers, and librarians from endorsing Wikipedia's content, a system of maintaining stability of articles has been proposed. A system need not stop anybody from editing, but should simply ensure that readers have an option to view "stable" versions of Wikipedia articles. A MediaWiki extension called "flagged revisions"[114] was proposed to resolve this issue by allowing users to mark whether a version of an article was free of vandalism and of generally acceptable quality.

In May 2008, the German Wikipedia community turned on the flagged revisions feature, allowing users to tag articles as "sighted." In an impressive display, 16 percent of the articles in the first week were sighted. Within four months, more than 70 percent were. It's invigorating, and it was driven not by the enormous English-language Wikipedia editors, but the smaller and more nimble German community.

Building on the idea of designating certain "finished" versions of Wikipedia articles is the concept of selecting stable versions of articles to be published on a static Web site protected from editing, such as http://en.veropedia.com/Veropedia. While this could solve many of the problems that readers have with quality, it could take away from people's usage of Wikipedia. This would lead to fewer donations, and fewer updates with current information, one of the main features of an online encyclopedia. But it might just be this maturation process that is needed. For example, the Linux operating system, which inspired the Wikipedia development model, has a robust marketplace creating multiple stable distributions built off a shared central base of computer code. Most users experience Linux through packages such as Ubuntu, SUSE, Debian, and Fedora, each one with different characteristics—ease of use, variety of features, look and feel, etc.

This might be a model of Wikipedia, where people experience Wikipedia's content through multiple "distributions," and not necessarily through Wikipedia's continuously shifting state as we see it today.

Conclusion

Perhaps no better quote sums up Wikipedia's challenges than "The greatest enemy of a revolution is its success." Wikipedia initiated something new and unprecedented, and for the better part of a decade, it led the way in demonstrating that the collaborative accumulation of knowledge was not only feasible, but desirable. Its neutrality policy, combined with a global team of volunteers, helped make Wikipedia not just a clone of existing encyclopedias, but an encyclopedia that made recording human history a revolutionary, collaborative act.

It was, however, inevitable that other groups and organizations would learn from the Wikipedia experiment, emulate the good, and resolve its problems. Britannica's move in early 2008 to quicken their editing process and to accept user contributions shows they are not sitting still. They announced on their blog their intention to "promote greater participation by both our expert contributors and readers. Both groups will be invited to play a larger role in expanding, improving, and maintaining the information we publish on the Web under the Encyclopaedia Britannica name."

Wikipedia faces two possibilities: It can remain complacent with what it has achieved, or it can attempt to find innovative ways to remain on the cutting edge of collaborative Internet projects. The former is essentially a recipe for stagnation. One can only wonder whether there is enough creativity left to adopt the latter path and whether a community of Wikipedia's size can manage the task.

Britannica is learning from Wikipedia. What is Wikipedia learning from Britannica?

Notes

Chapter 1. THE WIKI PHENOMENON

1. According to ComScore (http://www.comscore.com/press/release.asp?press=1049) and Alexa (http://www.alexa.com/data/details/traffic_details/wikipedia.org).
2. http://www.reason.com/news/show/36969.html.
3. ComScore, April 2008, http://www.comscore.com/press/release.asp?press=2160.
4. *Reason* magazine, June 2007, http://www.reason.com/news/show/119689.html.
5. Thomas Friedman, *The World Is Flat* (New York: Picador, 2007), p. 124.

Chapter 2. A NUPEDIA

6. http://www.pbs.org/wgbh/amex/quizshow/peopleevents/pande02.html.
7. http://www.enewscourier.com/homepage/local_story_224212506.html?keyword= leadpicturestory.
8. http://www.stallman.org/archives/2007-may-aug.html.
9. The Early History of Nupedia and Wikipedia: A MemoirSlashdot, April 18, 2005, http://features.slashdot.org/article.pl?sid=05/04/18/164213&tid=95.
10. http://web.archive.org/web/20010410035607/www.nupedia.com/steering.shtml.
11. http://www.nupedia.com/write.shtml.
12. The Early History of Nupedia and Wikipedia: A MemoirSlashdot, April 18, 2005, http://features.slashdot.org/article.pl?sid=05/04/18/164213&tid=95.
13. "Know It All: Can Wikipedia Conquer Expertise?" *The New Yorker,* July 31, 2006, http://www.newyorker.com/archive/2006/07/31/060731fa_fact.

Chapter 3. WIKI ORIGINS

14. C2 Wiki, http://c2.com/cgi/wiki?WikiWikiHyperCard.
15. Wikimania 2005, keynote speech, Ward Cunningham.
16. C2 Wiki, http://c2.com/cgi/wiki?WikiWikiHyperCard.
17. Gillies, James & Robert Cailliau. *How the Web Was Born: The Story of the World Wide Web.* (Oxford: Oxford University Press, 2000), p. 214.

18. C2 Wiki, http://c2.com/doc/etymology.html.

19. http://sunir.org/sunir/.

Chapter 4. WIKI INTRODUCED

20. Larry Sanger, "Let's make a wiki" (email), Nupedia-L mailing list, Nupedia, January 10, 2001, http://web.archive.org/web/20030414014355/http://www.nupedia.com/pipermail/nupedia-l/2001-January/000676.html (retrieved on May 1, 2008).

21. http://en.wikipedia.org/wiki/User_talk:Mark_Richards/Archive_2#The_.22Encyclopedia_that_Slashdot_Built.22_Awards.

22. Simon Winchester, *The Meaning of Everything* (New York: Oxford University Press, 2003).

23. Ibid, p. 108.

24. Ibid, p. 57.

25. Ibid, p. 200.

26. http://huettermann.net/index.php/?cat-2.

27. 2006 figure.

Chapter 5. COMMUNITY AT WORK (THE PIRANHA EFFECT)

28. CNN, December 5, 2005, http://en.wikipedia.org/wiki/User:SushiGeek/Wales_interview_transcript.

29. http://en.wikipedia.org/w/index.php?title=Wikipedia:Be_bold&oldid=38947.

30. http://lists.wikimedia.org/pipermail/wikien-l/2003-February/001149.html.

31. http://en.wikipedia.org/wiki/Wikipedia:Advice_for_new_administrators.

32. http://en.wikipedia.org/wiki/Wikipedia:Awareness_statistics.

33. http://stats.wikimedia.org/EN/TablesWikipediaEN.htm.

34. 4,687 editors made more than 100 edits each that month.

35. http://wikisummaries.org/index.php?title=The_Death_and_Life_of_Great_American_Cities&oldid=5639 (retrieved June 8, 2007).

36. http://en.wikipedia.org/wiki/User_talk:Rambot/Delete 17:32, 11 Sep 2003 (UTC).

37. http://en.wikipedia.org/wiki/Wikipedia:Bots#Restrictions_on_specific_tasks.

38. http://en.wikipedia.org/wiki/User:Seth_Ilys/Dot_Project.

39. http://en.wikipedia.org/wiki/User:Seth_Ilys/Dot_Project.

40. http://en.wikipedia.org/w/index.php?title=Wikipedia:Ignore_all_rules&oldid=54587.

41. http://en.wikipedia.org/wiki/Wikipedia:Neutral_point_of_view.

42. http://en.wikipedia.org/wiki/Wikipedia:Notability.

43. Wikipedia has come so far that inclusion implies societal validation of a concept.

44. http://lists.wikimedia.org/pipermail/wikien-l/2003-November/008153.html.

45. http://en.wikipedia.org/wiki/Wikipedia:Edit_war.

46. http://en.wikipedia.org/wiki/Wikipedia:Three_revert_rule_enforcement.

47. Gdansk, from Wikipedia, 19 September 2007, http://en.wikipedia.org/w/index.php ?title=Gda%C5%84sk&oldid=158792453.

Chapter 6. WIKIPEDIA GOES INTERNATIONAL

48. Marshall McLuhan, *Understanding Media: The Extensions of Man*, the MIT Press (October 20, 1994).

49. http://osdir.com/ml/science.linguistics.wikipedia.international/2002-02/msg00018 .html.

50. http://osdir.com/ml/science.linguistics.wikipedia.international/2002-02/msg00037 .html.

51. http://osdir.com/ml/science.linguistics.wikipedia.international/2002-02/msg00038 .html.

52. http://www.ojr.org/japan/internet/1061505583.php.

53. http://stats.wikimedia.org/EN/ChartsWikipediaDE.htm.

54. http://en.wikipedia.org/wiki/Wikipedia:Flagged_revisions/Sighted_versions.

55. http://toolserver.org/~aka/cgi-bin/reviewcnt.cgi?lang=german&action=images.

56. Editors making more than 100 edits per month, http://stats.wikimedia.org/EN/ ChartsWikipediaDE.htm.

57. The fine distinctions between Mandarin, *putonghua*, and *hua yu* are too exhaustive to cover in this text. Please see: http://en.wikipedia.org/wiki/Standard_Mandarin.

58. http://sr.wikipedia.org/wiki/%D0%97%D0%B5%D0%BC%D1%99%D0%B0.

59. http://kk.wikipedia.org/wiki/%D0%96%D0%B5%D1%80_(%D2%93%D0%B0%D0 %BB%D0%B0%D0%BC%D1%88%D0%B0%D1%80).

60. http://lists.wikimedia.org/pipermail/foundation-l/2006-September/023408.html.

61. http://wikimediafoundation.org/wiki/Press_releases/Wikipedia_Academies.

62. http://guaka.org/2008/01/16/idlelo3-dakar-march-18-20-wikipedia-in-west-african-languages/.

63. http://www.economist.com/search/displaystory.cfm?story_id=11484062.

64. http://en.wikipedia.org/wiki/Wikipedia:Wikipedia_articles_per_population.

Chapter 7. TROLLS, VANDALS, AND SOCK PUPPETS, OH MY

65. http://curezone.com/forums/troll.asp.

66. http://nostalgia.wikipedia.org/w/index.php?title=The_Cunctator/How_to_destroy_ Wikipedia&oldid=49164.

67. From "The Cathedral and the Bazaar," p. 65.

68. http://www.firstmonday.org/Issues/issue8_12/ciffolilli/.

69. http://www.wired.com/wired/archive/13.03/wiki.html.

70. http://en.wikipedia.org/w/wiki.phtml?title=Albert_Einstein&diff=2380047&oldid=2380036.

71. http://wikimania2006.wikimedia.org/wiki/Proceedings:MP1.

Chapter 8. CRISIS OF COMMUNITY

72. http://wwwtcsdaily.com/article.aspx?id=111504A.

73. http://ascii.textfiles.com/archives/000060.html.

74. http://www.news.com/In-search-of-the-Wikipedia-prankster—page-2/2008-1029_3-5995977-2.html?tag=st.next.

75. http://en.wikipedia.org/wiki/Wikipedia:Semi-protection_policy#Semi-protection.

76. http://chronicle.com/wiredcampus/index.php?id=1909.

77. http://freakonomics.blogs.nytimes.com/2007/02/28/wikipedia=oops/.

78. http://en.wikipedia.org/w/index.php?title=Talk:Imprimatur&diff=prev&oldid=12614544.

79. http://en.wikipedia.org/w/index.php?title=Wikipedia:Administrators%27_notice board/Incidents&diff=47360865&oldid=47360559.

80. http://en.wikinews.org/wiki/Jimmy_Wales_asks_Wikipedian_to_resign_%22his_positions_of_trust%22_over_nonexistent_degrees.

81. http://en.wikipedia.org/wiki/Wikipedia:Wikipedia_Signpost/2007-03-05/Essjay.

Chapter 9. WIKIPEDIA MAKES WAVES

82. http://www.comedycentral.com/colbertreport/videos.jhtml?videoId=72347.

83. http://www.sfgate.com/cgi-bin/article.cgi?f=/c/a/2008/03/30/BUQLUAP8L.DTL.

84. http://news.cnet.com/2100-1038_3-5186012.html.

85. http://www.google.com/explanation.html.

86. http://www.webpronews.com/topnews/2004/04/16/googlebombing-of-jew-keyword-continues.

87. http://www.informationweek.com/news/internet/policy/showArticle.jhtml?articleID=212300138.

88. http://www.copyright.gov/fls/fl102.html.

89. http://en.wikipedia.org/wiki/What_wp_is_not#Wikipedia_is_not_censored.

90. http://www.worldnetdaily.com/index.php?pageId=63722.

91. http://www.iwf.org.uk/media/news.archive-2008.251.htm.

92. http://www.smh.com.au/news/technology/web/wikipedia-added-to-child-pornography-blacklist/2008/12/08/1228584723764.html.

93. The six ISPs were Be Unlimited/O², Virgin Media, EasyNet/UK Online, PlusNet, Demon and Opal Telecommunications (TalkTalk).

94. http://www.guardian.co.uk/technology/2008/dec/08/amazon-internet-censorship-iwf.

95. http://www.amazon.com/Virgin-Killer-Scorpions/dp/B0000073NL.

96. http://en.wikipedia.org/wiki/Wikipedia:Wikipedia_Signpost/2009-01-03/Virgin_Killer.

97. http://theridiculant.metro.co.uk/2008/12/interview-with.html.

98. http://theridiculant.metro.co.uk/2008/12/interview-with.html.

99. http://en.wikipedia.org/w/indexphp?title=User_talk:Jimbo_Wales&diff=256862858&oldid=256836841.

100. "Share Your Knowledge," Encarta Blog, March 23, http://encarta.spaces.live.com/?_c11_BlogPart_BlogPart=blogview&_c=BlogPart&partqs=amonth%3d3%26ayear%3d2005.

101. http://encarta.spaces.live.com/blog/cns!77B9D618E03238CC!179.entry.

102. http://en.wikipedia.org/wiki/Wikipedia:Wikipedia_Signpost/2005-06-20/Wikitorials_and_Wikipedia.

103. http://ross.typepad.com/blog/2005/06/open_letter_on_.html.

104. http://www.nature.com/nature/journal/v438/n7070/full/438900a.html.

105. http://www.nature.com/nature/britannica/index.html.

106. http://www.britannica.com/blog/2008/06/collaboration-ownership-and-expertise/.

107. http://forms01.britannica.com/help/blogwebmasterform.html.

108. http://www.britannica.com/blogs/2008/06/britannicas-new-site-more-participation-collaboration-from-experts-and-readers/.

109. http://www.britannica.com/blogs/2008/06/collaboration-ownership-and-expertise/.

110. http://www.calacanis.com/2007/02/15/why-wikipedia-doesnt-have-advertising-hint-follow-the-money.

AFTERWORD

111. http://www.theglobeandmail.com/servlet/story/RTGAM.20080526.wrwikipedia26/BNStory/Technology/home.

112. http://features.slashdot.org/article.pl?sid=05/04/19/1746205&tid=95.

113. http://www.latimes.com/news/printedition/california/la-me-briefs31-2008may31,0,6581366.story.

114. http://www.mediawiki.org/wiki/Extension:FlaggedRevs.